Dyadic
Communication

DYADIC COMMUNICATION

Third Edition

William W. Wilmot
University of Montana

Random House
New York

For Joyce, Carina, and Jason

Third Edition
98765432
Copyright © 1987 by Newbery Award Records, Inc.

Library of Congress Cataloging-in-Publication Data

Wilmot, William W.
  Dyadic comunication.

  Bibliography: p.
  Includes indexes.
  1. Interpersonal communication. I. Title.
BF637.C45W54 1986   302.3′4   86-29648
ISBN 0-394-35826-0

Manufactured in the United States of America

COVER ART
NAUM GABO
Linear Construction In Space No. 1
(Variation) C.R. 53.1
Collection: Mr & Mrs Raymond D Nasher, Dallas
Photographer: John Webb, England

Cover design by Dorothy S. Bungert

Preface

This book is appropriate for courses examining interpersonal relationships in detail. It presents a comprehensive relational view of interpersonal communication with a pragmatic, real-world perspective. The goal is to give the student an integrated view of communication concepts, both as intellectually exciting ideas and as practical insights for everyday life.

Since the first edition of this book appeared in 1975, the study of human communication has made dramatic advances. This third edition has retained the transactional orientation of the first edition but with significant improvements and updating, which parallel our understanding of one-to-one communication. In addition to incorporating the latest theory and research, the new edition includes new coverage, such as an extensive treatment of metacommunication and expanded coverage of relational competence and enhancement.

PLAN OF THE BOOK

The first chapter sets the foundation for studying dyadic pairs. It presents an expanded treatment of relationship functions and explores dyadic relationships within their contexts—groups of people in families and organizations. The chapter overviews the nature of dyadic communication and concludes with an historical view of the importance of two-person relationships.

The second and third chapters illustrate the centrality of communication in how we perceive ourselves and others. The more we study perceptions, the closer we must examine the centrality of communication. For example, the perceptual biases we use when perceiving others are based on the communication cues we interpret coming from then, and this notion is given expanded treatment in Chapter 3.

Some exciting new notions are introduced in Chapter 4, "Perception of the Relationship." This chapter examines the mutual influences between communication behavior and relationship definitions. And, it illustrates how communication and relationship definitions are mutually influencing—the core elements in all relationships. In addition, it discusses how people distinguish between different kinds of relationships. This comprehensive treatment of the relational perspective expands on the important information in the earlier editions that many readers enjoyed.

Chapter 5, "Relational Intricacies," was one of the favorite chapters for many readers of earlier editions. This chapter explores some

v

intriguing concepts about the maddening, complex, intriguing events that occur in two-person relationships. A new section entitled "Dyadic Dialectics" is a valuable addition to these topics and looks at the opposite needs we have in our relationships with others. For example, we need to be open and disclosive yet not share all information with the other. These dialectics are at the core of the decisions we all make in our communication exchanges with others.

Chapter 6, "Relationship Development and Dissolution," has been updated with the latest research on these processes. An improved section on "Stabilized Definitions" charts the fluctuating dynamics of stable relationships, and a section on "relational oscillation" illustrates the recycling many people go through when attempting to dissolve an important relationship.

The final chapter has been retitled and expanded to treat both relational competence and enhancement. The importance of communication skills in both conversations and ongoing relationships is highlighted. Specifically, suggestions are made for the enhancement of relationships—how to improve them over time. The chapter ends with a retrospective view of the philosophy of communication presented throughout the entire book.

Readers interested in tracing references will find the extensive author and subject indexes helpful. The author index is keyed to the text where either the name is cited or the work is referenced by number in the discussion. And, as with the earlier editions, references are cited by number in the text to improve readability for the student, yet retain the information necessary to trace ideas.

ACKNOWLEDGMENTS

I appreciate the careful reviewers who read and critiqued the cut and paste manuscript. Special thanks go to Leslie Baxter, Lewis and Clark College; Sheryl Perlmutter Bowen, University of Delaware; Thomas Frentz, University of Arkansas; Lawrence Nadler, Miami University; Malcolm Parks, University of Washington; Laura Stafford, Ohio State University; Sally Jane Widenmann, University of California at Santa Barbara; and Katherine Yost, Rutgers University. Their keen analysis coupled with a desire to improve the book are greatly appreciated. The jokes especially kept me going when I thought the tasks would never end. Any error or misstatement is probably the direct result of my not following someone's advice!

The students in Interpersonal Communication 234 at the University of Montana continue to be delightful, critical, and understanding. Teaching them remains a pleasure and source of renewal for me. When those students react to the concepts and examples in this book, it convinces me of the importance of teaching a comprehensive view of interpersonal communication.

I, too, have some important dyadic relationships. I am fortunate to be married to Dr. Joyce L. Hocker. She is both colleague and spouse, and continues to provide insight and understanding of communication in both personal and professional realms. She has taught me much about how to have a successful, challenging, and growing dyadic relationship and her influence on me cannot be overestimated. Jason and Carina, in addition to providing examples for the book, both invest effort at continuing our relationships, and I marvel at their growth and change. Two better children can't be found—may we backpack forever!

Kathleen Domenig and Brian Henry served as my links with Roth Wilkofsky and Random House. They are a first-rate group who kept encouraging me without bludgeoning me over the head about deadlines. Special thanks to Brian, for he dealt with all the details of getting the book into production, while being upbeat and of good cheer. Finally, all those unknown people behind the scenes at Random House—copy editors, artists, compositors, and others did a splendid job. I only wish the manuscript editors could read the essays my high school English teacher had to read!

Pam Mangus, niece and communication graduate, gave timely and high-level help with references and index. Thanks, Pam.

I appreciate those of you who have shared kind comments about the previous edition with me. They have been more influential than you would ever guess. Your interest in the accuracy of text and adaptation to student needs has helped motivate me to undertake this edition. Some of the more extensive responses have come from Thomas Frentz, University of Arkansas; Kathy Adams, California State University, Fresno; and Glen Hall, Montana State University.

Finally, one cannot write without some spiritual replenishment that comes from sources other than relationships. Special acknowledgment to Kitaro for his melodic compositions—Silver Cloud and Oasis (among others) helped me transcend the hours spent and float above the mundane. My other source of renewal comes from the clean air, lofty mountains, and wild animals of western Montana. May they always remain free and as close to their natural form as possible.

Finally, I am proud to be a member of the communication profession, composed of disparate individuals in a variety of institutions and private practice. In this academic discipline, theoretical notions are developed in conjunction with an active concern for the pragmatic effects on people's lives. One would be hard pressed to find a more balanced group of professionals.

Bill Wilmot
Missoula, Montana

Contents

Dyadic
Communication

Chapter 1

The Nature of Dyadic Transactions

. . . much of the social activity of individuals can be described as search behavior—a relentless process of social discovery in which one seeks out new friends to replace those who are either no longer present or who no longer share the same interests.

—ALVIN TOFFLER, *FUTURE SHOCK*

In our highly mobile society, our relationships with others are continually changing. Whether you leave home to attend college, change jobs, get married (or divorced), or join new groups, your friendship patterns change. As your close friends of yesterday become more of a memory, you replace them with others. It is, in fact, rather unlikely that your best friends of five years ago are the same ones you would mention as being your best friends today.

The degree of change we experience in our interpersonal relationships can be, from one point of view, cause for concern. It may be that we have entered a "psychological ice age" and that, except for "occasional bursts of warmth, often fueled by sex after a few cocktails, truly intimate encounters have begun to disappear from civilized life" [17]. Certainly in many of our day-to-day communication transactions, we operate in "reciprocal ignorance" of each other [231]. Do you know anything or care about the lives of the people who sell you groceries, clothes, and gasoline, and do they know anything at all about you? If the people in your life are transitory, why should you attempt to establish any meaningful communication with them?

On the more optimistic side, our degree of autonomy and anonymity can provide benefits. If you are unhappy with your situation, you can often change it. A new job and friends can provide "breathing room" for you to maximize your potential and lead the type of life that suits you. And just because you slide by hundreds of thousands of people daily does not mean that you are incapable of forming meaningful relationships with select people. It may be that our mobility provides us with more acquaintances and fewer friends but the friendships we do have are highly engaging and meaningful [148]. Whatever your position is on this issue, it is clear that communication relationships are a very significant part of our lives. In almost all professions, for instance, "people spend approximately three-fourths of their waking time communicating with others" [429]. Even in highly technical occupations such as research and development, "communication with people, not equipment, is the principal focus of activity" [250]. Communication with others is an inescapable factor of our existence.

DYADIC RELATIONSHIP TYPES AND FUNCTIONS

This book focuses on dyadic communication—transactions between two people. Any communication transaction, whether it be fleeting or

4

recurring, face-to-face or mediated, is a form of dyadic communication. The pure form of dyadic communication occurs when the two participants are in a *face-to-face* situation, where both are attending to the other's communication cues, and it takes place in a variety of contexts and relationships. Talking over a cup of coffee, having an intense argument with a loved one, greeting someone on the sidewalk, or purchasing a new coat from a clerk are all forms of dyadic communication.

The basic dyadic processes occur in all types of contexts and within an incredible array of relationship types. The following is a small listing of some of the possible types of relationships.

I. Romantic relationships
   A. Cross-sex relationships such as husband or wife, fiance, lover, boyfriend or girlfriend, spouse, paramour, beau, steady, flame, mate, sweetheart, or just a casual dating partner.
   B. Same-sex relationships such as gay and lesbian relationships, which use labels such as partner, lover, friend, and roommate.
II. Friendships
   All friendship types, cross-sex or same-sex, using such labels as best friend, close friends, "just friends," casual friends, pal, confidant, buddy, and others.
III. Family relationships
   All types where the participants are called brother, sister, aunt, uncle, grandparents, parents, stepparents, siblings, stepsister and stepbrother, among others.
IV. Work and function-based relationships
   Examples are such relations as professor–student, co-worker, colleague, schoolmate, pastor–parishioner, and supervisor–subordinate, among others.

Obviously, the list of possible relationships is almost endless, with new terms often being coined to capture the diversity of relationships. For example, with the blending of families, do children have four sets of grandparents or two sets of grandparents and two sets of step-grandparents? As Knapp, Ellis, and Williams [261] have noted, the array of relationship types is quite diverse. In their research they used sixty-two different labels for dyadic relationships. Providing an exhaustive list of such relationships is unnecessary, but the point should be clear. We have a diversity of dyadic relationships available [513].

Dyadic relationships can also be examined from the perspective of the *functions* that they serve, rather than on the basis of the category of the relationship. The functional bases of dyadic relationships are complex and varied, but we can find some provocative results in the research that is available. Friendship, for instance, can serve a lot of different functions. Caldwell and Peplau [88] found that for women friendship serves the primary function of the "sharing of feelings." For men, however, friendship is oriented "more towards the sharing of physical activities," such as skiing together. To be sure, not all men

Relationships between co-workers may serve many functions, just as friendships and romantic relationships do.

and women pick friends for only these purposes, but the respondents in the Caldwell and Peplau study consistently noted that their friends served these functions for them.

Other dyadic relationships can serve diverse functions, just as do friendships. When I was an undergraduate student, there was one professor in particular who served an important function for me. Through my association with him—he was the debate coach and I was a debater—I began to identify with him. While Dr. Marsh served as an important role model for me and greatly influenced my own decision to become a college professor, for my debate partner, Lynn, he served another function—that of getting us to tournaments. The functions he served for us were quite different, yet he was the debate coach for both of us. The functions that one can serve for another in a dyadic relationship are influenced by, but not totally determined by, the category of the relationship. In my small city there is an organization devoted to linking volunteer counselors with delinquent boys and girls. The program is modeled after the "partners" approach and stresses to the volunteers that their role is to form a "friendship" with the younger kids. Although the relationship is one of "assistance" or "helper–helpee," it serves functions that are a blend between friendship and big brother or sister.

A number of scholars have attempted to pinpoint the functions our relationships serve for us. Weiss [524], for instance, stresses that relationships provide for intimacy, social integration, opportunity for nurturant behavior, reassurance of worth, assistance, and guidance. For

Weiss these functions are served by a variety of relationships, ranging from friendships to work relationships to helper–helpee relationships. One of the most straightforward treatments of the functions that relationships serve is from Bennis et al. [48], who suggest that our interpersonal relationships serve the four following functions:

1. *Expression of feelings.* The relationship allows the participants to express their emotions, both about the outside world and the relationship itself.
2. *Confirmation.* This function is served in a relationship when your sense of self is confirmed by the other. It answers the question "Who am I?" in relation to others around you.
3. *Change or influence.* In this type of relationship, the participants come together for the primary purpose of change—having impact on one another. Influence situations can range from persuasion to therapy.
4. *Creation and work.* These relational functions are instrumental— some goal or task outside the relationship itself is served.

Other scholars have addressed the functions served by specific types of relationships [554, 523, 104, 547, 560]. Skipper and Nass [462] for instance, deal with the functions that dating relationships serve for people. They speculate that dating serves one or more of these functions for the dyadic partners:

1. A form of recreation.
2. A form of socialization.
3. A means of status grading and status achievement.
4. A form of courtship.

Clearly, one category of a dyadic relationship can serve a variety of functions for either the same individual or for distinct persons. If person A is dating someone, it may be as a form of "raising his status" while another may simply see dating as a form of recreation—better than playing cards. While research on the functions served by our dyadic relationships is rather scattered, we can provide three conclusions about dyadic functions.

First, there are some consistent differences between the types of relationships [216]. For instance, there are differences between romantic relationships and kin or family relationships. Similarly, there are general differences between relationships with your peers and your family members. These generalized differences between relationships are used to distinguish between them. For instance, when we talk of close personal relationships involving sharing important information with others, close friends and romantic partners might qualify as people with whom we would share such information, but others, such as the neighbor we seldom see, would not. Second, even though there are global differences between relationship types, a given function can be served by more than one relationship [545]. A woman's husband may provide for some of her intimacy needs, such as close contact, sexual expression, and commitment to another human. And her close friend may provide for all the same intimacy needs except sex. In addition, one's closest confidant could be a same-sex friend, lover, twin sister, or someone sharing one's hobbies. Finally, a relationship can serve a variety of functions [216]. For example, in a relationship with one's employer, one's self-esteem and sense of self-worth may be bolstered at the same time that work is accomplished. Many of us have had a relationship that began on a limited basis and then expanded to other realms over time. Such is the case when a student becomes a friend of a former teacher.

The finest distinctions between relationships occur when we examine the *functions* rather than the *category* of the relationship. The actual quality of a relationship is more dependent on the type of interaction than it is on the category of the relationship [348]. One way to distinguish between dyadic relationships is based on the degree of pair

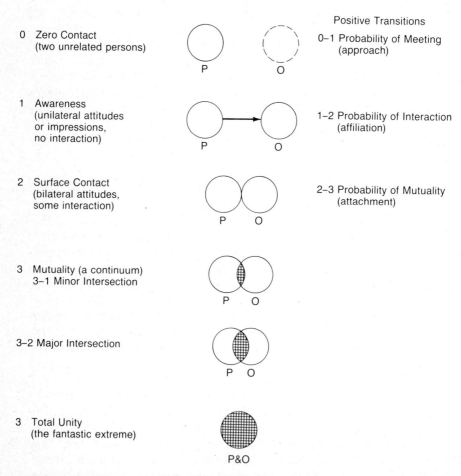

Figure 1-1.   Degrees of pair relatedness. *Reprinted by permission of the authors from George Levinger and J. D. Shoek,* Attraction in Relationship. *Copyright 1978 by George Levinger and J. D. Shoek.*

relatedness, or the interconnectedness of the two participants. Figure 1-1 from Levinger and Snoek [294] illustrate some of the diversity possible in relationships between two people. Each circle represents one person, with the amount of overlap symbolic of their degree of interdependence. Our dyadic relationships are diverse in terms of the amount of contact and interdependence. As Figure 1.1 illustrates, once both participants are aware they are in a relationship, that relationship can vary from surface contact and mutual exchange to the total blending of both people into one.

It is functionally impossible to relate to each person on the basis of a close, intimate relationship. In fact, we all need a wide range of relationships in order to keep our lives flowing smoothly. We need nonintimate work relationships just as much as we need intimate ones. Since our relationships serve a variety of functions, and since we all experience wide degrees of relational functions, this book will not be limited to the most intimate or profound dyadic relationships. All dyadic relationships will be used as examples to illustrate communication principles. The fundamental processes of relationships will be examined and illustrated, drawing upon romantic relationships, work relationships, family relationships, friendships, and others. Some of the topics covered will be more relevant to fleeting, one-time encounters between two strangers, while others, such as the more intricate processes discussed in Chapter 5, are found only in more enduring, recurring dyads. But throughout, the fundamental processes of dyadic communication remain the focus.

DYADIC COMMUNICATION DEFINED

What is this process called communication? The word *communication* is bandied about (and claimed as their own property) by public speakers, advertisers, specialists in audiovisual aids, human relations trainers, and even college professors. To some people, communication occurs when a TV station sends signals from its tower; for others "real" communication occurs only when two people reach perfect understanding. In a face-to-face context, the process of communication entails each person (1) emitting cues and (2) assigning meaning to her own and the other's cues. The communication process encompasses behavior and the meanings attached to it.

As an outsider looking in, it is difficult to specify when a participant in a transaction has assigned meaning to the behavior of another. But when you are in a dyad as a participant, you are usually aware of it. When you take cognizance of the other person and react, you have assigned meaning. For example, consider two college women "studying" together. When their eyes meet and woman A makes a face, woman B assigns meaning to it and she breaks out laughing. Clearly, each is assigning meaning to the other's behavior.

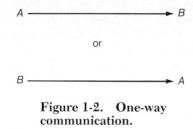

Figure 1-2.   One-way
communication.

One partner in a dyad does not have to "send a message" consciously to the other. If woman A had been daydreaming when woman B looked at her, communication still would have occurred. Whatever woman A does or does not do in the presence of woman B potentially has meaning for woman B. Put bluntly, when you are in the presence of another, *you cannot not communicate* [552]. Everything you do, or do not do, may have meaning for the other person. Take the case of two men having a coke together. One man says, "Hey, Charley, I've just been put on a retainer for a life insurance company and it will be a fantastic opportunity to pick up some much-needed money." Charley just sits there, thinking to himself what a greedy fellow his friend is. The first man tries again. "Charley, this is really a lucky break, isn't it?" And Charley just sits there. Is Charley communicating to the first man? He certainly is! He is shouting loud and clear, without making a sound, that he is not interested.

The assignment of meaning to someone's behavior is not an objective, fixed event. It happens within people's heads; it is a personal process. No matter what you do or say, you *do not* control the impressions others may have of you. You may react to your own behavior and see yourself as poised and competent. But other people may see you as aloof and distant. *Each* person assigns his or her *own* meaning to your behavior; it may or may not be similar to yours or to other people's assessments.

In a two-person context if only one person assigns meaning to the other's behavior, communication has occurred. For example, take two people, A and B. When A perceives B (even if B doesn't see him), communication has occurred. Likewise, when B sees A, communication has occurred. Figure 1-2 shows that communication occurs whenever one person assigns meaning to the communicative cues coming from the other. If A is watching B, but B does not see A, then the actions of A cannot influence B. Rambunctious grade school students use this principle as the guide for when to stick out their tongues at the teacher.

Figure 1-3.   Dyadic communication.

Aside from those teachers who have eyes in the back of their heads, if the teacher cannot perceive their behavior, they escape being sent to the principal's office.

In the preceding cases, we have cues being processed by only one participant at a time. As a result, we have communication occurring, but not *dyadic* communication. When both A and B are aware of the other and aware that the other is aware of him or her, the *dyad functions as a unit.* The two of them are then functioning in relationship to one another when the "actions of each person affect the other" [514], when there is the "perception of being perceived." This is shown by the model in Figure 1-3.

Not only is an awareness of when a relationship is created instructive, but it can be fun. For those people who want to watch you and *not* enter into a relationship, your recognition of them can be embarrassing. The next time you are stopped at a traffic light in your car and the person in the car next to you is staring at you, just turn, face her, give a friendly smile, and wave. You are saying, "Aha! I see you seeing me!" She quickly turns away and pretends that she was not seeing you. (But she saw you seeing her see you, and she is trapped! Your response to her created a relationship that she did not want to occur.)

Unfortunately, the other person doesn't always respond to the "I see you seeing me" tactic. I recently was sitting in a local coffee spot and noticed that a young man just off to my right side was staring at me. I shifted positions in my chair and turned slightly away from him to indicate that I did not want to make any contact. Three minutes later, I glanced back. He was still staring intently at me. So I turned my chair back and started returning his gaze every few seconds. He still stared intently. After playing this game for a few minutes, though it seemed like an hour, I couldn't stand it any more. I gave him a good strong glare and left for class. My awareness that he was still looking at me as I left only increased my sense of frustration. He made his awareness felt and since I didn't want to engage him in conversation, I felt uneasy. We were functioning in a unit that I did not want!

DYADIC COMMUNICATION IS TRANSACTIONAL

Dyadic communication requires (1) the existence of some cues, such as talking, gesturing, or lack of movement and (2) the assignment of meaning to the cues. Each of us processes cues in a different way. For example, look at Figure 1-4.

What do you see in the first figure? A new game, like LaCrosse? Two chicken tracks and a rock? A terribly skinny man reaching for a baseball? Two Montana trees on a clear winter day?

What about the second illustration? Is it a fledgling weightlifter who couldn't hold up a big rock? Two one-legged men diving into a swimming pool together? The newest form of UFO? Two apples placed one behind the other?

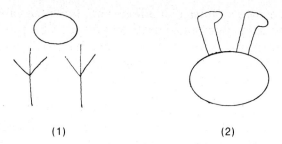

(1)   (2)

Figure 1-4. Perception objects. *From* Po: A
Device for Successful Thinking, *Edward de
Bono, New York: Simon & Schuster, 1972, p.
195. Copyright © 1972 by European Services
Ltd. Reprinted by permission of Aitken &
Stone, Limited.*

Whatever you do see, the meaning you have for it is a product of
(1) the cues you see and (2) your individual interpretation of them.
Each perception we make of our environment is a transactional process
between us and what we perceive. What we see "out there" is as much
a *function of us as it is of the object.*

The process of human communication has an added element that
renders it decidedly transactional. Our perceptions of people, as with
objects, are filtered through our interpretations. But in addition, our
perception of another and our subsequent behavior can actually
change the behavior of the person we see. Your own behavior affects
the behavior of others around you. If you are in a bad mood and are
walking around with a scowl on your face, such an approach will affect
someone you meet for the first time. If you are projecting hostility, the
other person is likely either to be very withdrawn or to give back some
of the hostility. Whatever the other person's reaction, you will form
an impression of his or her personality—which was partially produced
by your own behavior. When you perceive a mountain, you will have
your own meanings for it. When you communicate with a person, part
of what the person does will be a reaction to you.

Because each participant is affected in a dyadic transaction, dyadic
communication is *not* a linear, one-way event. You do not communicate *to* someone as if he or she were an inert blob of clay; you communicate *with* another. You do not originate communication; you
participate in it [519]. Some people erroneously think that
communication is a tool, something to be turned off and on at will, to
be used or not. Such a view is shortsighted. If, for example, you are a
salesperson and your task is to sell a product, it is easiest to see yourself
communicating to someone. You are giving the message and the client
is absorbing it. You are the "seller" and the client is the "sellee." This
point of view ignores two important points: (1) One cannot *not* communicate (*both* of you are attaching meaning to the transaction), and

(2) when you create a message it affects you, too. One cannot create a message without it affecting himself or herself. The process of your creating a message may affect you *more than* it does the person receiving it. Your participation in an encounter means that it will affect you, whether you are primarily creating or primarily deciphering the verbal message.

An experiment with behavioral modification vividly demonstrates the joint effects present in a communicative transaction [184]. In Visalia, California, students who had behavior problems were placed in a special class for "incorrigibles." In this particular instance, the students were given training in behavior modification. When they returned to their regular classes, unknown to the regular teachers, they engaged in a systematic attempt at behavior modification. The goal was simple—to encourage positive teacher behavior toward themselves. Some students had such long histories of receiving only negative teacher behavior that they could not identify positive behavior when it occurred. After training with videotapes and role playing, they had become skilled in identifying positive teacher behavior. The students systematically praised and encouraged the teachers whenever the teachers gave them a positive response. The results were fascinating. The teachers' behavior changed dramatically; they became more positive. And the student behavioral engineers began enjoying school and performing more successfully.

From a transactional point of view, the crucial question is who changed whom? The students thought the teachers changed and the teachers "tended to think of the projects as having changed the children rather than themselves" [184]. The transactional point of view stresses that to describe communication accurately, we need to think of people together rather than of each person separately [274]. Their relations are interpenetrative; *each person influences and is influenced by the other* [508].

Since the process of dyadic communication is transactional, some of the terminology applied to communication is inaccurate. For instance, numerous writers on communication refer to "senders" and "receivers." But in any dyadic transaction each participant is simultaneously sending and receiving. For instance, when you are engaged in conversation with someone, while you are creating cues (talking, sitting erect) you are attaching meaning to the cues sent by the other (she is looking at you and twirling a pencil). Likewise in that same frame of time, the other person is both sending and receiving cues. You are both participating, and in this book the term *participant* is used in place of *sender* and *receiver*.

A related point must also be made. A transactional event cannot be adequately characterized from the action–reaction perspective. A pool game, in which the cue ball is the action (stimulus) and the eight ball in the corner pocket is the reaction (response), can be adequately viewed from the action–reaction perspective. But human beings are not billiard balls. The analysis of a pool game is not sufficient to describe a communicative process. But obviously it may be useful for purposes of partial description to label some elements of a transaction as causes or stimuli and others as effects or responses. For example, if a young man is attractive, then a person meeting him may respond favorably to his attractiveness. We can label the attractiveness as the independent variable to see what behavioral effects it produces. If we do, we have specified an independent variable (attractiveness) and a dependent variable (the responses to attractiveness). Our distinction may be instructive because we can conclude that attractiveness produces particular effects. The important point to note, however, is that we could just as easily have specified attractiveness as a dependent variable. If we did, then we would be concerned with questions like, "What produces perceived attractiveness?" Regardless of what we select as the independent and dependent variables in a communication transaction, we have made an *artificial distinction.* In any communication situation, any variable can be seen as independent *or* dependent, contingent on your point of view. But whatever choice you make, the distinction is a function of you rather than of the communication event. Communication is more complex than the listing of independent and dependent variables would make it appear. There is a "loss of clear separation between independent and dependent variables" because, "Each subject's behavior is at the same time a response to a past behavior of the other and a stimulus to a future behavior of the other; each behavior is in part dependent variable and in part independent variable; in no clear sense is it properly either of them" [502].

In summary, the following statements best characterize the assumptions about dyadic communication:

1. Dyadic communication is transactional.
2. Each participant simultaneously creates and deciphers communication cues.
3. Each participant affects and is affected by the other.
4. In a communicative transaction, any action can be seen as cause or effect, contingent on your point of view.
5. When viewing dyadic communication, an appropriate unit of analysis is the series of patterned relations between two people—the relationship itself.

From the transactional perspective, the simplicity of a dyadic relationship disappears, and communicative transactions are seen as in-process, circular, and unrepeatable. This book will illustrate the transactional, relationship-bound nature of the dyadic communication process. °

°For more detailed treatments of the transactional point of view see [126, 386, 463, 508].

CHARACTERISTICS OF DYADS

Imagine yourself sitting alone in the library or at home and a friend approaches. Whether you are reading, daydreaming, or simply gazing at the sky, a reorientation is necessary with the arrival of your friend. You have to take account of the other person's presence; there is a change "away from the comfort and safety of self-preoccupation and toward a more inclusive frame of reference that embraces the experiential field of another person" [344]. The presence of the other person constitutes another, entirely different social situation. The ensuing discussion, therefore, is qualitatively different from your intrapersonal communication. Both you and your friend have altered your behaviors because of each other's presence. As Von Wiese [513] noted, "the pair always behaves otherwise than either member would if alone. . . ." A distinctive communication system has been set into motion, a dyadic system. Each subject's behavior is at the same time a response to a past behavior of the other and a stimulus to a future behavior of the other; each behavior is partly dependent variable and partly independent variable; in no clear sense is it properly either of them [502].

Although it is tempting for us to ignore the joint influences in dyadic encounters, it is clear that the participants co-determine their relationship. For example, even in ordinary conversations, what you send forth (questions or statements) has a direct influence on the other's response [475]. Similarly, parents and babies influence each other's communication [142, 200]. In one review of over 200 studies, Capella noted that there is strong evidence of "interspeaker influence" across many relationships and contexts [90, 91]. As Kelley summarizes, "events associated with one person are causally connected to those associated with the other person" [248].

Of all forms of communicative exchange, dyadic communication is the most prevalent. Wheeler and Nezlek [528], for example, had college students record who they talked with for a period of two weeks. Almost half of their total interactions were in a one-on-one situation. Similarly, observations of people in playgrounds, train depots, shopping malls, and other settings have confirmed that most groupings of people are dyadic [238]. Paul Fischer [149], after a study of college student communication, concluded that the "great bulk of human interaction is dyadic in nature." If you keep a diary of the number of communicative contacts you have with others, you should not be surprised to disover that you have more dyadic contacts, and of longer duration, than any other single type of exchange. Although participation in small groups, public gatherings, and mass-media arenas is certainly frequent, it is usually less common than dyadic transactions. In fact, as we will see, dyadic pairings are so pervasive that small groups and larger gatherings contain multiple dyadic relationships.

Not only are dyadic relationships most prevalent, but our earliest human relationships are dyadic. In early childhood, from the ages of two to five years, a person has the ability to engage in communication with only one person at a time. It is not until later childhood, from six to twelve years, that one can engage in communication with several persons at a time [421]. Chronologically speaking, dyadic communication is the primary form of social exchange. As noted earlier, even after we reach maturity dyadic relationships are so primary that very few individuals live apart from dyadic relationships. In fact, husband–wife, friend–friend, and other social pairs are so prominent that one sociologist concludes that the "human pair is the structure upon which a great many social processes are based, and may be regarded, metaphorically speaking, as the cell-unit in the social structure," [513]. Dyadic groupings can be characterized as offering four aspects—uniqueness, allowance for intimacy, completeness, and operation as a fundamental unit.

Each Dyad Is Unique

The functions that one person serves for you will be somewhat different from those served by another. In one employment context your employer will only provide you with a paycheck, yet in another the employer may serve as a friend as well. Similarly, one counselor may serve a variety of functions for you, whereas another meets a more limited range of needs.

Each dyadic relationship develops its own *culture*, a system of rules and rituals unique to it. Just as a nation has a culture, each relationship develops its own particular dynamics. I remember one of my most distinctive dyads, which occurred when I was in the eighth grade. Jack and I, both loudmouths, sat next to each other in all our classes. In one class we would giggle no matter what the teacher did. The more inappropriate it was to laugh, the more uncontrollable the urge to giggle. Finally the teacher, being of rather keen insight, got the best of us. He told me that if Jack giggled or spoke out of turn in class, I could hit Jack on the arm. Jack was given the same instruction. We both adopted the suggestion and there we sat for the rest of the year—perfect gentlemen with striking arms poised. Each dyad develops its own rule of behavior, whether they are adopted from the outside or generated internally. These norms for behavior may often run counter to social norms. In fact, many people form friendships because the standards they adopt as a pair are unconventional or improper [147]. The unique nature of dyadic transactions makes it possible to develop and maintain the way of life that one chooses.

Each relationship we have is unique because we invest different parts of ourselves in it. To illustrate how we adjust to the presence of others, imagine that you are a college student living with someone of the opposite sex. Even the words you use to represent that pairing are different in each of your dyadic situations. To a close friend you may discuss your living arrangement by speaking of your "roommate." To a passing acquaintance you may speak of your "boyfriend" or "girlfriend." To your father you may speak of your "friend." Even the ways we describe dyadic events change as the context changes. Can you imagine, for example, using the same tone of voice and words to express the same idea to a friend, your parents, and your favored loved one? What is appropriate in one case is inappropriate in another. What is a good response from you in one situation would be considered a rebuff in the next. And as everyone who is in love knows, there has never been a relationship quite like theirs [315]. All our dyadic pairings are unique, and the more intimate the relationship, the more unique the dyad. As each person gives more of himself or herself, more uniqueness is created. Every intimate relationship with a romantic partner or close friend is more unique than every nonintimate relationship with a grocery clerk.

Dyads Allow for Intimacy

It is within the one-to-one situation that the most personal aspects of each participant can be presented. The informality of the dyadic context allows the uniqueness of each person more expression than does any other communication context. As a result, intimate behavior that is appropriate within a dyadic context is often disapproved of in public settings. Watch the reactions of people who encounter a romantic pair embracing and kissing while on a heavily traveled public sidewalk. Some onlookers laugh and others are offended, but both reactions arise from dyadic intimacies being displayed in public.

Dyadic intimacy has its consequences. The intimacy brings with it the potential for ecstasy or agony. In all types of pairs—love, friendship, family, or common interest—treating the other with respect and warmth is a common occurrence. A close friend, with a touch on our shoulder, can "break down isolation" and change our "condition of solitariness for one of personal intimacy" [513]. In the dyadic transaction, each person can assimilate much of the other's personality and meet needs. It is no coincidence that relationships formed for the purpose of helping someone are dyadic in nature. Institutionalized programs such as Big Brother and Crisis Center set up pairs for the purpose of helping. Other dyadic helping situations are priest–confessor, counselor–client, father–son, mother–daughter, and teacher–student, to name only a few. In all these cases, the pairing can provide for personableness and warmth that would not occur so effectively in other groupings.

A pair can also plunge to the depths of conflict and unfulfillment. A casual visit to married friends who are "on the outs" can make a miserable evening for anyone. When a dyadic relationship is disintegrating and the participants are in open conflict, the intimacy of the dyad becomes ugly. Spoken endearments give way to blows below the belt. Because the participants know each other well, they know where to strike in anger. The classic confrontations in our society—son and father, husband and wife, employer and employee, lover and lover, child and child—are dyadic. The close bond of the pair can work against them, and the intimacy and personableness of their transactions makes for serious conflict. Dyadic transactions, then, because of their intimacy, have the potential to be the most and least pleasant of situations. You may not always "hurt the one you love," but you have more ability to harm that person than someone with whom you are not on personal terms. Having a significant effect on the other, whether it be pain or pleasure, comes about through the intricate web that dyadic communication spins.

Dyads Are Complete Units

Dyadic groupings can bring with them a sense of completeness. This characteristic of dyads is reflected in two ways: (1) A dyad often functions as a completed unit, and (2) a dyad cannot be subdivided. Once you and another person have formed a pair, a unique and complete social system results. People both inside and outside particular pairs recognize that the pair can be addressed as a complete unit. Marital pairs, for example, often present a united front to the world—if you want to deal with one member, you have to deal with them both. Such alliances, even if they are temporarily frustrating to outsiders, are very functional. One of the advantages of dyadic relationships is that the strength of both members is pooled; they form an intact unit.

A couple, however, may resent being treated as a single, intact unit rather than as two separate individuals. Some married couples try to remind others that they are separate individuals by keeping different last names and refraining from using the terms *my wife* and *my husband.* Instead, one says, "I'd like you to meet Lynnette. She is an investment counselor, and the woman to whom I am married." And the other repays the courtesy by a similar choice of words.

Seeing two people as an intact unit is a shorthand way to deal with them—a way that has both advantages and disadvantages. In fact, we are so accustomed to reacting to a pair as a pair that totally individualistic behavior of pair members causes us to wonder. Take, for example, a married "couple" that rarely acts as a pair. Each person goes his and her own way; rarely, if ever, is a united front presented. Many people, in reacting to such married arrangements, typically ask, "Why are they married? They certainly do not act in any way committed to each other." Obviously the marriage meets certain needs or it would not continue. But in any event, we expect dyads to act at times as units because dyads typically do.

When a pair acts as an intact social unit, the members can collectively resist outside social pressure. The chosen living styles of a woman and a man can, if the pair chooses, go against accepted standards. If they as a pair support each other and treat the unit as inviolate, then it will probably be so. On the other hand, if a partner does not actively work to support the pair, severe strains will develop. Take the case of two close friends. If one member of the pair seizes every opportunity to criticize the other, to talk "behind his back," such behavior is seen as destructive. If a pair is to remain strong, the members must support each other. Sometimes the mutual support may be a false front. A pair may appear close-knit to others outside it, even though they are not really close. Such cases of "shoulder to shoulder when attacked" and yet "civil war when the outer danger passes by" [513] demonstrate the utility that dyadic bonds have. Dyads are intact units; they can resist social pressure and be a separate social system apart from all others.

Dyads also have a completeness about them because they cannot be subdivided. Each person is confronted only by the other. If you are member of a pair and are frustrated by the other's behavior, you have limited options. You can deal with it yourself, forsake the relationship and destroy the dyad, or introduce new members. Basically, however, you really have only two choices. You can deal with it yourself or change the dyad. If you introduce a third party, you have dramatically altered the fundamental pair—you have made it a triad and changed the entire system. An important feature of a dyad, therefore, is that if it is to remain intact you *cannot appeal to majority opinion.* There are only two of you and you cannot appeal to others to put pressure on your partner, as is possible in a small group. Importantly, each person "possesses power to influence the decision by withdrawal or veto" [18]. There are only two of you, and with the withdrawal of one from the relationship, the pair will cease to exist. In all other forms of social intercourse, the loss of a member will not necessarily mean its destruction, although it will undoubtedly change the system. Even an important position such as president of the United States is easily filled once it is vacated. Larger organizations have a collective identity that keeps them going after an individual is lost. Granted, the character and style of the organization will change with the new replacements, but its life will continue. In a sense, it is immortal. Not so with the dyad. It has no "super-individual structure" to maintain it after one participant leaves [92, 513, 548].

In a dyad, the loss of one is the loss of all. The marked degree of interdependence each member of a dyad has on the other is often only fully realized with a sudden loss. The unexpected death of a loved one can be a shattering experience. The other person is irreplaceable; no other partner can be to you what this one was. As Von Wiese [513] notes, "Occasionally, the survivor and his intimates realize for the first time how far-reaching the effect of the deceased partner upon their previous behavior had been." Unlike a corporation or other large group that finds a replacement for the lost person, the dyad is dead. The surviving member has to initiate a totally new system, complete with new behaviors and adjustments. In sum, each individual is vital to the dyad; it cannot be subdivided.

Dyads Are Fundamental

The dyad is the building block of other communication contexts. Within small groups of people, each individual engages in a global relationship to others and specific dyadic relationships [498]. Our shifting dyadic relationships allow us to select manageable sets of relationships within a complex social structure. In large, complex organizations such as the military, there is a recognition of the importance of dyadic components. The buddy system flourishes within the confines of a larger grouping. But as fundamental as the dyad is, it also has some characteristics that make it distinct from groups that have more than two members. These features can be highlighted best by specifically comparing dyads with small groups.

A collection of three or more individuals constitutes a small group. And although the dyad is obviously the "scheme, germ, and material" of small groups [548], it is *qualitatively different* from them. We have already noted the intimacy characteristic of dyads. Compared with small groups, therefore, dyads provide each participant with more involvement, more satisfaction, and more participation [379].

In addition, when a group numbers three or more, the basic properties of all larger groups begin to emerge. Leadership functions become more identifiable, communication networks are established, and coalitions or subsystems are formed [379]. And importantly, majority opinion can be appealed to as a tactic to change another participant's point of view. The addition of new members to a face-to-face transaction dramatically changes the nature of the system.

Let's examine a bit more closely some of the consequences of adding more people to a social setting. To begin with, as the number of people increases arithmetically, the number of possible relationships

Size of group	Potential relationships
2	1
3	6
4	25
5	90
6	301
7	966

Figure 1-5. Potential relationships within groups.°

°The formula to determine the number of potential relationships as a consequence of group size:

$$PR = \frac{3^N - 2^{N+1} + 1}{2},$$

where PR is the number of potential relationships and N is the number of persons in the group.

increases geometrically. With three people A, B, and C, there are six possible relationships between individuals and subgroups (A–B, A–C, B–C, AB–C, AC–B, and BC–A). Hare [197] has conveniently figured out the potential relationships in groups from two to seven (see Figure 1-5).

It is no wonder, then, that as the number of people increases, the situation becomes considerably more complicated than any relationship between two individuals [277]. Each individual has more relationships to maintain in a given amount of time. And it is not surprising when you look closely at Figure 1-5 that many neurotics and psychotics are able to maintain one-to-one situations but "are unable to consider multiple relationships simultaneously" [425]. Such an array of possibilities is difficult enough for a "well-adjusted" person to comprehend.

The increase in the number of potential relationships is handled in a typical manner by most groups. Since it is unlikely that all the members can "share the same mood or enter into synchronized sets" [502], two things usually happen. First, as noted earlier, leadership emerges because it can reduce the psychologically complicated relationships. Group transactions can be reduced to a series of pair relationships of each member with the leader [194], thereby simplifying the communication process. Second, a group typically gains stability by breaking into smaller groups, usually of even-numbered sizes [149].

As the group size increases, the degree of intimacy decreases. The dependency of the group on each individual decreases; a member or two is easily replaced. And the consequences of alienating a single member become less severe [463]. While each member must fit into a more elaborate structure, he or she gains psychological freedom and may even "withdraw from the fray without loss of face" [463].

Although the dynamics of social groupings change as the number of people increases, the fundamental element within the larger group is the dyad. In fact, the basic dyadic bond sets forces into motion that affect groups of three, four, and more. These dynamics are so important that the next section examines in detail the forces at play within larger groupings.

THE TRIAD: A DYAD PLUS ONE

The distinctive characteristics of dyadic transactions have been sketched by comparing two-person exchanges with those in small groups. The smallest of small groups, the triad, will now come under intense scrutiny as a backdrop for our continued analysis of the nature of dyadic transactions. It will soon be apparent that one of the most prominent features of triads is the presence of dyadic transactions.

Transactions in Triads

A triad is a social system composed of three people transacting face to face. On the surface it would appear that a triad functions as a complete entity—each person transacting with each other one. We all know of triads that exist on a permanent basis. For example, in families where there are two parents and one child, a triad exists. Similarly, many work groups are composed of three people who gather together to perform a given task. The three people are obviously intertwined.

A distinction must be made at this point between (1) the number of people defined as part of a group and (2) the actual communication behavior that transpires in the group. Whenever there are two people together, the "ability to communicate with one person requires a highly idiosyncratic, well tuned, and synchronized communication system" [6]. Similarly, the presence of a third person puts even more demands on the communication abilities of the participants. Try this exercise to illustrate to yourself the difficulties of fully communicating to more than one person at a time. Sit in the middle of two friends. Have the first person talk to you in a regular manner as if the two of you were all alone in the room. She will ask questions, probe your answers for more detail, and carry on a normal conversation such as two people would have at a kitchen table. Instruct the second friend to engage you in conversation, too, as if he were the only person in the room with you. As the two of them begin talking at once, you will probably find yourself attempting to tune in at a superficial level to each one. While catching a phrase in your left ear in order to provide some answer to her question, you are looking at him and finishing your short answer. After trying this for a couple of minutes, ask your friends how it felt to attempt to get your attention as a dyadic partner when you were distracted by another. It is not very satisfying for the two of them and is frustrating for you. And if you do not try to communicate simultaneously with both of them, you put one of them "on hold" while relating to the other.

This example makes an important point. In a dyad, the two members can fully focus on one another, exchange freely, and become finely tuned. A triad, however, in which the "power and influence of all three of the members are equal, is not normal, but on the contrary is extraordinarily rare" [513]. When a group of three comes together, the communication relationships evolve so that it is normal for one member to be isolated, suppressed, or excluded from complete participation. A primary dyad plus the third person usually evolves. One of the persons, over time, gets closed off so that the other two persons can form a dyadic bond, complete with all of its advantages. Friends, for example, close off others in some respects; otherwise their relationship cannot become special in its own right. "If friends invite all others into their private morality, then they lose the very special covenant they have authored" [488]. Look at your own relationships for a moment. Do you have two friends who are also themselves good friends? Do the three of you enjoy doing things as a threesome? If two of you are together, does the sudden appearance of the third make the friendship really blossom, or does it cause an uneasy feeling in you? Probably the latter case is true.

From a functional standpoint (looking at the relationships) a triad is usually composed of a primary dyad plus one. There is no triadic relationship that is so stable and complete that "each individual may not, under certain circumstances, be regarded by the other two as an intruder . . ." [461]. Further, it is rare and difficult for three people to come into a "really united state of feeling, which, however, may occur with relative ease between two" [461]. Even our English language makes it difficult to deal with a triadic relationship. We speak and write in first, second, and third person: I am; you are; he is. But this is not the case in face-to-face communication.

> I speak to you, and you speak to me, but even by our language, he is sep-
> arated from us. You and I, if combined, become we. The only way a third
> person can become one of us is to cease to be a third person; that is, he
> must join us (first person plural), or he must become one of you (second
> person plural). By this process, any three people in a persistent situation
> must form, not a triad, but a dyad of me and you (plural) or you (singlular)
> and us [109].

The most comprehensive treatment of the nature of triads is by Caplow [92]. His position is that the "most significant property of the triad is its tendency to divide a coalition of two members against the third." When a primary dyad forms within the framework of three people, it is not necessarily permanent, however. A father, mother, and child, for example, probably will experience shifting alliances. Father and mother may unite against the child to discipline him or her, and the next moment mother and child may argue together for a trip to the forest. Or father and child may join forces in order to go fishing together. The important point is this: When three people are in a face-to-face transaction, the transaction *at any point in time* is composed of a primary dyad plus one.

A Triad Dissected

Let's take a look at what relationships can be formed within a triad. The three individuals will be labeled *A*, *B*, and *C*. Caplow [92] states that every triad has three relationships: *A–B*, *B–C*, and *A–C* (see Figure 1-6).

You will recall that earlier, however, the small group of three people was said to have *six* relationships [194]. Caplow is referring to only

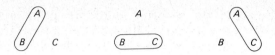

Figure 1-6. Dyads within a triad.

the basic dyadic bonds. In a triad, there are combinations of relationships such that a dyadic pair can relate to the third person. Figure 1-7 shows the range of possible relationships in a triad.

In a triad there are actually seven possible relationships, but the seventh relationship, in which all three members are equally joined, is so scarce and unusual that any of us would be hard pressed to supply an example of one. A related point needs to be made. Diagrams 4, 5, and 6 in Figure 1-7 show that a triad functionally may consist of *two dyads.* In diagram 4, for example, person *C* is trying to communicate with *A* and *B*. If *A* and *B* have formed into a strong coalition, then *C* has to treat them as a *single unit. A–B* as a unit makes joint decisions and *C* has to relate to them as if they were a single person who has gained extra strength. The *A–B* bond is one dyad and the *AB–C* relationship is the second.

The triad has a tendency to resolve itself into the basic form of a dyad plus one. Because of this tendency, *a triad is less stable than a dyad* [499]. There is an innate tendency toward discord.

Enter the Third Party

The presence of a third person always has an effect on an existing dyad. Whether the dyad is permanent or transitory, the presence of a third person brings *change* [513]. That third person alters the existing "habits in perception, evaluation, and transmission" [421]. We have all experienced the intrusion of a third party into dyads that are transitory. Have you ever been with a close friend having coffee and engrossed in a conversation when a third person approaches? You are stuck. You can tell the third person, "Beat it, I don't want you destroying our dyad!" or do as most of us and say, "Oh, no, you aren't disturbing us. Pull up a chair." There you are, in the middle of a conversation, and you are suddenly faced with a choice. You can ignore the third person, thereby making her feel uncomfortable, or you can stop

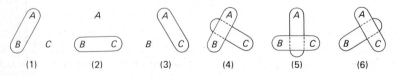

Figure 1-7. All possible relations in a triad.

the conversation and try to bring the third party up-to-date and include her in the conversation. Either choice poses difficulties. One way of coping with the situation would be to do what a friend of mine did. Bob was talking with Cinda when Jeanne joined them. He stopped his conversation right in the middle of a sentence and changed topics as a way to adjust to Jeanne's presence. When she left in a few minutes, he turned to Cinda and completed his unfinished sentence, their conversation only temporarily interrupted. It is an ingenious way to deal with an intrusion, but few of us develop such an ability.

When third parties enter existing dyads, whether they are transitory or permanent dyads, they "exert pressures that tend to develop, arrest, maintain, and dissolve . . . the relationships" [274]. One of two things happen: Either the existing dyad is *strengthened* or it is *weakened* (and maybe destroyed).

One for Two: Strengthening the Dyad
The presence of a third party can often be the impetus needed for cementing a dyadic bond. When marital couples seek the assistance of a marriage counselor, they are trying to find a third party who can intervene and strengthen their marriage. The presence of the third person provides enough change in the original dyad to allow the partners to reform on a different basis. For example, if the counselor intervenes into a marital dyad in order to provide new ground rules for how the couple is to conduct its conflicts, then the imposition of the new rules may provide for a healthier relationship when the couple is alone. One word of caution is in order, however. If the therapist or counselor is not aware of the tendency of a triad to dissolve into a dyad plus one, he or she can create other problems due to the intervention. Say, for instance, that persons A and B go into therapy with person C. For a period of time, the therapist, C, can side with partner A to hear his complaints about B's behavior. But, as Haley [193] warns, a "good therapist will avoid consistently being in a coalition." In fact, the tendency for coalitions to form is so great that Haley further cautions therapists that a "comment by the therapist is not merely a comment, but also a coalition with one spouse in relation to the other or with the unit against a larger group" [193]. Even in cases where a third party is being sought in order to strengthen an existing dyad, the pressures toward dissolution of the triad into a dyad plus one are ever present.

Often couples have children in the hopes of strengthening their dyadic bond. On the surface, it may appear that if a dyad adds another to their unit it will automatically create discord between the parents. But the influence of children on a marital relationship is not all negative. Sometimes the introduction of a child can have more beneficial than harmful effects on the married couple's permanence as a couple. For even if the presence of the child changes the daily dyadic exchanges, the child might strengthen the marriage by providing a

When a third person joins a dyad, creating a triad, the relationship between the people in the existing dyad is altered.

common goal for the parents. In addition, the joy of helping a young child develop can add to the happiness of the original dyad. In these days of a rapidly climbing divorce rate, and with a large proportion of children being raised by one natural parent and one stepparent, or by other adults, the entire question of how the presence of a third (or more) person affects a dyadic bond is a central one [503]. And, as noted, the presence of the third person can provide other bases for the original bond to be strengthened. A child can, in some cases, provide a bridge over the troubled marital waters.

An original dyad, such as two friends, can be strengthened when a third person serves as a "common object of opposition" for the dyad [336]. Whether it is the landlord trying to promote marital disharmony or a third "mutual friend" always getting in the way of two good friends, the original dyadic bonds may be strengthened by the intrusion of the third person. Many human relationships are formed and strengthened because of a mutual dislike for a third party. Many a student has found a new friend because of a mutual dislike for the professor in a required class. The effect of such rejection of a third person is to make the dyadic bond stronger, becoming the justification for it. If *A* and *B* reject *C* and feel closer because of it, then they can easily conclude that because they feel close to each other, they should not let *C* into their inner circle.

Two Against One: Fighting It Out

The other major effect of the presence of a third person is the destruction, or attempted destruction, of the existing dyad. The third party often tries to "divide and conquer" the dyad so he or she can have a partner. The third person attempts to replace one of the original members. This type of situation has two main variants: "Either two parties are hostile toward one another and therefore compete for the favor of a third element; or they compete for the favor of a third element and therefore are hostile toward one another" [548]. Whatever the chain of events, if the original dyad is disrupted, the third person finds a partner and a new pair is formed.

Most of us have participated in triadic situations when the presence of the third person causes disruption. For example, have you ever had a younger brother join you when you were having a romantic conversation with a boyfriend or girlfriend? Or have you ever tried to have a meaningful talk with a boyfriend or girlfriend with your mother in the room? Such feelings of discomfort are not limited to romantic pairs. Richard and Bob were close friends but Bob had another very close friend, Wes. Once when Richard was upset over something about Bob, he remarked, "I don't like the way Bob acts when he is with Wes." In other words, Richard did not care for the Bob–Wes dyad because it meant that Richard was the third person, the outsider.

Two close friends commonly become disrupted when one of them falls in love with a third person. Judy and her roommate, Sue, were very close friends; they went almost everywhere together. Then, during their senior year at college, after rooming together for three years, Sue entered into a romantic relationship that was very important to her. She and Brad just could not see enough of each other. Rather rapidly, Sue began spending more time with Brad than she did with Judy, and Sue and Brad began talking about marriage. One night when Sue came home after an evening with Brad, Judy unleashed a torrent of anger at her. She screamed, "You are such a slob. You leave all your dirty clothes around and expect me to pick them up. If you can't do your fair share here, I don't want to live with you anymore." Translated into relationship terms, the outburst can be seen as saying, "Why have I been replaced by Brad? I thought *we* were the primary dyad."

One of the most intriguing cases of the entrance of a third person into a coalition occurred with Mike and Sarah. They were married and Sarah formed a close friendship with another woman, Toni. After about a year's time, it appeared that the Sarah–Toni friendship was a love affair. Mike, who not too surprisingly was disliked by Toni (since he was competing for her romantic partner), soon became aware of the intensity of the Sarah–Toni relationship. A showdown ensued, and Sarah and Mike moved from town and began to work on rebuilding their dyadic bond. The thing I found fascinating is that within one year after moving away they had a baby. They replaced the disruptive third person, Toni, with a third person whom they were both equally invested in.

One of the truisms about the entrance of a third person is that it will affect the dyadic bond, even if that bond is not totally destroyed. The common example of a married person having an outside relationship is a prime point. The third person causes some realignment of the bonds of the person he or she is involved with. Often the person who gets involved has some dissatisfactions with the marriage. And as the dissatisfactions continue slowly to increase, that person is more likely to seek an outside relationship involving sex [140] With the outside involvement, of course, comes the increasing possibility that the original bond will be weakened further. When these triadic situations come to light, there is a period of difficult decision making for the partners. Often the original partners can reform their bond with new commitments and realignment of priorities. But whether they reform or dissolve, the third preson has had a significant impact on the original dyadic bond.

When a romantic dyad such as a married couple has suffered from a splitting of loyalties and affection, there must be some effort made to reestablish the ties if the relationship is to grow. Haley [193] notes that sometimes a couple wants to live apart while "working on their marriage." In his experience, therapeutic help for people who prefer this mode for reestablishing their ties is usually a waste of time. The reasons are simple. The dyadic ties, while strong and ever present, are also fragile. When the dyadic bond has been stretched too thin, it cannot return to its original shape.

To pretend that the introduction of a third party will not affect an existing dyadic relationship is sometimes to court disaster. A husband and wife who are very close, enjoy hiking together, and do other things on the spur of the moment are kidding themselves if they think having a child will not affect their relationship. The child may cause the father to compete for the mother's affection (or vice versa), thereby introducing an entirely new dimension into the relationship. When the child gets older it is distinctly possible that one parent will form a more or less permanent bond with the child, excluding the previous partner. To pretend that the arrival of a baby will not affect the couple's relationship is to ignore the reality of all triads. At a given point in time, *someone* is the excluded third party.

In societies where polygamous marriages are the rule, one might expect these principles of triadic dissolution into a dyad plus one not to hold true. It appears on the surface that the husband can deal successfully with more than one wife at a time. Even in cases where there are multiple wives, however, the "co-wives are set up in separate establishments, which enables them to enjoy a relative autonomy with respect to one another, and to their husbands" [101]. It becomes clear that the successive dyadic coalitions are what keep the marriages functioning, rather than "one big, happy family." The separation of the wives even carries over to the raising of children. They are either raised independently of each other, under the supervision of the senior co-wife, or raised jointly, with a system of rotation [101]. Notice that they are not all lumped together with more than one wife at a time. Dyadic coalitions occur within most groupings of three, or even more, people.

DYADIC COALITIONS

Dyadic coalitions lie at the heart of triadic groups. In any group of three, when we coalesce with another and create a close bond, the coalition influences the entire system. Triangles, such as love triangles, are well known for the difficulties they spawn. For example, Craig is an outdoors person who loves to ski with his friend Steve. This year he and Amy were romantically involved and decided to spend Christmas break skiing in Glacier Park. Craig, not wanting to drift away from his friend Steve, invited him to go too. The three of them roomed together and spent the entire vacation skiing—and having difficulties. Triangles such as this cause so many complex situations that they need to be examined in a bit more detail.

Triangles and Tangles

Within larger systems, such as organizations and families, triadic relationships "obscure and complicate things" [433]. Triangles are important because a family or organizational operation depends on how triadic dynamics are handled [432, 433]. When triangles become rigid or toxic, the negative effects are felt throughout the entire system. One prominent example is the Rescue Triangle (see Figure 1-8).

The Rescue Triangle [477] is composed of three people, bound together in a system that is not healthy for any of them. There is the Persecuter, who picks on the victim. The Persecuter might be an older brother, or sister, who constantly tries to embarrass, make fun of, or physically bully the smaller or younger child. The Rescuer, sometimes

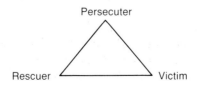

Figure 1-8.   Rescue triangle.

the mother, tries to protect the "Victim" and continually interferes in the relationship between the Persecuter and Victim. The Victim, of course, looks innocent and complains about being powerless and at the mercy of the Persecuter. The three people are stuck in their roles. The Persecuter receives negative attention from the Rescuer (which of course is better than no attention at all!), the Victim continues to need the intervention of the Rescuer, and the Rescuer feels trapped into the continual bickering and conflict. Of course, each person contributes to the ongoing rounds, and the pattern continues only because each person refuses to change his or her part in it. In this example the triangle occurs in a family where the younger daughter is the "Victim" being "picked on" by the older brother. One alteration will stop the recurring cycles of Persecuter–Victim–Rescuer responses—the daughter can learn and use karate! Of course, the Victim is not powerless and often provokes attack so that (in this case) she can form a coalition with mom. The Victim and Rescuer also come to rely on the Persecuter. If he didn't cause difficulties, maybe the mother and daughter would not be able to relate to one another.

Triangles such as the Rescue Triangle are destructive when they become rigidly repeated within a system [433, 337]. As Fogarty says, "when triangles are used by the family to deal with a problem, symptoms show up all over the place" [156]. For example, if the system is composed of two parents and a child, the victim may become one of the parents, with the other parent forming an iron-clad coalition with the child. Usually, when this happens, the parental coalition is further weakened, putting even more stress on the already troubled family system. Similarly, one can be involved in a secret triangle that contributes to situations that are difficult to understand. Carla was in a romantic relationship with Curtis and couldn't understand why he was so "flakey." Every time things would go well for awhile and the two of them would get close, Curtis would pick a fight. Once they had drifted apart for a time, he would search her out to get close and spend more time together. After a couple of months of this, Carla discovered, quite by accident, that Curtis had another romantic involvement. She was caught in the throes of a triangle without knowing it.

Predicting the Coalitions

The dyad that forms within a triad does so for specific reasons. When a person pairs up with another, it is clear case of choice because, theoretically, each person has two partners from which to pick. A dyadic coalition arises in a triad so that paired members can affect the outcomes. Two children gang up against a third precisely because they can, by joining together, increase their influence over the third. A husband and wife pair up so as to better discipline their child (and the child tries to pair up with one parent to avoid discipline). A close dyadic friendship, regardless of whether it forms within a triad or not, serves the same function as a coalition in a triad. We know that a friend will come to our aid, and we will to hers. In effect, we form a coalition so that power resources of the friendly pair can be mobilized against an external threat [502]. A dyad can be viewed as a coalition formed for the purpose of maximizing desired outcomes.

Within a traid, what types of coalitions will form? One study demonstrated that the two more active members form the pair, and the isolated individual is the one who is least active [336]. Within families where sibling rivalry is present, the typical coalitions involve siblings of the same sex and children closest in age [92]. Overall, peers often select each other on the basis of likeness; those who are the most alike form pairs [92]. In purely economic terms, a person wishing to maximize his financial gain is often confronted with a choice. He can choose a less effective coalition in which he is powerful or a powerful coalition in which he is less effective [502]. One person expressed her choice this way: "I'd rather have ten percent of a million dollars than one hundred percent of ten dollars."

Predicting coalition formation is still far from an exact science. The most comprehensive treatments of available research do not set forth definitive conclusions. Some experimental work on dyadic formation is worth examining, however. In laboratory simulations, persons with excessively high or excessively low power (assigned weights) do not form coalitions. The coalitions that are formed are usually on the basis of the "cheapest winning coalition," where the person's share of the payoff is proportional to her contribution to the success of the coalition [163]. The situation is analogous to two business partners who have equal time and ability to contribute to the business but have unequal amounts of money to invest in it. In such cases the profits are usually divided in proportion to each contribution. In both experimental situations and real life the "equity norm" operates—a desire to form coalitions so that each gets a fair and equitable share [81].

Considerable experimental work is now being done in an attempt to understand further why people pick the coalitions that they do. Most of these approaches stress the players' orientations to the payoffs of the game [363, 364]. Many factors relevant to coalition formation in the real world, however, cannot be accounted for in an experimental study that observes people competing for points. First of all, in real life the "payoffs" we receive are rarely specified. When you gang up with your sister against your younger brother, no one is standing there saying that "that coalition is worth ten points." Furthermore, if you choose to unite with your sister against your brother, the act of bonding means that you are losing something from not uniting with the younger brother. In real life, one of the important considerations is what we lost by not joining with the unchosen partner. And a host of other factors operates. Have you formed coalitions with the person in the past? What success did you have? If you form a coalition, will the person try to freeze you into a permanent coalition? Will being in this particular coalition demand too much from you in terms of time and energy? At the present time, very little is known about coalition formation in natural settings [109, 433, 337]. It is to be hoped that this extremely important topic will be widely investigated with a focus on the communication behaviors that facilitate the formation, maintenance, and destruction of dyadic coalitions in triads.

Dyadic coalitions in triads are *not necessarily permanent.* Toxic or rigid triangles are instances of where the coalitions are fixed and enduring. For example, if a dyad is permanently formed against a third person in a family, the prolonged rejection of the third person can be devastating. However, such repetitive coalitions are not always the case. As Hare [194] says, "Members tend to switch coalitions from one disagreement to another simply to maintain solidarity and avoid the permanent exclusion of one member." Similarly, most of us can cite instances of dyads we enter into and exit from periodically. One point seems clear, however. A triad functions with a coalition, but it cannot function with two coalitions at the same time [92]. A husband–wife–wife's mother coalition is a case in point—when all three people are transacting, the wife cannot be a partner with both husband and mother at the same time.

Dyads always form within triads. In fact, because the dyad is the basic unit of social exchange, it is the fundamental building block upon which triadic relationships form.

Coalitions in Larger Groups

When coalitions form within a triad, they must be dyadic in nature. If one member is excluded, that leaves only the other to be your partner. In larger groupings, however, dyadic coalitions are supplemented with the possibility of larger subgroupings. In the tetrad, a group of four, two distinct features alter the shape of the dyadic coalitions that are formed. To begin with, it is within this group size that the first possibility for *countercoalitions* arises. If person A lines up with person B, that leaves C and D to form their own coalition. The excluded third party has someone available for a different coalition. Take the case of Sharon and Owen. They had three children who continually rotated their coalitions, working all the while to make the outside child miserable. The three children continually squabbled. Sharon reported that she and Owen had a fourth child so that the excluded third child, whoever it was at a given time, could have a partner. In this case, it happened to be a good decision. Whenever any two of the children would form a temporary coalition, the other two would also do so, thereby partially equalizing the power. Countercoalitions mitigate many of the adverse effects of the original dyadic coalitions. That is why the husband or wife who is not involved in an outside relationship while the other is, quite often subsequently seeks a relationship of his or her own. It tends to counterbalance the lopsided triad.

At the level of the tetrad (four people), one other development occurs. Here the coalition size first becomes an issue [542]. Within a group of four there are three possibilities: (1) there can be no coalitions, (2) there can be two dyadic coalitions, or (3) there can be one three-way coalition and an excluded person. While there is little data available on which type occurs most frequently, it seems that the second type—two dyadic coalitions—probably does. In groups of four it is unusual for no coalitions to form. Further, since any three-way coalition is inherently unstable, it too has a tendency to dissolve into its dyadic components. As a result, in a group of four, two dyadic coalitions typically arise. When choosing between the potential coalitions each person must keep in mind "(1) the strength of the coalition relative to a possible countercoalition, and (2) his bargaining position within the coalition" [542]. Once the coalitions are formed, they serve the function of helping manage the conflicts that arise in tetradic groups [512, 220]. When members team up together, they influence the decisions that occur within the family structure.

The process of trying to predict which dyadic coalitions form within a larger family unit is slippery. It appears that the most common coalitions are those between siblings closest in age and sex. The experimental literature tends to support the notion that coalitions are formed on the basis of power such that a "winning coalition" is formed in the multiperson context. However, Willis [542] notes that "these results can be more satisfactorily accounted for on the basis of shared interest than differences in power." And coalitions shift with the changes in circumstances. Two persons who work in the same department may have little overlap of their lives. But when circumstances change and they are both fired through a cutback of all recently hired personnel, the two gravitate together. Their coalition is sponsored by a change in external circumstances. Similarly, a brother and sister who are one year apart in age may form a coalition, leaving out another sister who is several years older. But with the passage of time, the younger sister and the brother may have a "falling out" over choices of lifestyle. Then if through some fortuitous circumstance, the older sister and the brother form a business partnership, this shared interest tends to override the effects of the earlier coalition. With changes of locale, interests, and values, coalitions within families shift over time.

Likewise, when another member is introduced into the family unit, fresh coalition material is available. One young lady in a family of five was the "outsider" until the mother remarried. Now she and her stepfather have a happy coalition that she reports is the "first one I have ever formed in my family." Similarly, the marriage of a brother or sister can provide an in-law who is available for coalition formation. The manner in which coalitions are formed, the choices that individuals make to select some coalitions over others, and the functions that coalitions serve are ripe for considerable speculation. Perhaps as the process of coalition formation becomes more understood and the consequences of coalitions on the subsequent entire family structure become clear, the subject of dyadic coalitions in larger groups than three will receive more systematic investigation.

THE ECOLOGY OF DYADS

Within larger systems such as families and work environments, two interrelated processes are at work. First, each coalition is embedded within a larger social framework that also affects the dyad; second, establishment of coalitions affects all others in the system.

Hinde argued that, "Each individual has relationships with many others, and each relationship he has will be affected by the other relationships that he has and the other relationships that his several partners have" [216]. Whether we are talking about organizations, families, or romantic and friendship ties, all of one's relationships are mutually influencing. Jablin [234] has demonstrated, for example, that as the size of an organization grows and the interpersonal relationships become more complex, one's communication with the superior becomes both more frequent and less open. Similarly, our friendships with others are affected by their other relationships. If a close friend falls in love with someone and moves toward marriage, it usually has some impact on the friendship.

Parks and others studied college students' romantic relationships to see if they were directly affected by the network in which they were embedded. Since, as they argued, "relationships do not spring from a social void" [379], we would expect the overall constellation of relationships to affect the romantic dyad. Romantic dyads who communicated more with their partner's networks both were more romantic and had a lessened chance of "breaking up" three months later [380, 379].

Not only does the overall constellation of relationships affect the dyadic coalition, but the effects are reciprocal—the dyadic coalition impacts on the system as well. In a typical American middle-class family, for instance, the mother is often the "heavy communicator," keeping track of the children, relaying messages, and being the communication switchboard for the family. Her dyadic bonds with each child, of course, have an effect on the father's ability to form separate coalitions. In many families, by the time the children reach their teens and twenties, the tight coalitions reinforce the father's isolation in the family. He often gives up on forming effective relations with the children and the mother often feels overburdened with the heavy demands of keeping track of everyone and passing messages. The coalitions of the heavy communicator, who sometimes is the father or a child, help put some other person in the role of family isolate.

When they work with distressed families, many family therapists try to reform some of the dyadic bonds [432, 433, 537]. For example, if the father–mother subsystem is weak, it sets up one or both of them for strong coalitions with a child, which then reverberates back into the system, further weakening the parental bond [171]. The tight cross-generational coalitions, then, put more forces into motion that further damage the family. Most evidence indicates that the parental coalition should be the strongest one, because a weak parental bond affects everyone else's coalitions [171, 501, 451].

The mutually reinforcing effects of the system and the coalitions within the system can be kept from becoming destructive. Satir's work on the Identified Patient (I.P.) [171, 506, 451, 501, 506] shows rather clearly that systems sometimes elect one person to bear the brunt of the distress [432]. Often this is a child who is easily picked because of some physical difference (e.g., being the only child with red hair, being the shortest in the family, or having a deformity) or some other prominent characteristic, such as being the only adopted child. The I.P. then attracts the energy of others toward him or her and keeps the parents from strengthening their marital coalition. In some organizations, the same dynamics occur, but the person gets labeled as the "turkey," or as I call it, the I.T. This "Identified Turkey" likewise becomes the brunt of others' dissatisfactions with work, and their bondings against him keep the relationships from improving.

Stated succinctly, *coalitions provide for their own justification.* If three teenagers in a family are in a pattern of Sue being the "odd one out," she will probably engage in communication behaviors that are unproductive. Any excluded person will cause disruption, act in an unappreciative manner, or withdraw for self-protection. Of course, what happens is that the members of the group form an even tighter coalition and say something like, "If Sue would just be more responsible, we wouldn't have any difficulties." They exclude her; she reacts in inappropriate ways, which justifies the exclusion.

USING COALITIONS PRODUCTIVELY

Recognizing the powerful impact that coalitions have on both the ones who coalesce and the one (or more) excluded can provide optimistic insights. If you are in a family where one member is the only one not in the ongoing coalitions, then you can grasp the opportunity to form a coalition with the excluded party. There will be some resistance from others for doing this, because most systems of relationships become invested in maintaining the present status even if it isn't working for one of the members. Suppose, for example, that your mother is the one who is always alone at family gatherings and is seldom spoken to. When you begin paying attention to your mother, others in the family might actively try to siphon off the energy you direct toward her. The key to making coalitions work in larger groups such as families is to *shift coalitions* so that the members get a chance to experience the best of each other. The positive effects of coalitions can be used to overcome the negative effects by occasionally shifting them. Spread the warmth and love around by seeking out the isolates or the members who are typically in coalitions other than your own. It can have very surprising results.

As an outside party to a multiperson system, whether it be a family or work group, you can sometimes facilitate the shift in coalitions. In one case where a mother and son had an airtight coalition and the father was peripheral, a therapist structured the situation so that the father had to get involved with the mother. Their redefined relationship served to help strengthen the overall family unit by providing a new coalition [193]. It has been demonstrated that the parental dyad must be strong to deal with family decisions [171].

If nothing else, a knowledge of the existence and effects that coalitions have can prepare you for situations that arise in the future. More and more single-parent and parent–stepparent families are being formed every day [177]. These departures from the typical American family model call for an increased sensitivity to the need that people have to form bonds with a significant other person. And when old bonds become strained because of the altered circumstances, you can help others to understand the natural flow of these changes. For instance, when a couple gets a divorce, their relationships with their spouse's family undergo dramatic change. It seems especially true that divorced and remarried women are unlikely to contact or receive help from their former spouse's family. Each person brought into the marital dyad a network of interpersonal linkages, and once the original bond is severed or redefined (such as getting a divorce but remaining friends), the linkages with the relatives become realigned. Each set of parents usually keeps their primary alliance with their own children.

One young woman, Marcy, worked overtime to overcome the effects of coalitions that could have been destructive. She was dating a fellow (and liked him a lot), but then he became attracted to her roommate. Before he actually began dating the roommate, the three of them, meeting separately in groups of two, talked and worked on the relational hassles involved. Marcy took the position that (1) she wanted the man as a romantic partner, but if he didn't want her, she wanted a friendship with him, and (2) she wanted to maintain her close friendship with her roommate. So she talked with her roommate and with the man. In turn, the roommate and the man talked to one another. They all recognized the strains involved and did not want any of the relationships to suffer because of the shifting romantic interest. Much to their credit, and after many weeks of difficulty for Marcy, the three of them managed to allow the coalitions to shift by recognizing that the pressures, hurt, and anger were natural by-products of a shifting dyadic coalition in a triad. Significantly, the three of them never tried to operate as a three-person group. As far as I know, these agreements were successful. Although Marcy didn't retain her desired romantic partner, she would not have kept him by forcing a showdown. She kept her relationship with her roommate, maintained an ongoing friendship with the man, and the roommate and the man became romantic partners. Their awareness of the natural pressures involved in coalition shifts allowed them to work through the changes.

Jennifer, who has two daughters, ages ten and seven, provides another example of how to use coalitions productively. In this family of three, it would be very easy to lapse into a rescue triangle and pick out one child as the identified patient. However, the three of them have an imaginary person, "Kooch," who can be called up by anyone. If someone feels outnumbered, she can say, "Well, I'm going to have Kooch help me," and proceed to bring Kooch into the discussion. The rules are that Kooch is imaginary and that the child who is being put upon must begin a discussion of the things Kooch has done (which were really done by her). The entire group then decides how Kooch can improve, what Kooch's positive qualities are, and how situations such as this can be avoided in the future. Since Kooch is imaginary, once his purpose has been served, he is retired until needed again.

Dyadic coalitions are bondings that occur within the context of three or more people in the same group or system. They occur naturally, shift over time, and can be put to productive use. With sensitivity, the negative effects from coalition formation can be mitigated.

DEMANDS ON THE DYAD

The demands we place on our personal relationships are higher than they ever have been in Western history. In the colonial time, personal life was not private, the "colonial house was a business, a school, a vocational institute, a church, a house of correction, and a welfare institution" [160]. However, with the advent of the industrial revolution and the growth of urban centers, the home was no longer the center of all social ties. Whereas the community life previously had provided both support and constraint, couples were left to generate the "bases of their relationships from the dynamic of the relationship and their personal feelings" [160].

Given the level of demands on the important two-person systems, it is no wonder that popular magazines and college courses focus on issues of improvement and preservation of the dyadic groupings. In the 1970s the focus on "me," with concern for personal growth and change, sharpened our awareness that relationships were fragile. Many individuals put considerable effort into self-improvement only to discover that the changes could not be sustained within the context of their important relationships. As a result, we are now shifting from the "me" concerns to consideration of "we"—how to maintain and enhance realtionships [45]. Relationships per se are now a topic for discussion and analysis as never before.

As we experience social changes and our dyadic relationships also undergo transformation, we have to be careful to not confuse changes of *style* of living with *quality* of living. For example, in small-town environments, people tend to be more involved with their relatives, but in large, urban environments, people spend more of their quality time with nonkin [148]. Whatever the future alterations in our social environment may be, it appears that dyadic relationships will remain central to our happiness and quality of life.

SUMMARY

Dyadic communication is a transactional process. Each participant's perception of the other is a transaction between the qualities of the other and the unique interpretation of them. Furthermore, when the two participants are in the presence of each other, they are both creating and deciphering communication cues. As a result, each participant affects and is affected by the other.

While dyadic encounters are distinct from larger groupings of people, they do form the building blocks of larger groupings. The triad consists of a primary dyadic coalition plus another person who has not entered fully into the coalition. Even larger groupings are also characterized by shifting dyadic relationships.

The influence of dyadic coalitions and the larger constellation of relationships is reciprocal—coalitions affect the larger groupings and the other relationships affect the primary dyad. Basic dyadic relationships take a more important role in people's lives as we demand more and more from them. We can expect the emphasis on the quality of relationships to continue for the foreseeable future.

Chapter 2

Perception of the Self

When she was three years old my daughter Carina was sitting with me on the couch when she looked down and noticed that her shoe was untied (a not uncommon condition). She lifted her foot, showed the dangling laces to all within viewing range, and made it clear that she needed help. I reached over to her and said, "Here, let me tie your shoe for you so you won't trip over the laces." Carina looked intently at me, then conveniently ignoring the fact that she did not know how to tie shoes yet, exclaimed in a loud voice, "I can do it *myself*!" She was at the age where she was beginning to be fully aware that she had a self—that she was a separate human being who could do things her own way.

Carina, like the rest of us, acts toward herself and others based in part on her self-perception. For all of us, the meanings that we have for ourselves are derived from our transactions with others. The basic components upon which all dyadic transactions are structured, perception of the self and perception of the other, are the topics of this and the following chapter.

We have the ability to attach meaning to our own behavior. The ability to analyze oneself may, in fact, be a human's most distinctive characteristic. While other members of the animal kingdom can respond, it is not at all certain that they can be self-reflexive. The ability to engage in self-reflexive acts is best stated by Allport [1], "We are not only aware of what is peculiarly ours, but we are also aware that we are aware." Whether people are the only creatures capable of self-reflexive thinking or not, this ability has a profound effect on all dyadic relationships. As this chapter will demonstrate, our self-concepts are inextricably bound to our relationships with others, both influencing them and being influenced by them.

The self-concept is a generalized view of oneself, or as Rosenberg defines it, the "totality of an individual's thoughts and feelings having reference to himself as an object" [411]. One's concept of oneself is obviously subjective, for whatever an individual thinks she is, to *her* this is what she is [504]. Outsiders do not know your level of self esteem, and their evaluations of you will be quite different from your own. Most work finds little agreement between how others view a person and how the person views himself or herself. Interestingly, though, there was agreement between how people *think* others view them and how they perceive themselves. Similarly, it has been demonstrated that self-ratings and others' ratings of one's communication style are unrelated [491, 56].

The subjective nature of self-concept can be illustrated with the case of Mike, a student in an interpersonal communication class. He is, in his words, an "upper-middle-class black with connections." He is very bright, outgoing, and genuinely friendly to others in the class. It came as a shock to us to discover one day that Mike saw himself as shy and afraid to talk to people. He was quite serious; he really saw himself as shy and retiring. His meaning for himself was not at all what any of us would have guessed.

The subjective nature of the self-concept is manifested in other ways as well. For instance, two individuals can have similar experiences yet have totally different meanings for them. One student can flunk a test and it will signal for her that, "It's time to get busy," whereas a second person will interpret the same grade as meaning, "You are no good." One self-concept has been bolstered and the other has been badly shaken because the meanings are subjective and internal to that particular person.

COMPONENTS OF THE SELF-CONCEPT

Each person's self-concept is subjective primarily because (1) there are differing degrees of awareness of the self, and (2) we each have "multiple selves" from which to choose.

Degrees of Self-awareness

Most people accept their lives and the meanings of their lives as given, reflecting on these meanings only when a novel situation develops. Novel situations that promote reflexive thinking are quite disparate. If, for example, you have just experienced a disruption in a relationship, self-reflexive thinking occurs. A newly divorced man or woman, or someone who finds herself the outsider in a romantic triad, is typically the one who begins to question her self-concept. Questions like, "If I'm normal, then why didn't it work?" are quite serious at such times. Even the disruption of a potential relationship can lead to self-examination. The person who asks a romantic partner to live with him or her and is refused will probably engage in some self-examination. If the smallest boy in a high school class is the only one who did not make the basketball team, he may subject himself to intensive personal questioning. While the others are on the court giving the game their utmost, he is on the sidelines in personal doubt.

Of course, not all novel situations are negative, nor do they all produce a weakened self-concept. For instance, if a woman applies for her first job outside the home, having spent the preceding time as a full-time homemaker and child raiser, she will probably undergo many self-reflexive moments. If all goes well, she will probably experience an improvement in her self-concept. Abilities she was not quite certain she had prove to exist. Similarly, a move to a new city can bring new friendships and a heightened feeling of personal worth. Whenever novel situations arise, whether they be disasters or good fortunes, an individual typically becomes more self-aware.

One other type of novel situation is worth mentioning because it so frequently occurs. When there is an inconsistency between what you believe and what you have done, awareness of the self is prompted. If you do not believe in stealing but are "talked into it" by some friends, personal examination will be the next step. Or if you do not believe in premarital sexual relations but find yourself engaging in them, self-reflexive thinking will closely follow. Whether you become entangled in personal remorse or spend your time trying to rationalize your behavior, your concept of yourself will undergo some degree of examination.

Not only does our awareness of self change as a result of a novel experience, our own usual degree of awareness may be quite different from someone else's. A self-proclaimed "Mr. Know-it-all" who has no periods of reflection projects quite a different communication behavior from "Mr. Shy," the fellow who rarely speaks. The first fellow may take a close look at himself only once a week, whereas the second fellow scrutinizes himself periodically. And these "peeks at the self" may be quite different. The first undergoes a simple check to see if he put all his clothes on and is still breathing. The second examines himself to the point that he is trapped into reflections about his reflections. He thinks, "Gee, I sure don't impress people with my communicative ability. Anybody who has no ability to communicate has nothing to contribute. And if I have to worry about my communicative ability, I really must be messed up." His reflections about his reflections keep him so internally occupied that his shyness is accelerated.*

Objective Self-awareness

One of the few systematic treatments of the amount of self-awareness that we each have has been supplied by Duval and Wicklund [139]. They proposed a theory of objective self-awareness, which specifies two major states that we all experience: (1) subjective self-awareness and (2) objective self-awareness. When in a state of subjective self-awareness, the person feels "at one with the environment" such that he or she is not aware of the self. In the state of subjective self-awareness, the self is not the object of attention. For example, if you are sitting in class and absorbed in taking notes on that day's lecture, you are focusing outward, toward the outside environment, and are in the state of subjective self-awareness. Similarly, if the professor is totally involved in answering student questions, then she also would be in a state of subjective self-awareness. When you are not focusing on yourself, you are in a state of subjective self-awareness, which is the more common state [139].

---

*This example is only for purposes of illustration. It may not be at all true that vocal and socially aggressive people are less aware of themselves than are more timid folk. Likewise, shyness or lack of social exchange does not necessarily lead to reflections about reflections.

When, on the other hand, you turn inward and begin to examine yourself, you are in the state of *objective self-awareness*. You treat your "self" as an object to be perceived and reacted to: "the individual views himself as another object in the universe—not at one with the environment and not subject to forces that move the environment" [139]. You are the *object* that you are focusing upon, thus the term *objective* self-awareness.

The state of objective self-awareness typically brings with it an experience of self-evaluation. The person who is examining the self is often doing it in comparison to some "ideal" self. If you are up late at night studying for the test over this material the next morning, then when you begin thinking, "A good student would have read this stuff earlier than the night before the exam," you are in the state of objective self-awareness by comparing yourself with some ideal student. And you can get into a state of objective self-awareness by comparison with your own past performances. In most cases, this initial surge of self-evaluation for people is negative—we examine our shortcomings and deficiencies and see that we fall short of our ideals. Or we see how we are "out of step" with others [506].

Focusing upon ourselves may have some positive features, however. If we perform better at a task than we thought we would, for example, the rush of evaluation can be positive. I recall during a winter vacation in Colorado when, for the first time in eight years, I attempted to downhill ski. I was afraid of being unable to get down the mountain without breaking my neck or leg. Fortunately for me, I skied better that day than I ever had in my life. During my third run down the mountain, I stopped on the hill and found that I was thinking about myself. I was thinking, "I sure am doing a better job than I thought I could. Maybe I ought to take up downhill skiing again if I can do this well." This particular state of objective self-awareness had positive results.

What are the conditions that lead to an examination of the self? As stated before, whenever an unusual event happens, one tends to examine the self. Also, whenever a person is reminded of being an object in the world, objective self-awareness is prompted [139]. The triggering situations can be impersonal—looking into a mirror, hearing a tape recording of your voice, seeing a photograph of yourself, or experiencing a novel situation where the norms for participation are unknown to you. I know one woman who best exemplifies how objective self-awareness can be caused by mirrors. Although she is very attractive, when she got her first contact lenses she suddenly began acting as if she had some contagious disease. She wouldn't look at people, started avoiding some of her closest friends, and generally acted as if she were unworthy. Her contact lenses enabled her to see herself clearly in mirrors for the first time in her life. Every little imperfection that was previously just part of the blur in the mirror now was visible to her. It took her weeks to adjust to her increased visual accuity.

Not only do impersonal events promote objective self-awareness, but interpersonal events are also a prime producer. The presence of others is so strong a trigger to objective self-awareness that just the anticipation of meeting someone will cause one to examine the self. Most people who are meeting their romantic partner on an arriving plane find themselves combing their hair at the last minute, adjusting their tie, fixing their makeup, or even popping breath mints as the ultimate guarantee. Just think back on your own behavior immediately before a date or outing—it usually involves a very self-conscious state of preparation. One of my students was so concerned with how she looked and with what to do that she had difficulties moving into action. She had a date with a man from another university and wanted to structure their future time together so that she could get to know him better. Their previous date had been in the presence of four other people and she wasn't confident that he had the chance to see the "real" her. So she asked me, "What can I do so that he will like me, yet not think that I am hustling him?" She was so aware of herself that she was afraid to telephone him. She finally did call him, however, and learned that he too was self-conscious around her. The impending contact had made both of them self-aware.

Objective self-awareness can be triggered interpersonally whenever you are aware that another person is examining you. If you walk in front of the class and everyone looks at you, self-awareness is triggered. If you are a professor and find yourself stammering and the class goes quiet, you are usually aware of your performance. If you are in a public place and laughing loudly and then notice that everyone in the place is looking at you, you become self-aware.

Focusing attention on ourselves has its benefits and its liabilities. Baron and Byrne [23] note that focusing on ourselves yields increased self-understanding. By treating ourselves as objects, we can learn more about how we react to various situations. It is through objective self-awareness that we come to know our "self." Obviously, if you spend all of your time examining yourself, then you can become bogged down in the cycle of examination. If you are unable to take any action whatsoever, then you have no new information about the "self" that you examine. We have to keep our self-awareness within bounds. If we are too self-aware, or are self-aware in inappropriate circumstances, then we can become dysfunctional. For instance, if you are engaged in a conversation with someone and show a high level of self-consciousness, you disrupt the communication transaction. I know one person who, while talking to others, holds his hand in the air and turns it slowly over and over, focusing his attention on it. As Goffman [178] noted, this self-consciousness is an inappropriate monitoring of the self when the situation demands that the other person focus on you. We all have to abandon some of our self-awareness in order to function as effective communicators in the presence of others.

Self-perception Theory

I have discussed the issue of how one becomes self-aware and have shown that awareness can have positive or negative consequences. Bem's self-perception theory carries these concerns a step further and specifies that we draw conclusions about ourselves in systematic ways [46]. He says that we come to know our own attitudes, emotions, and other internal states by inferring them from observations of our behavior and the circumstances in which this behavior occurs. We come to know the internal states of others ("Sally really dislikes me") by inferring these states by the others' actions. Similarly, if our internal cues are weak, ambiguous, or uninterpretable, we are in the same position that we are when we observe some outside person [46]. If our internal cues are strong, we label them and use them as a guide. For instance, if you are dating someone and find yourself sexually aroused, this usually gets interpreted as, "I think I really like him." But if your internal cues are unclear ("I can't tell what I feel toward her"), then you look for situational cues as a more reliable guide to interpreting your "self." In this case, if you are spending a lot of time with the person, you might conclude, "I must like her. I spend all of my available time with her." The confusing internal cues are interpreted by using the external cues. Many a stale relationship is kept together because the participants say, "I don't feel anything, but since I am still with the person after three years I must love him."

We spend only a small portion of our time examining ourselves, but even when we do we are usually unaware of the factors that lead to how we judge ourselves [46]. If your university has suffered severe faculty cutbacks, that external factor can have a considerable impact on how you feel about yourself. The morale of the faculty sags, and fellow students dislike being around school. But if you forget that the entire university is like a morgue, you might conclude, "I'm depressed. I guess I don't like being a student anymore." The internal cues were strong, so they take precedence in the interpretation of who you are. Nisbett and Valins [356] conducted some experiments in which they found that if the subjects were artificially stimulated in an experimental situation they inferred they had strong feelings. The subjects interpret their arousal as a strong emotion. Similarly, if you are in an appropriate environment for "feeling love" and have some strong physiological response, you label it as "being in love" [60]. One intriguing experiment demonstrated that if a man was interviewed by an attractive female on a dangerous suspension bridge, he was likely to label his strong emotional feelings (fear) as romantic interest and would call the young woman back later to discuss the experiment. If, on the other hand, he was interviewed on a very low, safe bridge in the same general area, he would not call her back to "discuss the experiment."

We are not very accurate interpreters of the causes of our emotional states. And we often cannot just "look inside" to see what we are feeling and how we are reacting. We have to rely upon both internal and external cues to determine what we think we are thinking. Using this information, we label our emotions. One man I know is aware that the labeling of an emotion is crucial to its interpretation. Therefore, when he is depressed, he dresses himself up in his finest clothes and stands in front of the mirror. Then, gazing intently at himself, he says, "Ohhh, my good man, how can you be feeling so bad when you are *looking so good*!!!!" He focuses on the external cues in order to override the internal cues, and convinces himself to feel better.

Multiple Selves

> "You should have seen Ed at the party. He was so blasted he picked a fight. He wasn't himself for two days."
>
> "I don't know about Carrie. She is going to a nude marathon to try and find herself."
>
> "I wish Sam would quit playing games on our dates. He is always trying to impress me with his intelligence. If he would just be himself, we'd get along a lot better."

What are you *really* like? Your teacher thinks you are too easygoing, your friends feel you take life too seriously, and your parents quite probably think you are too rebellious. How do you go about finding the *real* you? Is it the *real* you showing when you are drunk, stoned, or in love? Or is it the *real* you sitting under a tree all by yourself thinking about life?

There is no real you, and a search for it is doomed to fail. A complex human being, subjected to different people and pressures, is no solitary blob of identity. Each of us is complex; the person one is on the job or at school with is different from the one in the company of a close friend. The impressions others have of us are, at best, incomplete and slightly faulty, and so are the impressions we have of ourselves.

Obviously all of us are complex, and there are innumerable components or parts of our lives that affect our self-concepts. As an example, let's take a superficial look at Tom. For his self-concept, he can pick from any or all of the following characteristics (plus many more):

- Short
- From Pittsburgh
- Friendly
- Has a scraggy beard
- Working on his B.A.
- Husband
- Hard-working
- Mountain climber
- Needs others
- Has tattoos
- Mill worker
- Poet

- Father of two girls
- Drives a VW Bus
- Others need him
- Photographer

The list could include thousands more items. And Tom can choose from all his attributes, possessions, and experiences (and future goals) to make up his self-concept.

We all have multiple selves. One general semanticist makes the point that self should be represented as Self-1, Self-2, Self-3, Self-4, . . . , Self-n, ad infinitum [10]. In the case of Tom, we see only sixteen aspects of his life. These sixteen qualities could be rank ordered in importance to him and then combined in all possible ways. For instance, let's say his self-concept was most dependent upon (1) driving a VW bus and (2) being a photographer. These two items would be the most crucial determiners of how he sees himself. He could, however, have the qualities combined in other ways. Another combination might be (1) mountain climber, (2) mill worker, (3) poet, and (4) photographer. The number of possible combinations that one can make is very large. If we put together all possible permutations of just these sixteen items, there would be 20,923,000,000,000,000 possible configurations he could select from for his self-concept. And that is only from sixteen qualities!

For purposes of understanding, it is useful to look at the components of the self-concept from a broader framework. After all, no one wants to list all possible aspects that can contribute to a generalized view of oneself and then try to figure out all the possible combinations. One of the earliest category systems for describing the self was offered by James [239].* His list was composed of three items:

1. Material self.
2. Social self.
3. Spiritual self.

According to James's point of view, each of us has these three as separate components of our self-concept. The *material self* consists of our body, clothing, and other trappings or material possessions that we see as part of us. The importance of clothes to many people is obvious. Some find it necessary to always "dress to the hilt"; to others it is important that their clothes *not* be important to them. The importance of the material self in developing the self-concept is easily observed in children. Children extend their sense of self by identifying with material possessions [5]. Give a young child a set of pistols, boots, and a

---

*Numerous other classifications are available. For example, see [4, 5, 165, 166]. James writes that the material, social, and spiritual selves constitute the empirical self, or "me." I have taken the liberty of interpreting the empirical self to be the generalized view one has of himself—the self-concept.

cowboy hat and shirt, and the child may try to convince you he or she *is* a cowboy. My own son, Jason, went through a trauma when he was three because his material possessions did not match one aspect of his self-concept. We had just returned from vacationing in Wyoming, where he had ridden a horse for the first time. With boots borrowed from a cousin and other appropriate gear, he rode "his" horse. Everything was fine until we returned home and prepared to go to a small-town rodeo. All of a sudden he realized that he no longer had his borrowed boots. He promptly informed me that "*all* cowboys wear boots," making it perfectly clear between tears that without boots he could not be a cowboy. Luckily I was able to convince him that new boots would be forthcoming next year prior to his being a cowboy again in Wyoming.

The material aspects of some people's lives are so prominent that the material self is a significant portion of their entire self-concept. The individual who buys objects because of their "image" is simply saying that she wants you as well as herself to conceive of her in a particular way. The overweight man of thirty-three who buys a Porsche may be trying to change his self-concept. He may actually become young and sporty (in his eyes) by the purchase. Many people define themselves by what they own rather than by what they do. After all, if you own a $200 high-light tent, a pair of expensive hiking boots, and appropriately faded cut-off jeans, you *must* be an experienced backpacker and hiker. Most of us, whether we go to this extent or not, can find material objects we own that are central to our material self. Whether it be a professor's books, a banker's Cadillac, or a student's stereo set, we all have a material self that is part of our overall self-concept.

The second contributor to each person's self-concept is the *social self.* The social self is the recognition one earns from others, arising out of dyadic and other transactions. (The social self is so crucial to each person's self-concept that the next section in this chapter deals specifically with it.) Our social self develops from how others see us. If, for example, you are a "hard worker," you learn to see yourself this way because of how others have reacted to you. Our social selves, of course, are developed in all our dyadic contexts, ranging from our personal, intimate relationships to our family relationships to our work associations. The social self, then, arises from others' conceptions of us that we see as an accurate reflection of ourselves. The key point to remember is that our self-conception develops from our communicative interchanges with others.

The third and final aspect of the self-concept is the *spiritual self.* For James [239], the spiritual self includes the actions of the psyche, the process of introspection, one's thinking. The spiritual self is made up of all one's intellectual, moral, and religious aspirations. From it arise the sense of moral or mental superiority and, conversely, the sense of inferiority or guilt. Although James interpreted the spiritual

Our material possessions are part of our self-concepts. We may also select material possessions, such as a particular kind of automobile, to reinforce or alter our self-concepts.

self in very broad terms, its existence is most easily observed in the narrower sense of religious belief and action. Individuals' self-concepts are affected by how they perceive themselves in the overall scheme of things. For instance, people are often concerned with events that happen before and after death. Your self-concept is affected by how you believe your behavior fits with your spiritual convictions. A person maintains a positive self-concept as long as he or she maintains a belief system that is perceived as giving approval [9]. A central belief in God and an adherence to the principles of behavior that one perceives as associated with such a belief can play an important role in one's overall self-concept.

The material, social, and spiritual selves combine in unique ways to constitute each person's estimation of himself or herself. For one person a belief in a personal savior may be the component of his self-concept most crucial to his life. For another person the spiritual self may be relatively unimportant in shaping her overall view of herself. One of the freeing aspects of a complex society is that we can choose between several goals. We each can set our own goals, each one related to different components of the self, and evaluate our success at them. One person can be a poor typist, yet his self-concept does not flounder. Another may be overweight, but unless she sets being slim as a worthy goal, her self-concept will not be damaged. We don't all have to be athletes to feel important—neither do we all have to fix a car, take a thirty-mile hike, or write a book. We can select an appropriate goal for ourselves, perform well at the task, and have a feeling of worth.

As noted, the self-concept is composed of the material, social, and spiritual selves. When one particular goal becomes important to you (fixing a car, having a lot of friends, or attending church), your performance in achieving that goal constitutes your self-esteem. Self-esteem is your feeling of worth arising from a specific situation, and the combination of all cases of specific self-esteem makes up your self-concept. Self-esteem and, in the long run, the self-concept are determined by (1) the goals (pretentions) you set and (2) your success at accomplishing them. James [239] put it most succinctly:

$$\text{Self-esteem} = \frac{\text{Success}}{\text{Pretentions}}$$

According to this formula, the person who wants to be a millionaire and makes $40,000 a year will be less happy than a person who wants $20,000 a year and makes $18,000. Interestingly enough, the person who has the most may be less happy because of her lofty goals. And the person who has minimal goals may feel the best about himself. As an individual who wants to increase your self-esteem, you have two options available: (1) increase your success at the chosen goal (pretention) or (2) lower the goal.

The occupational choice that people make reflects an intuitive understanding of James's formula. It is no accident that people try to pick jobs where they will have some measure of success—for success at goals builds self-esteem. If you find yourself frustrated over your choices (such as attending college and not performing well), then you can go in two basic directions: (1) change the goals or (2) increase your successes. Either approach will serve to bolster a faltering self-image.

We have examined numerous aspects of the self-concept. People are aware of themselves to differing degrees and enter into both objective and subjective self-awareness states. Further, proponents of self-perception theory note that we interpret our behavior as a guide to what we are like. Finally, there are multiple selves, highlighted by the material, social, and spiritual components. Of all these, the social self is the one most central to dyadic communication.

THE SOCIAL SELF

Each to each a looking glass
Reflects the other that doth pass [106].

Cooley's famous two-line poem expresses the fact that self-concepts are essentially social. Although the material and spiritual selves contribute to the self-concept [239], social life is the beginning and sustenance for all the components of the self-concept. The material and spiritual selves have meanings for us because of others around us. Why be concerned with clothes (part of the material self) if others are not around to see them? The meanings one attaches to herself or himself (the spiritual self) are likewise molded in society. Frankl [157] goes so far as to say that the "true meaning of life" is to be found in the world rather than in one's psyche or spiritual self. In any event, *our communication transactions with others* mold our self-concept. In fact, our self-identity is carved within our relationships [58].

Many social scientists agree in principle with Cooley's notion of the "looking-glass" self. Following are some short statements that emphasize that our communicative transactions are the cornerstone of the self-concept.

> . . . the sense of identity requires the existence of another by whom one is known.
>
> —R. D. LAING

> The self may be said to be made up of reflected appraisals.
>
> —H. S. SULLIVAN

> It is well to remember that all the information a person possesses about himself is derived from others. His impression of the impact he had upon others is what makes up the picture of himself.
>
> —J. RUESCH

> . . . will conceive of himself as he believes significant others conceive of him.
>
> —C. GORDON AND K. GERGEN

> The becoming of a person is always a social becoming: I become a person as I progress through social situations.
>
> —TIRYAKIAN

> . . . we maintain our natural level of self-esteem so long as we do not lose the approval, affection, and warmth of those around us.
>
> —L. WOODMAN

> We are who we are only in relationship to the other person(s) we're communicating with.
>
> —J. STEWART

I am not what I think I am. I am not what you think I am. I am what I think you think I am.

—BLEIBERG AND LEUBLING

This vitally important social self is built primarily in three ways: (1) by the reflected appraisals of others or the "looking glass" self, (2) by the comparison of the self with others, and (3) by the playing of social roles.

The Looking-Glass Self

That the appraisals of others affect us has been demonstrated time and time again. Rosenthal [415], for example, showed that if teachers expected students to be intelligent, the latter performed better in school. Tell someone he is untalented enough times and he will begin to perceive himself that way. Guthrie [190] and Kinch [257] both relate similar stories that demonstrate the impact that the evaluations of others can have. In the Kinch example, five males in a graduate-level class wanted to see if the notion of the "looking-glass" self could be put to use. Their subject was the woman in the class who could be described at best as "plain." They planned to respond to her as if she were the best-looking girl on campus and to watch the effects of the treatment. Here is how it went:

> They agreed to work into it naturally so that she would not be aware of what they were up to. They drew lots to see who would be the first to date her. The loser, under the pressure of the others, asked her to go out. Although he found the situation quite unpleasant, he was a good actor and by continually saying to himself "she's beautiful, she's beautiful . . . " he got through the evening. According to the agreement, it was now the second man's turn and so it went. The dates were reinforced by the similar responses in all contacts the men had with the girl. In a matter of a few short weeks the results began to show. At first it was simply a matter of more care in her appearance; her hair was combed more often and her dresses were more neatly pressed, but before long she had been to the beauty parlor to have her hair styled, and was spending her hard-earned money on the latest fashions in women's campus wear. By the time the fourth man was taking his turn dating the young lady, the job that had once been undesirable was now quite a pleasant task. And when the last man in the conspiracy asked her out, he was informed that she was pretty well booked up for some time in the future. It seems that there were more desirable males around than those "plain" graduate students [257].

Besides the poetic justice involved, the impact of others' views is clear. The girl perceived the actual response of the men such that she had to change her self-concept, which in turn changed her behavior. While this example is one of the best to illustrate how the views of others can affect one's self-concept, I do not endorse it as a *modus operandi*. Clearly, there are some sexist implications in it that cause one to doubt the wisdom in performing the experiment. However, the point is clear—the way we see others seeing us greatly influences how we see ourselves. It is so important that "no more fiendish punishment could be devised" than to be "turned loose on society and remain absolutely unnoticed by all the members thereof" [239].

The Self by Social Comparison

The second subcategory of the social self is the image we build of ourselves by comparison with others. More often than not, the comparison is made with peers. Sally, a young woman who is concerned about her attractiveness, wants to be invited to an upcoming party. If Sue gets an invitation and Sally doesn't, Sally is painfully aware of how she compares. Similarly, Joan knows she is an excellent student only if she can compare herself with other students for some idea of her relative standing.

A formal theory of social comparison processes has been offered by Festinger [146]. The aspects of the theory that are relevant to our discussion follow. We all have a basic drive to have correct opinions about the world and for accurate self-appraisals. When objective, nonsocial means of evaluation are not available or are ambiguous, we evaluate our opinions and abilities by comparison with others. We often choose peers for comparison because they closely approximate our ability and opinions.

By recalling James's formula for self-esteem, the impact of social comparison on our self-concepts can be made evident. If self-esteem equals success divided by pretentions, determination of degree of success is crucial. How does one arrive at some estimate of his or her success? By comparison with others. In addition, how does one establish goals or pretentions? By comparison with others. The entire process of establishing self-esteem is dependent upon our comparison with others.* This process takes place in every activity from school, to skiing, to selling life insurance. In fact, when "objective" standards are established for performance (every tenderfoot Boy Scout has to be able to tie a square knot), these standards arise from the past performance of others.

As a side comment, a person's level of pretentions or goals is affected by past performance in trying to attain a goal. Furthermore, a person's criteria for degree of success will be modified if he is told of

---

*Obviously, a large part of the comparison with others is based on their reactions, their evaluation of our performance. Even here the "looking-glass" nature of self-concept plays a part.

someone else's performance. If he finds that his performance is below that of someone he considers to have little ability, he will raise his expectations. Conversely, if one is performing above another who is thought to have a great deal of ability, aspirations will be lowered. Whichever is the case, the social comparison with others is another social aspect central to the self-concept.

The Playing of Social Roles

> . . . a man has as many social selves as there are individuals who recognize him.
>
> —W. JAMES [239]

The complexity of modern society places us in situations that demand widely different behaviors. When our society was more agrarian, an individual's niche in the social order was rather firmly established. The family was the basis of one's identity, and job and home were closely meshed. Now, however, it is not unusual that our family members do not even know the people we work with. We are expected to be effective people in the hustle and bustle of city life and then, as if by magic, transform ourselves into fully functioning family members. To our parents we are one person, to our co-workers or fellow students another, and to our closest loved ones still a third.

An alarm bell has been sounded. Many people perceive our social lives as tearing us apart, as making us into social chameleons who change personality with every new situation. Goffman [178], for example, perceives a person as running around trying to "convey an impression to others which is in his interests to convey." From this point of view, we conduct our social relationships as types of calculated performances. We are always playing roles in order to make the proper impressions. As a result, there is little left in the way of an identifiable self-concept. The person wears masks and plays his socialized role "so well that he forgets who he is or what he looks like when the staged performance is over" [174]. According to this view, we have an "other-directed" culture where we conform to others' expectations rather than to any inner sense of values [403]. We become "yes-men" in the organization by adopting the correct lifestyle and adopt "Yes, J.B., you're right!" behaviors just to please our superiors [534]. We sell ourselves out to the social order.

However, we do have to adjust to the presence of others to lead successful social lives. Can you imagine a marriage, for instance, in which the husband wears a tuxedo to breakfast every morning? We have different relationships with different people—we rarely kiss the boss good morning. The question is whether one's degree of adaptation is so far-ranging as to cause psychological trauma. Our behavioral change in the presence of another is not necessarily calculated like a stage play; it can be an honest adjustment to the other's style. In a very honest sense, we are not the same to all people. Different relationships conceal and reveal different aspects of our personality [316].

We all have different roles or role identities that are prominent at different times. Your adjustment to the demands of being a student requires different behaviors than those expected during a long holiday at home. Based on a number of factors, the role identities are called into prominence [316]. Based on the importance to you of a given role, you do develop some consistency in your communication behavior. Within a particular relationship, some consistency must exist or else no trust or enduring relationship can result. In fact, when your actual behavior is consistent with your self-perception, then those communicating with you are also perceiving you in that role. But when your behavior seems out of line with the role others ascribe to you, they regard you as playing a game. A student who has attended college and undergone dramatic changes in interests and lifestyle is often accused of "putting on airs" or being a "smart college kid" upon returning home. His behavior is no longer consistent with their images of him, and that is disrupting to them.

Hart and Burks [198] have extended the notion of successful role playing. They term someone who can adapt to the complexitites of modern life as a *rhetorically sensitive* person. The rhetorically sensitive person tries to accept the necessary demands of different roles as a natural part of human existence. The choices facing us are not whether to play a role, but in which role to play. We literally "select those aspects of ourselves which will best meet the social conditions we face," in order to be socially competent. As we noted earlier, "each new relationship requires a unique form of adaptation" [167], and as a result, to become rhetorically sensitive means that one is capable of adaptation to those demands. This is *not* to say that people should be chameleons—changing complete colors at the alteration of the surroundings. Rather, we each select and adapt the parts of ourselves that are appropriate to a given situation. The parts of your "self" that you reveal to your best friend are not the same parts that you reveal in a class of thirty people—yet both are parts of you that you select for the circumstances.

Often our self-concept is so discrepant from how others see us that we must convince them that our view of ourselves is accurate. People who are successful in convincing others that how they perceive themselves is accurate have been called self-confident, autonomous, strong-willed, or persuasive. All of us have degrees of conviction and strong will, yet we are affected by others' views. One of the most dramatic attempts to assert independence from the roles others assign for us is demonstrated in Frederick Perls' poem:

> I do my thing
> and you do your thing.
> I am not in this world
> to live up to your expectations
> And you are not in this world
> to live up to mine.
> You are you
> and I am I
> and if by chance
> we find each other,
> it's beautiful.
> If not, it can't be helped.°

In a sense, it is inaccurate to talk about "hiding the self" or "staging a presentation." We do not have some *real self* that we can hide or reveal. We don't have some entity that we dress up and dress down for display. In a given situation, we have a set of behaviors that we consider to be (1) appropriate to the situation and (2) consistent, to some degree, with the self-concept we have. If we violate our expectations or personal desires too much, then we feel that we have played a game in that situation. Take the student, for example, who feels that he has received an unjust grade on an essay test. He sits up late at night outlining his arguments and rehearsing the defense he will make to the instructor. Just before entering the instructor's office, he wipes his sweaty brow, takes a deep breath, and then marches in. Once in the presence of the instructor, he is about one-fourth as self-assured, logical, and bombastic as he wanted to be. He is self-conscious, awed by the instructor's knowledge, and unable to hit hard verbally. The instructor, regrettably, cannot be budged from her evaluation and the student returns home with the same grade. Was the student untrue to himself? Was he playing a game? No—he was simply adjusting to the presence of the instructor and setting forth appropriate behaviors. Even in more extreme cases, such as job interviews, when individuals are consciously planning to present only their best aspects, they are not violating any real self. They are simply selecting an appropriate repertoire of their possible behaviors.

The "looking-glass" self, the self built by social comparison, and the demands of our social roles are all interrelated. They are variations on the same theme—our self-concept is formed by our social relationships with others.

°From *Gestalt Therapy Verbatim* by Fredrick S. Perls © 1969 Real People Press. Reprinted by permission.

SELF: A RESIDUE

It should be clear by now that one's self-concept is formed in social contexts. The examples used to illustrate the development of the self-concept, however, may make it appear that one's self-concept changes in every different social situation. A short description of the *residual self* is therefore in order.

Our self-concept is built by the meanings we attach to all our experiences—those of the past and those we are engaged in now—and the meshing of those meanings with our future aspirations. Faules and Alexander [144] said it well. The self is the person's "organization of accumulated experience . . . which provides the basis for personal action." When we have a communication experience, the interplay between our expectations and how we see people reacting to us adds another element to our self-concept. It must be stressed that the meanings are constructed through selective perception, which is partially governed by our past experiences of social acceptance. It is this *residue* of past experiences, which we retain as meanings, that influences our current reactions.

No one enters a communicative exchange without a previously formed self-concept. Our views of ourselves are never blank; we always possess a residue of past experiences. If people react to your behavior in consistent ways, then there is no discrepancy between (1) how you saw yourself before the transactions and (2) how you see yourself during and after the transaction. In other words, your self-concept was reinforced in that social relationship [452]. And as Woodman [551] says, we maintain our natural level of self-concept "so long as we do not lose the approval, affection, and warmth of those around us." Even though the self-concept is situationally determined, as long as it is supported it *appears* to be a stable personality trait.

The interplay between the self-concept and a given social situation can be sketched as follows.°

1. You enter a situation with a residual self-concept.
2. Your behavior is experienced by others; their interpretation of your behavior influences theirs.
3. You interpret (attach meaning to) the others' behavior.
4. You view yourself as you think others do based on your meaning for their behavior.
5. When necessary, you reconcile the two views of yourself: (a) the residual self-concept and (b) number 4 above. You arrive at a slightly revised self-concept which is a new residual of the two meanings. And the process continues.

°This is an expansion and revision of the paradigm suggested by Heine [200].

Our relationships with others affect our self-concepts, which, in turn, affect our future transactions. This student's perception of how well she has done in past job interviews is likely to affect her behavior in this interview.

Put simply, the residual self-concept from your previous experiences is balanced against the view of yourself that you have in a particular transaction.

Clearly, though the process is the same, each person we encounter does not have the same effect on our residual self-concept. Early life experiences greatly affect our self-view. When you are four years old each interaction you have with someone is a large share of your experiences. But as you advance in age and experience, each event assumes a smaller proportion of your total experiences. A similar thing happens with the perception of time. One year at age four is one-fourth of your life, but when you are fifty, one year is only one-fiftieth of your life. Likewise, the reaction of your partner in your first love relationship may have more impact on your self-concept than the reactions of later partners.

The sheer number of experiences is, of course, not the only factor influencing the impact of people on our residual self-concept. One crucial element is the importance of the person to you. If you go to K-mart and a cashier whom you do not know says, "You are selfish," it probably would not ruin your week. Yet that same comment from your best friend, closest family member, or romantic partner could have considerable impact on how you see yourself. Finally, one central determinant of the impact of others on your self-concept is how you interpret the reactions of others. If you are feeling down on yourself and someone says, "Go away—give me some space," the comment probably will have a negative effect on you. On the other hand, if you are in a jovial mood, such a comment may be the beginning of a friendly and humorous exchange.

CYCLES AND THE SELF

Self-concepts and transactions are bound together in a cyclic process. One's self-concept grows from transactions with others, and transactions with others are influenced by one's self-concept. The cyclic nature of the transaction between each person's self-concept and dyadic exchanges has been diagrammatically presented by Kinch [257]. Take a moment and carefully study Figure 2.1.

The self-concept influences one's behavior, which of course has an impact on the actual responses of the other participant. In turn, your perception of the other's responses develops your self-concept, *ad infinitum.* As Kinch states, "The individual's concept of himself emerges from social interaction and, in turn, guides or influences the behavior of that individual" [257].

This is the process of interplay as sketched from the viewpoint of one participant. There are two participants engaged in the process, and as a result, a similar description should be provided for the second person. *Each person's view of himself affects his as well as his partner's behavior.* Stated another way, each self-concept influences and is influenced by the communicative transaction.

Very little empirical work has focused on such cyclic processes. For one thing, such a view has yet to gain any general acceptance; its advent is relatively recent. For another, it is difficult in experiments

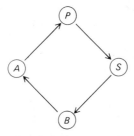

P = perception of other's responses toward him
S = self-concept
B = his behavior
A = actual responses of others toward him

Figure 2-1. The cyclic nature of the self-concept.

that are designed to ferret out cause–effect relationships to consider the same variable as both independent and dependent. One interesting although not conclusive investigation has paved the way for such approaches. Coombs [107] tested the cyclic model by examining the relationship between social participation, self-concept, and interpersonal valuation (receiving a favorable evaluation from others). Specifically, dancing was the index for social participation, self-concept was measured, and the favorable or unfavorable evaluations of dancing partners were assessed. The partners were paired for the dance on the basis of computerized selection. Coombs discovered that, in general, "previous dating experience increases the probability of being favorably evaluated by a dating partner; favorable evaluations foster a favorable view of self; and a favorable self-concept leads to more participation in dating" [107].

The Coombs investigation was inventive in that it attempted to test empirically the cyclic point of view concerning self-concept and transactions with others. However, it does leave many unanswered questions. For example, while the cyclic point of view does indicate mutual influences of concept and social transactions, it does not specify that those influences are of equal magnitude. Specifically, your residual self-concept has been formed over so many transactions that it is relatively stable at any point in time. It is rare that a single transaction with another will precipitate a dramatic shift in how you view yourself. An intense encounter, however, can propel you into an extended balancing act—comparing how you thought you were with the incoming information. If, for instance, you are in a committed relationship with someone of the opposite sex and he or she suddenly writes you a letter telling you that the relationship is "off" and that you are a "snob" and a "socialite," you will probably undergo the following sequence of reactions: (1) accept part of the definition along with severe hurt and pain, (2) seek out friends and others who know you and ask them if you are a "snob" or "socialite," and (3) come to realize that in most of your transactions you certainly could not be called this type of person. The residual self, in this case, will rear up and fight against the blatantly negative evaluation. Whatever the specific scenario of the interplay between the residual self-concept and your current transactions, it is clear that the process is cyclical. You enter each situation with the residual of what went before, and some elements of the current transaction either reaffirm or modify the view you have of yourself.

THE STUCK SELF: DO-LOOPS

Our self-perceptions may become self-sealing and self-validating. If, for instance, you see yourself as a person who is socially competent, relates well to others, and has a good time in life, then those definitions provide forces for their own fulfillment. Similarly, if you feel that you are socially inept and apt to make mistakes, then you may set yourself up to do just that. A student came to me the other day explaining his own form of an intrapersonal self-fulfilling prophecy. He had been silent in a class full of rather open, attentive students and was troubled because he had a lot to say but did not speak up. During high school he had been very outspoken in class until one teacher had continually called on him when he wasn't prepared to respond. As a result, he found it difficult to speak up in my class. He was so worried about why he "couldn't just say what he wanted to" that he was unable to say it. His fear of making a mistake kept him from breaking his self-definition of having nothing to say.

Unfortunately, negative views of the self can set one up for some rather intricate forms of being stuck. For example, Seligman [471] notes that "learned helplessness" sometimes develops where the person feels ineffective and, as a result, is depressed. Of course, if one is depressed, it is difficult to operate effectively, thereby reinforcing the belief that one is not effective.

The most extensive analysis of being stuck in a negative view of oneself is provided by Woodman, who uses the term *do-loops* to describe this process [551].* He notes that the human mind has the ability to metacommunicate, to communicate about communication. The mind is self-reflexive; it can turn upon itself and, using its processes, examine its own processes. This self-reflexiveness can sometimes pose problems. For an individual who simply experiences life and never reflects on it, do-loops pose no problem. But when one "goes beyond simple experiencing and making statements about his experiencing to new levels where he thinks about the way he thinks about things," do-loops can set in [55]. Do-loops are situations of "infinite regress," a spiraling to higher and higher levels of abstraction. The process of self-analysis can end up just like two mirrors facing each other and endlessly reflecting the other's reflections. A do-loop is an expanding cycle of reflexiveness that "continually tries to encompass itself, a kind of Alice-down-the-rabbit-hole spiral" [551].

Do-loops can occur for a variety of reasons. One of the most common is that an individual tends to apply labels rigidly to his or her behaviors and then begins reacting to the labels. For instance, one man takes a trip instead of giving vacation money to his brother's widow for hospital expenses. He then "misconstrues the meaning of such an act as indicating once and for all that he is a tight, selfish, and money-grabbing person . . . " [327]. As a result:

---

*I have chosen to retain the term *do-loop*, borrowed from Woodman, although technically, a do-loop in the computer world has a command leading one into and out of the algorithm. The do-loops illustrated here are essentially ones without an exit command.

A kind of rigid logic then takes over in the mind of the helpless victim and starts him thinking what he is and what he should be, the ways in which he can look like what he should be, how he can *try* to actually *be* what he should be, and perhaps mistakenly, thinks he is not; he develops new and more complicated ways of thinking about himself and the world; he becomes compelled to block out whole areas of his most basic experiencing; he becomes frightened of finding out who he *really* is; his mind goes beyond simple experiencing and making statements about his experiencing to new levels where he thinks about the way he thinks about things; and it is not long before he finds himself entertaining and rejecting the same ideas over and over again, caught in circles and eddies of reasoning he is incapable of getting out of [551].

Woodman's solution to do-loops is for the individual to seek freedom from the rigid set of categories. By giving oneself the "permission" to follow those feelings regardless of how illogical or unreasonable they seem, the pattern of infinite regression can be halted. One must try to discard rigid categories that create do-loops; one must experience openly and let in new meanings for one's behavior.

Do-loops caused by one's self-reflexiveness going into deeper and deeper levels are a communication situation that Frankl has also dealt with. His psychiatry has focused on individuals who perpetually are caught in do-loops. In a typical case, the burden of "unavoidable unhappiness" is increased by "unhappiness about being unhappy" [526]. Or take the case of a patient who cannot sleep at night. The fear of the sleeplessness results in a "hyperintention to fall asleep, which, in turn, incapacitates the patient to do so" [157]. Frankl's logotherapy (meaning therapy) is used to break the self-fulfilling do-loops and free the patient of the concerns. The technique is that you engage in "paradoxical intention"; you try to do the very thing you are trying to change [157]. If you can't break the spiraling effects of unhappiness, you try to be as unhappy as possible. If your problem is sleeplessness, you apply paradoxical intention and, upon going to bed, try to stay awake. One client had a problem with sweating when others were around, and, of course, his anticipation of it caused him to sweat all the more. Frankl advised him to deliberately show people how much he could sweat, and the do-loop was broken.°

A do-loop is an *intrapersonal* self-fulfilling prophecy; it occurs solely within the thinking processes of one person. Do-loops do, however, have an impact on one's dyadic transactions. In its most extreme form, it is a completely debilitating form of self-reflexiveness. One becomes so engaged in the intrapersonal transactions that it is impossible to respond fully or appropriately to the dyadic partner. Look at the following example of do-loops that R. D. Laing supplied in his book

---

°See also similar suggestions discussed in [192, 193, 519, 520].

Knots [272]. It demonstrates how one's thinking processes can affect a relationship.

Jill

I don't respect myself
I can't respect anyone who respects me.
I can only respect someone who does not respect me.

I respect Jack
because he does not respect me

I despise Tom
because he does not despise me

Only a despicable person
can respect someone as despicable as me

I cannot love someone I despise

Since I love Jack
I cannot believe he loves me

What proof can he give?

When Jill is in such a do-loop, Jack cannot give any proof of his love. As a result, her preoccupation with herself blocks an appropriate communicative exchange with Jack.

When a do-loop involves only you, the analysis spirals down into deeper and deeper levels. When a do-loop involves a definition of yourself that you communicate to others, you place the other person in a position such that he or she cannot alter your intrapersonal definition. A particular graduate student illustrated this phenomenon very clearly for me. She was a "late bloomer"—she was convinced that she was not a good student until suddenly she began getting high grades and producing outstanding work. She came into our graduate program and did outstanding work in her first graduate seminar. At the end of the course, I encouraged her in her writing, for she showed great promise as a clear, cogent thinker and a fine researcher. Then, two quarters later, she came to talk to me about finishing her degree. At the end of our session, in which we planned the nuts and bolts of what she had to do to graduate, she said, "There is something else that I'd like to talk to you about. When you gave me that positive feedback in the course two quarters ago, were you just doing that because you saw that I had a low self-concept and needed encouragement? Or do you really think that I have talent?" I assured her that the feedback was honest and that I wasn't trying to convince her of something that was untrue. Just like Jill in the preceding example, her self-definition set her up to reject any positive responses from outside. She looked for confirmation of the low self-concept.

A few more examples will illustrate how a negative loop can keep others from affecting our self-concept. The first one shows the thoughts of a person who feels overweight.

- I am dissatisfied because I'm fat.
- I'm fat because I eat too much.
- I eat too much because I'm dissatisfied with myself.

The following illustrates the mechanism that allows this loop to continue in spite of others trying to help:

CRAIG *(thinking to himself)*: I'm really fat.
GIRLFRIEND: Gee, you look nice today!
CRAIG *(thinking to himself)*: I must be so fat that she feels sorry for me and tells me I look nice to cheer me up. Whew! I'm even fatter than I thought if others notice it too.

The same pattern can occur with other beliefs about oneself—thinking one is unlovable, weird, or anything else. Whenever a person engages in such self-blame, it erects a barrier to positive feedback and distorts what others say to the person [68].

How does one get out of such loops? Woodman and Frankl both offer similar solutions. Because it is the person's view of the behavior that sets up the loop, one way out is to refuse to use global negative labels. For example, one can simply refuse to use a rigid label for one-self, discarding such self-descriptive terms as *fat, oversensitive, selfish, procrastinator, flakey,* and the like. Each behavior we engage in can be cast in positive or negative terms, and we can refuse to allow for extreme negative, global classifications if they put us in loops. The "aggressive" person can also be characterized as strong-willed, relia-ble, willing to put it on the line, and not wishywashy!

Watzlawick et al. [520] call the relabeling of behavior "reframing." They tell of a person who stammered a lot but wanted to make his living as a salesperson. He got to the point of being so worried about stammering that he could not sell. Worrying about the stammering made him stammer all the more. Watzlawick and his co-workers got the man to "reframe" his definition for the behavior. The stammering was redefined into an advantage by convincing the person that he actually had an edge on other salespeople because he stammered. They convinced him that people listen very intently to a stammerer because they feel sorry for him and wonder how he could possibly make a living at being a salesperson. As a result, people would be more persuaded by someone who "bumbled" than by someone who was overly smooth. Paradoxically, the stammerer did not feel tension about how he talked and then stammered less.

Another technique that is useful in breaking out of do-loops is to turn the analysis into a humorous event. One fellow I know has had trouble with a loop of being "too sensitive" and too easily rejected. He was able to break the loop one day when he felt rejected by his loved one by saying, "Well, I'll just crawl into the closet and eat worms." It was so absurd that both he and his lover laughed for fifteen minutes.

It has been noted that Frankl used "paradoxical intention" (doing the very thing you were trying to change) as yet a third way to break out of loops. Paradoxical intention works well for some forms of loops, such as not sleeping at night, but like any attempt, is not equally successful for some other loops.

This discussion of the entrapment power of loops is not meant to imply that all self-analysis and labels are negative. If one's label is positive and if one sets up circumstances where one's view of oneself elicits positive responses from others, it is obviously very healthful. Becoming stuck into a negative loop, however, can be delibitating and set off a chain reaction of low self-concept and unproductive communication with others, leading to a reinforcement of one's lowered self-concept.

ENHANCEMENT OF THE SELF-CONCEPT

People do, of course, take steps to improve their self-concepts. It has been argued that people have a "self-esteem motive," a desire to maintain and enhance a positive conception of oneself [411]. It can take many forms, from taking responsibility for positive outcomes and denying your role in negative events, blocking out counterinformation about yourself you do not want to hear, and selectively perceiving events from your past.

One concept encompasses all these mechanisms—*selectivity.* Selectivity takes many forms, all of which serve to give some stability to the self-concept. In general, (1) we can selectively expose ourselves to individuals who support our self-concept, (2) we can selectively interpret either our or the other person's behavior, and (3) we can selectively choose the goals we wish to achieve [282, 411].

We expose ourselves to individuals who support our self-concept. We choose certain people to associate with because they are the ones who think well of us. In a time of personal crisis, which is one of the situations that prompts self-awareness, we go to a friend because of the support we expect to obtain. Put bluntly, "friendship is the purest illustration of picking one's propaganda" [411]. Even on a day-to-day basis, our continuing transactions with our friends lend support to our self-concept. Quite clearly, the more people attribute traits to you that you feel you possess, the more your self-concept will be resistant to change [3]. If your most personal dyadic contacts are with people who react to you in very stable ways, your self-concept will appear to be stable.

Selective interpretation of your own and other people's behavior is another mechanism that lends stability to your self-concept. When we are exposed to situations that can threaten our self-concept, we selectively interpret the information [452]. As Rosenberg says, "There is scarcely any behavior which cannot be interpreted as admirable in some way . . . " [411]. The operation of selective interpretation can be observed most vividly in individuals with high self-esteem. Such individuals tend to respond to a specific failure by evaluating themselves higher [180]. One of the most intriguing statements regarding the maintenance of the self-conception I have ever seen came from a poem written by a student in one of my classes. He wrote it in response to a guest lecture that stressed that too many of us see ourselves as losers (frogs). Rather, we should see ourselves as winners (princes):

Frogs and Princes

Since we are here for only a short time
And while we're here we earn some dimes
These precious dimes may be many or few
It depends a lot on our personal views.

And if I'm a frog and you are a prince
And you have brains and I lack sense.
You will be a winner and I will lose,
But aren't most frogs faithful and true?

And suppose frogs are faithful and true,
Can't I as a frog become a winner, too?
And if a frog can win at this game
Who can say frogs and princes aren't really the same?°

The third major way people can selectively protect their level of self-concept is by a choice of goals. A person typically values those qualities and abilities in which he or she excels and devalues those qualities in which he fails to excel. Further, we will selectively expose ourselves to situations in which we will excel [411]. The boy who did not make the basketball team may suddenly develop an interest in debate activities. The girl who is not invited to many social gatherings may develop a heightened interest in being a good student. The college professor who puts students to sleep in class may become more absorbed in research activities. We all seek some degree of consistency between our goals and our degrees of success. After all, if you are 5

°Reprinted by permission of Stephen J. Wallace.

feet, 3 inches tall and weigh 100 pounds, it is rather foolish to continue getting smashed playing football when you have the option of selecting new goals.

The selectivity that we can exercise in order to maintain our self-concept does have its limits. Otherwise everyone would have a good self-concept that continually received support from other people. Circumstances are often such that we are restricted from having options from which to choose. Especially at an early age, we cannot choose who our parents will be or in what neighborhood we will live. If someone is disparaged and rejected by parents and friends, a weakened self-concept is likely to result. Often too, choices are made that bring totally unexpected consequences for the self-concept. One can be placed in a situation where one's talents and resources are not appropriate. The person starting a different job or the student attending a different college may experience a total lack of positive social support that obviously affects self-concept. We often do not realize that degree of dependence we have on other people until they are gone. One friend of mine experienced a precipitous decline in self-concept. She entered one social situation and for seven months experienced positive social support for her creativity and insight. She also became involved in a romantic dyad that was very meaningful to her. As a result of accepting a job in a new location, she had to change her residence. Much to her dismay, she discovered that she had no close friends nearby, her working associates did not provide the support to which she was accustomed, and she missed her romantic partner. During the months she remained there, her positive self-concept eroded to the point where the once self-assured, confident, friendly person became moody, depressed, and felt very inferior. After she returned to her previous place of residence and once again received a healthier dose of positive responses, her self-concept began the long climb to its previous level. Although her experience is a bit more dramatic than most, it does demonstrate that the freedom to choose one's social support is sometimes limited.

If you desire to change your self-concept, for better or for worse, you might change environments and transact with different people. Cooley states that the chief advantage of travel and change is "to get away from one's working environment," which is, in a sense, "to get away from one's self . . . " [106]. As you enter a different social situation, because of the expectations and responses of others and the shifting, mutually adaptive, transactional nature of human behavior, your self-concept undergoes change [211]. The new environment may produce responses in you that you were not aware were there. For instance, you may find yourself for the first time in many years openly exploring new job possibilities, meeting people of diverse religious beliefs, or taking up new hobbies. Then, as Bem noted in his self-perception theory, our meanings for ourselves change as a result of looking at the behavior we engage in. The "stick in the mud" might really become the "life of the party," with a subsequent change in how that person sees himself or herself.

Whenever you develop a new view of yourself, whether it is a dramatic life change or some slight modification, it also puts pressure on others to see you that way. Take the case of Greg. A college student with average grades, he enrolled in a course that he really loved. As a result, for the first time in four years, he really began to hit the books. He studied consistently and read additional material for the class. As a result, he received his first A in a long time. He began to think, "Maybe I'm a better student than I thought." This slow change in self-definition then put pressure on others to begin seeing him as a good student. As McCall and Simmons tell us, if we conduct ourselves as if we were a certain kind of person, it puts leverage on others to act toward us as if we were that kind of person. Then if we can "avoid tripping ourselves up through our own performances," people are obliged to give us the benefit of the doubt. Greg began projecting his newfound confidence, asked more questions, and others did begin seeing him as a good student.

The self-concept, since it is the residual of our past experiences, is resistant to change because of the selectivity that we each utilize. But if you can change environments, alter your goals, increase your success at your chosen goals, or project a new image of yourself that is consistent with your behavior, the self-concept can slowly begin changing. Greg still does not see himself as a Rhodes Scholar, but he does see himself as a "late bloomer"—a student who has much potential that is yet to be tapped. The key to a positive self-concept is to match your talents, both in the work world and in your personal relationships, with the expectations of others. And even if you cannot totally shape the expectations of others, you can at least find people who will appreciate you. Then you can appreciate yourself.

An understanding of the process of forming the self-concept is essential for an accurate view of dyadic communication. The cyclic nature of self-conception, influencing and being influenced by our dyadic relationships, highlights the central role it plays in all transactions. As might be expected, there is a high correlation between self-regard and regard for others [481, 555], because the two are inextricably bound together in our social relationships. Furthermore, self-acceptance is essential for psychological growth and health [406]. Individuals who feel accepted, capable, and worthy are not those in mental hospitals and prisons; such places are peopled by those who feel unwanted and unaccepted. It is precisely those with a low self-concept that find it necessary to reject others. As Sullivan puts it, "it is not that as ye judge so shall ye be judged, but as you judge yourself so shall you judge others" [481]. Or in more negative terms, "if you are a molehill, then, by God, there shall be no mountains" [483]. The self-concept is a potent perception influencing your dyadic relationships.

SUMMARY

People have the ability to think about themselves (objective self-awareness) and, as a result, develop self-concepts (generalized views of themselves). One's self-concept has multiple components and is basically social in nature. The prime determinants of one's self-concept are (1) the perceptions others have of one, (2) the comparisons one makes between oneself and others, and (3) the social roles with which one is identified. Although one's self-concept is shaped by communicative transactions with others, it also shapes those transactions. The self-concept is an inextricable element of the transactional communication process—it influences and is influenced by each dyadic communication event. The residue from previous events comprises the self-concept that one brings to each new situation.

Chapter 3

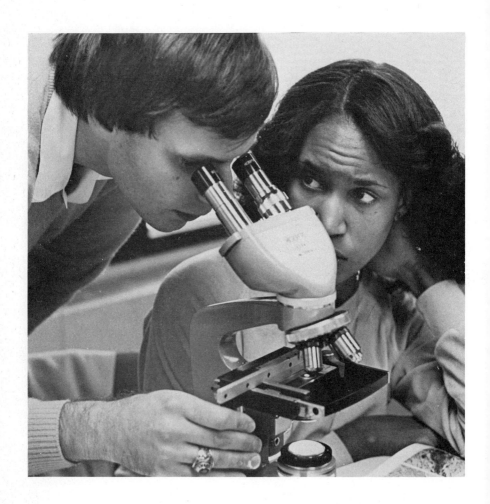

Perception of the Other

In Chapter 2 you read that the perception of the self is a vital component affecting your communicative transactions. Your perceptions of the other person—the crucial other half of the dyad—are no less important in determining the direction that the relationship goes. If you see your landlord as a tyrant, this perception will certainly affect the amount and kind of communicative experiences the two of you will have. Both the perception of the self and the perception of the other contribute to the meanings we assign to the communication situation [210]. And, of course, the meanings we assign determine our reactions. We act toward others based upon the meanings we have for them [316, 449].

Irrespective of your age, sex, or background, you attach meanings to the behaviors of others. For example, young children often perceive others' behavior as cooperative [236]. Similarly, if you have a job and see your supervisor as "cold, aloof, and uncaring," such perceptions will affect the way you work for him or her. In one organization with which I am familiar, the supervisor saw one key employee as "hostile, unhelpful, and critical," yet the employee saw herself as "unrewarded for all the extra work I do for free." Reciprocally, the employee saw the supervisor as "incompetent and lazy," whereas the supervisor saw herself as "trusting of others, and believing that people do their best work without close supervision." All of us "make meaning" continuously in our perceptions of others, and as the work example illustrates, the "meaning" we make about someone will diverge from how she sees herself.

The processes of perceiving others and perceiving ourselves have some similarities and differences, which then predispose us to communicate in particular ways. Perceptions tend to beget communication, so understanding the processes of self and other perception are central to understanding people's communicative choices.

SELF AND OTHER ATTRIBUTION

One of the most useful frameworks for discussing the perception of others comes from attribution theory, which deals with the process of attributing meaning to the behavior of ourself and the behavior of the other. As Shaver [449] notes, "people search for meaning in human behavior"; this search for meaning is the attribution process. When we observe our own behavior, as Bem argues in the preceding chapter, we attribute meaning to it. Likewise, we observe the behavior of others and attribute meaning to it.

Whether you are observing your own action or that of another, you make an attribution based on the available information that you have. For example, if you overheard a fellow student say, "That dirty crook. I'll never trade in that store again," you would probably feel that the store owner isn't to be trusted. However, if you read in the local paper the next day that the student you overheard had been found guilty of shoplifting from the store, it would alter your perception of both the store owner and the student. The evidence that we have for our attributions differs markedly, depending on whether we are attaching meaning to our own or the other's behavior.

The first difference is between *Insider vs. Outsider.*° If you just meet Sam on Tuesday, and on Wednesday you discover that he has terminated a relationship with a woman you like, you might well think he did a foolish thing. But because you are the outsider, you have no way of directly knowing what his thought processes were. And because you are an outsider, you don't know how hard he tried to make the relationship work. But if you are in a similar situation of saying goodby to a former intimate, you have all kinds of special, inside information on the effort you put into the relationship and the things the other person might have done to "deserve" the termination. This perceptual difference regularly happens in work situations also. If you are part of the "inside" crowd that makes decisions that affect others' lives, then there are "good reasons" for the actions you take. However, if you are standing on the outside watching a business executive fire an employee, you will probably be less charitable in your evaluation— seeing the actions as "unjustified" and "cruel." Although it isn't always true that the "inside" perspective on a person's or an organization's actions is necessarily more charitable, it does operate on different information than does the outside view. The inside information may be more negative than the outside perspective—but whatever the case, it will surely be different. The locus of your information, whether from the inside or the ouside, is the first central difference in how you attribute meaning to your own behavior compared with how you attribute it to the behavior of others.

The second element of difference between self and other perception is *Intimate vs. Stranger.* When we attribute meanings to ourselves, we have our past performance to use as a guide to the meanings. Let's say, for instance, that a student receives a *D* on the first exam in this course. If Jennifer is that student, you are likely to conclude that she didn't study very hard or that she "wasn't playing with a full deck." You simply do not know what her performance on the test was compared with other tests she has taken for fifteen years. But if you are the person who got the *D*, you probably will begin by comparing your performance on this test with those of all your other tests. If in the past term you had a perfect *A* average, this background information will

---

°For a fuller treatment of attribution theory see Shaver [449], Jones, and Nisbett [241], Jones [240], Baron and Byrne [23], and Bem [46]. The four-part distinction between self and other attribution is borrowed directly from Bem [46].

greatly influence how you attach meaning to the grade. Woe to the poor professor who gave you such an undeservedly difficult, tricky, and sneaky test.

The third central issue that divides self and other perception is *Self vs. Other*. Our meanings for ourselves tend to serve the function of protection of the self, as we noted in the last chapter on selectivity of self-concept. Bem [46] thinks that the notion of self-perceptions protecting the self is overrated but feels nevertheless that self-perceptions contribute to the differences between the meanings we have for our own and someone else's behavior. I'll never forget one day when I was a college undergraduate. Three men who ate together, slept in the same building, and went to the local bars together each weekend were walking across campus. As they approached three black men, they hushed their voices and resumed talking only after being out of earshot. Then one said, "I just can't stand those guys. They are such a clique; they go everywhere together."

The fourth difference is between *Actor vs. Observer*. Most of the time we are in the state of subjective self-awareness, unaware of the contributions our "self" makes to an ongoing communication transaction. As a result, our attention is focused outward—we are the actor in the social setting. But when it comes to perceiving the other person, we are in the role of observer. Our focus is on the behavior of the other, and we act as an observer studying him or her. This third party perspective, however, cannot be fully used when viewing ourselves—we are always the actor.

The interrelatedness of these four dimensions is readily apparent. The result is as Jones and Nisbett [241] specify: "Actors tend to attribute the causes of their behavior to stimuli inherent in the situation, while observers tend to attribute behavior to stable dispositions of the actor." Translated, this means that we tend to look for "personality traits" in the other that explain his or her actions, but when examining ourselves we tend to look for outside forces that explain our behavior. One of the more intriguing studies that demonstrate this principle was conducted by Nisbett [356]. He interviewed college males about their choices of girlfriends and also asked them about their best friends' choices of girlfriends.

The students reported that they choose their girlfriends because of their looks or behaviors, forces all external to the subjects themselves. Yet when asked why a friend had a particular kind of girlfriend, they said it was because the friend needed a particular kind of companion, or because he had strong personal needs—all personal attributions. When perceiving the self, people tend to underrate their personal dispositions that help account for their choices. When perceiving other people, the tendency is to underrate the situational forces that contribute to the choices. When we turn a paper in late, we are "overworked"; our friends hand in papers late because they are "lazy."

THE TRANSACTIONAL NATURE OF PERSON PERCEPTION

The psychologically naive individual operates under the assumption that he or she "perceives and observes other people in a correct, factual, unbiased way" [231]. If Charlie perceives Sam as dishonest, that means for him that Sam *is* dishonest. Such an approach, although it makes "reality" easy to deal with, ignores the transactional nature of perception. There is no objective world of persons. We each interpret others in different ways. To be sure, there is much agreement over evaluations. Two women may both agree, after each had to fight her way home, that Sam is "handy with the hands." But what does it mean? Sam needs affection? Sam is a male chauvinist? Sam's mother rejected him? Sam is overreacting because he's afraid of women? Sam would make a bad husband? Sam would make a good husband? Just as we can never know the real or ultimate self, we cannot know what Sam is really like. We can say, however, that, "This was my experience and this is how I reacted," recognizing that others experience a different aspect of Sam and attach their own meanings. The following anecdote illustrates the point that our meaning for another's behavior is subject to error.

The small son of upper-class parents worried them considerably. In the presence of strangers, the boy stammered, withdrew, and became quiet. When around other children he became afraid and nervous. The parents felt the need to secure some professional help for the boy but wanted to do it so that the boy would not be embarrassed or feel singled out. Finally they hit upon an idea. An old college friend of the father was a clinical psychologist, so they invited him to dinner. After the meal, they revealed the real reason they had asked him over—to diagnose the son's problem. He accepted the task of observing the boy the next day (after, of course, collecting appropriate information on history and behavior).

> He watched, unseen, from a balcony above the garden where the boy played by himself. The boy sat pensively in the sun, listening to neighboring children shout. He frowned, rolled over on his stomach, kicked the toes of his white shoes against the grass, sat up and looked at the stains. Then he saw an earthworm. He stretched it out on the flagstone, found a sharp-edged chip, and began to saw the worm in half. At this point, impressions were forming in the psychologist's mind, and he made some tentative notes to the effect: "Seems isolated and angry, perhaps overaggressive, or sadistic, should be watched carefully when playing with other children, not have knives or pets." Then he noticed that the boy was talking to himself. He leaned forward and strained to catch the words. The boy finished the separation of the worm. His frown disappeared, and he said, "There. Now you have a friend." [438].

Figure 3-1.   Disappearing dot.

The transactional nature of perception occurs in both the perception of objects and perceptions of people. You might think that objects, since they are "real" and objective facts, can be observed without interference of our own views. However, as Bateson says, "objects are my creation, and my experience of them is subjective, not objective" [29]. The meaning attached to an object is a function of (1) the perceiver, (2) the object, and (3) the situation. For an illustration of this, look at Figure 3-1.

Hold the book level with your eyes and close your left eye. With your right eye look directly at the asterisk and then move the book back and forth slowly about 12 inches away. You will notice that the spot, which you can first see, disappears at a certain point. The "disappearance" of the spot on the right occurs because we have an absence of photo receptors (rods and cones) at that point on the retina [511]. But this physical "blind spot" makes an important point as well. We all have "blind spots" in our perceptions of both objects and people, and even if we had all the physical equipment, we could not "objectively" perceive objects. For purposes of illustration, look at Figure 3-2 [509]. What do you see?

Figure 3-2.   Arrangement of dots.

Probably dots arranged in the forms of a triangle and a square. Look again! On the left are three dots and on the right are four dots. Why did they not produce the following shapes in your mind?

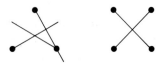

Or why were they not seen as totally unrelated to one another? Clearly, what you perceived was as much a function of you as of the arrangement of dots.

If the perception of objects is a "transaction between the brain and the environment" [382], the process of person perception is certainly no less a transaction. As a *minimum* in person perception, there is (1) the perceiver, (2) the person, and (3) the situation. In addition, some important elements are added in a dyadic relationship that are not present in the perception of objects. To begin with, there is a *mutually shared field* [494]. You see him and he sees you. The person you are perceiving is engaging in the same process you are. The complexity of the situation is described by Tagiuri [493]:

> The perceiver, in some sense aware of many of the general properties of the other person (consciousness, mind) or his specific attributes (for example, generosity), has to allow for the fact that he himself, with similar properties, is also the object of perception and thought and that, as such, he influences his own object of perception. Observer and observed are simultaneously observed and observer. Their reciprocal perceptions, in a continuous recycling but varying process during which each person uses the variations in himself and the other person as a means of validating his hypothesis about the other.

Your own behavior in a dyadic transaction produces reactions in the other, which you then use as the basis of your perception. And the same process is occurring for the other participant. The process of person perception is obviously more complex than is object perception because the object is not adjusting to our presence. Often the conclusion that another person's behavior is consistent simply means that we provide a "self-picture which remains relatively stable and coherent," which has consistent effects on the other's behavior [166]. The personality characteristics you perceive in a person may depend in part on the characteristics he or she perceives in you [311].

We can never perceive the "real" person because the concept of the "real" person is a myth. The other person's behavior is just as relationship-bound as ours is. For example, if you perceive a person to be acting in a hostile manner, her perception of your behavior as hostile could have triggered her response. Furthermore, we often project onto others. We see things in them that are not in them, but in us [231]. For instance, if you are feeling alone and bitter because of the recent loss of a romantic partner, you may tend to perceive other people as being lonely. And conversely, "when you're smiling, the whole world smiles with you."

At the very least, person perception is a transactional process because what we see *is as much a function of us* as it is of the qualities of the other person. For example, when you are really angry at someone, your reaction may say more about you than it does him. There is no "immutable reality" [126] of the other person awaiting our discovery. We attribute qualities to the other based on the cues we have available, and the unique way that we interpret them. Our perception of the other, while seeming certain, is grounded in permanent uncertainty.

Research dealing with person perception is beginning to recognize more fully the transactional nature of the process. For instance, Delia's work argues that the communicative transactions influence perceptions of others [117]. At this point, we can specify that there are some general principles about the process of attaching meaning to another's behavior, and they will be discussed under the topic of perceptual regularities. Two of the most important perceptual regularities occurring in dyadic contexts are (1) the imposition of structure and (2) the attribution of causality and responsibility.

PERCEPTUAL PATTERNS

Perceptual Sets

There are certain patterns that regularly occur in our perceptions of others. These "perceptual sets" arise because of our desire to "make sense" out of others' behavior—to place it in a category with a label. Perceptual sets are the result of these regularities: (1) imposing structure, (2) assuming consistency on the part of the other.

Just as we impose structure upon objects, such as seeing the dots of Figure 3.2 in a pattern, we impose a structure upon a person's behavior. We always have to act on the basis of incomplete information, and we make sense of the incomplete information *by going beyond it* [77]. We take the initial and incomplete information and use it to define the person, to place her in a particular category. We do this because our world of experience has (1) structure, (2) some stability, and therefore (3) meaning [202]. The Asch [11] study is one of the best examples of how we structure impressions of others based on partial information. Subjects were given a list of traits of an individual and were asked to write a paragraph describing the person. They also chose from a list of opposing traits those they felt characterized the person. Subjects formed overall impressions of persons based on such terse descriptions as *intelligent, skillful, industrious, warm, determined, practical,* and *cautious.* And furthermore, when the word *warm* was replaced by the word *cold*, impressions were considerably altered. Overall impressions of others are based on partial evidence; we translate the partial evidence, whether it comes from a list of words or from a short transaction with the other, into a meaningful structure. Once we construct this model of the other, we guide our responses appropriately [322]. For instance, if you interpret a new acquaintance's acts as generally morose, you will use this overall structure as the basis for your reactions.

The structure that we impose upon situations is uniquely ours. As Kelly [237] noted, we interpret information within the realm of our personal constructs. We "make sense" out of the other through our

Each person's interpretation of another's behavior is unique. If two people have enough in common, however, they may have similar impressions of a third person.

own personal experiences and ways of viewing the world [120]. In fact, the person's behavior is understandable to *us only to the extent that we can tie it back to our own experience* [514]—only to the extent that we have a construct for it. While the way each of us construes events is personal, there is enough commonality between two peoples' constructs to allow overlap in constructs [133]. Therefore, if you and Sharon both observe Bob in the same situation, your interpretations of his behavior may have enough commonality that you "agree" on what you perceive to be his personality.

The meaning that we impose on the behaviors of others has been termed the "implicit personality theory" that each of us has [113]. We each have an intuitive notion about which traits are likely to go together and use those ideas as a basis for judgment of others. If a car salesperson misrepresents some of the information about a car to you, you may well refer to him as a "shyster," imputing a definite personality trait. But some other person may say, "Hey, the person isn't a shyster. He is just required to turn the best profit possible. It's all part of the job." Each of you is imposing a different implicit personality theory on the behavior of the other. One research study in communication demonstrates that implicit personality judgments are made early in the course of our interactions with others. Berger [51] found that if people act somewhat consistently both early and late in their interactions with others, they are judged to have traits that carry on through the other interactions. If you meet your college roommate and she acts "warm and outgoing" toward you, you will probably conclude that she is a "friendly person." This early attribution will carry forth until there is compelling evidence to cause you to alter you attribution—such as her moving all your belongings out into the hall and changing the lock on the door.

As noted earlier, our perceptual sets about others involve imposing structure and "going beyond" the information about another. Paradoxically, not only do we "see more than is there," but we also "see less than is there." Once we impose a perceptual structure on another, it blocks us from seeing other attributes of the person. For instance, one man when asked what his ex-wife's name is says "FANG!" Such a label short-circuits our thinking about her, blocking us from seeing her other qualities as a mother, friend, or co-worker. I once had an experience of being stranded on a lonely Montana back road, about 20 miles from the nearest town. There was almost no traffic, it was dark, and the car engine had just had a major seizure. One car finally came over the horizon, and I managed to stand in the middle of the road and get the man to stop. As I sat in the back of the car, the driver said, "Hi—what do you do?" I said, "I'm a professor at the university." There was a silence, an "Oh," and then the conversation ended. The rest of the ride to Townsend was filled with the sounds of silence while I wondered what his perceptual set was for college professors.

One fascinating study with mental health workers also illustrates perceptual sets in action—blocking people from seeing other information. Over 100 mental health workers were shown a videotape of a therapy session with a female client. Half of the professionals was told that the client was lesbian and the other half was told that she was heterosexual. When the professionals were asked to assess her psychological adjustment, those who thought she was lesbian saw her as being more defensive, less nurturant, and less confident and having less self control and more negative attitudes toward men. On the other hand, those who believed her to be heterosexual reacted to her in a totally positive way and even wondered why she was in therapy, [299]. The label of *lesbian* activated a perceptual set that did not allow the mental health workers to see the behavior they could see in the case of someone else.

Perceptual sets permeate perceptions of others, and the imposed structure both adds and misses important information. These processes are so pervasive that you can be assured that someone's description of another person will not be accurate. The perceiver's imposed structure will not present an accurate picture to you of the other person no matter how hard they try. Our language gives us shortcuts for explanations, but unfortunately, it also guarantees misrepresentation of another.

A related aspect of our imposition of structure is that we assume personal consistency on the part of others. Because we attribute a "definiteness of attitudes, sentiments, and views" to others [231] when it is not there, we are often surprised. The young woman who had been a serious student shocks her parents by quitting her job and traveling alone around the world. The boy who had been a juvenile delinquent suddenly breaks his habits and spends his next few years helping others. And the freewheeling, loose bachelor joins the monastery. Research evidence does not support the notion that people are consistent in their behavior, yet we are often dismayed when they act inconsistently. As Mischel [338, 341] has pointed out, our behavior is a product of the unique combination of the people we are around and our adjustment to them and is not due to any inherent personality trait.

Often our expectation for consistency in others' behavior can produce humor. Joe was a semiserious student in one of my classes (he attended and participated, but did not study very hard). He was older than the other students, about thirty, and was the father of four children. All in all, I saw him as a responsible, hard-working student. One day during a rather rigorous final examination, he was sitting in the back of the room and like the other students, was intensely involved in the test. All of a sudden, when I looked his way his hand shot into the air with a huge middle finger extended—and a grin on his face. His gesture was so unexpected and so disruptive to my view of him that all I could do was laugh in front of a very puzzled class.

We often punish people who violate our conceptions of what they are. When we label someone's behavior as insincere or label her as a fake, we are only saying that she violated how we expect to perceive her. One study demonstrated that predictable people tend to be liked more than unpredictable ones [166]. Because (1) we want consistency in the other, (2) our behavior often produces consistency in the other's response, and (3) we construct a consistent view of the other, we have a tendency to evaluate him in terms of particular personality traits [231]. If someone always acts intelligently around us, we tend to ascribe it as a personality trait, when in fact it as well as all his other behaviors are situationally determined. The total mix of (1) your meaning and behavior and (2) his meaning and behavior produces the "personality" you perceive. There may be certain tendencies for response—he may wish to be a happy person—but the situation has to be appropriate in order to observe that quality in him.

Attribution of Causality and Responsibility

The second perceptual regularity characteristic of person perception is the attribution of causality. As human beings, we want to come to grips with our environment; we want to make sense out of the world. One of the techniques we utilize to this end is the attribution of causality. From the general view that events are caused, we view human behavior as being caused. Most of us feel we are in part responsible for our actions, and we impose this same perspective on others. We see them as at least partly responsible for their actions [493].

When we mentally attach causes to the behaviors of others, we essentially have two choices: attribution to *external* causes or attribution to *internal* causes; that is, we ascribe the behavior of another either to the actor (internal locus) or to the circumstances surrounding him or her (external locus) [440]. We tend to attribute the person's actions to external causality under the following conditions [23]:

1. *High consensus.* Other people also act in this manner in this kind of situation. For instance, if we think that most people will suffer depression when they lose a loved one, then person A's depression is seen as being caused by the loss of a loved one.
2. *High consistency.* If the person acts similarly to the way she is acting in this situation on other occasions, then we assume that the situational constraints produce the behavior.
3. *High distinctiveness.* If this person acts differently in other situations, then we assume that her depression has been produced by circumstances of this situation. For instance, if someone lies when interviewed by the police for a drug charge but does not lie in other situations, we would tend to see the lying as produced by the strong arm of the law, and not by some personality trait.

The conditions leading to an attribution of internal causality are the opposite of those cited earlier. If there is low consensus (others in this situation do not act this way), then we attribute the behavior to a personality, or internal state of the person. Suppose that an out-of-work, recently divorced friend of yours has been evicted by his landlord. During the process of moving, he physically harms his ex-wife because she had come over to claim some of the furniture. You will see your friend as "aggressive" or "hostile," because most people would not act violently in such a situation. Therefore, whenever attributing causes to the other, the more unique or bizarre the behavior, the more likely we are to attirbute it to some internal state. If there is low consistency (the person is in the situation often, but acts differently), we tend to attribute the behavior to internal states that are unpredictable. Take the evicted friend again. If he has been with his former mate many times before in dealing with the property, but this one time he assaults her, we are likely to conclude that he "has gone off the deep end," or some similar situation. Finally, if there is low distinctiveness (the person acts similarly in a number of situations), then we assume it is a function of personality not of the situation. If our friend has been in many physical spats with others before, we would see him as an aggressive person and would see his assault on his ex-wife as just fitting a firmly established pattern.

The key to attribution of causality is, as Kelley [247] notes, the amount of covariation. If the behavior occurs with the presence of the person and not when the person is not present, then we conclude that the person has caused it. With the man who assaulted his former mate, if the woman has been physically assaulted many times by many former romantic partners, we would conclude that something in her behavior toward men contributes to the responses that they have toward her [247].

When attributing causality, the judgment centers on whether we think the other has the power to create the effects. In most situations, we also attribute responsibility—where we impose an emotional or moral judgment along with the notion of causality. Researchers in attribution theory separate the two processes, but the preceding examples combine the notions of causality and responsibility because in most reactions to others, the two are intertwined.

The degree of responsibility we place on others for events depends on a number of factors. If external forces are not very strong or if the ability to withstand those forces is regarded as high, we tend to place causality and responsibility in the lap of the other. If the person has the ability to create effects, he is typically held responsible for those effects [492]. When observing a disintegrating marriage, for example, if we feel that one of the partners had it in his power to cause the demise of the marriage by having an outside relationship, we place the responsibility on him. Furthermore, if we see the person intending to gain the desired goal, we are more likely to assign responsibility to him. In sum, people are held responsible for the effects they intend to create and for effects they have the ability to create [210].

The crux of the matter is that in analyzing social situations, we usually have two choices. We can ascribe the effects either to the person or to the environment. If we see another fail at a task, we can attribute it to a lack of ability, "a personal characteristic, or to the difficult task, an environmental factor" [210]. Whichever path we choose has consequences for our transactions. If, in the preceding case, we see the person as failing because of a lack of ability, we may concomitantly perceive him as a weak-willed, nonpowerful person. Our tendency will be to blame him and to take the "he-had-it-coming" attitude toward his misfortunes. This attribution often follows the "belief in a just world" notion that many people have [449]. If a person is fired, has children in trouble with the law, or is experiencing any other difficulty, this belief allows people to conclude that if bad things happen to a person, he or she somehow deserves it. This attribution pins the effects of behaviors solely upon the person.

If, on the other hand, we ascribe his failure to environmental causes ("Anyone would have failed at that."), then we will see him in a friendlier light and be sympathetic to his plight. A special form of attributing causes to environmental forces occurs in the case of unconscious moti vation. If you see someone's behavior as caused by circumstances beyond his understanding and control ("He had a bad childhood and that is why he is insane."), you will absolve him of blame. Our courts of law recognize that environmental forces may be so overwhelming in some cases that the individual should not be tried.

The attribution process is central to the ongoing communication transactions we have with others. If we see someone as "trustworthy" and "having to slightly bend the truth," our communication behavior toward her will be markedly different than if we view her as a "liar who cannot be trusted in any situation." In our communicative transactions with others, we make attributions, attach meanings to their communicative behaviors, and take action based on them. The process of attribution, therefore, occurs constantly in our communication with others.

PERCEPTUAL BIAS

Our perceptual biases occur for a variety of reasons, with three prominent ones being (1) our past experiences unrelated to this person, (2) our repeated experience with one person, and (3) the nature of the relationship we have with the person.

We all learn from our previous experiences and sometimes carry over those learnings inappropriately. For example, one day I was walking with Betsy across campus, and I spotted an interesting-looking fellow. I pointed him out to her, and she said, "I wouldn't trust him as far as I could throw him." She had not met him before, nor had she heard of him, so I asked how she knew he couldn't be trusted. She responded, "Never trust a man with a beret!" Her past experiences with men with such hats must have been interesting. Our past experiences with people in similar categories can predispose us to see new people in terms of our already formed categories, whether they be teacher, student, preacher, housekeeper, railroad employee, or member of a particular racial or ethnic group.

Second, our previous experience with one particular person can predispose us to perceptual biases. Kellerman notes that when we initially meet someone, negative information is "weighted more heavily than positive information" and is more resistant to change than positive information [246].

Third, the nature of the relationship with another person will set some perceptual biases into motion. One of the most common events in organizations is the distrust of those in power over you; the nature of the relationship predisposes people to look for negative attributions about the powerful person.

Your *investment in the relationship* will also let bias blossom. Courting couples misperceive each other's faults (if love isn't blind, it is at least near-sighted!) because negative information would deter them from developing a romantic relationship [252]. Similarly, when someone experiences the termination of an important romantic relationship, you can certainly hear some interesting phrases to describe the other. If you know someone who has gone through an entire relationship with another person, you know that the early descriptions and the later descriptions are miles apart. People protect their self-view by disparaging the other [458]. As Sillars and Scott note, biases in long-lasting relationships may not disappear; they may "become more firmly entrenched" [460]. If you "fall out of love" you may be invested in showing to others that the decline in the relationship was not "your fault," so this investment deters you from seeing the positive characteristics of your partner.

Finally, during the course of a relationship, there may be changes in the communication that stir up perceptual biases [460]. If a couple is engaged in a conflict with one another, the emotional nature of the struggle can accentuate negative perceptions of the other [460, 458]. How can we correct inaccurate perceptions of others? First, we would see that our perceptions serve functions for us and do not accurately reflect the other person's qualities, and we should be willing to update perceptions. If you become more interested in forming good relationships than in being "right," it opens up new possibilities. For instance, if you get the opportunity to experience a person in a different context, new information can seep into your perceptions. I once went on an outdoor expedition with a person I didn't care for on the job. The result was that I began to see his humorous, fun-loving aspects, and I would expect he also saw a more positive side of me than he had previously.

Second, if you understand the transactional nature of human communication, you might be able to unfreeze some perceptions. Most people tend to see others as causing all the difficulties. ("She is crazy!") This is the "fundamental attribution error"—seeing your own behavior as a reaction to the other, and the other as manifesting stable personality traits [457, 354]. The transactional approach stresses the need to see that both of you are reacting to what the other is communicating—you are both influencing and being influenced by the other. If you accept the transactional notion, then the search for the "correct perception" of another is lessened and you can begin to focus on the joint product you both create.

Finally, if you have a close friend or intimate partner who will not accept negative personality labels you try to paste on him or her, it can be a source of both conflict and correction. Almost any adjective about another can be seen in positive or negative terms. Is someone "too sensitive" or tuned into others? Isn't a procrastinator one who takes time to make decisions so they will be more correct? Isn't someone labeled "flighty" really a person who is fun-loving, carefree, and not uptight and prone to ulcers? Whatever the negative personality description, it can be seen in more positive terms, and our close friends and romantic partners can often be a source of perceptual correction for us.

We humans respond to the behavior of another as if it were an index of his emotional state. From the time of Darwin, deciphering the process of assessing emotions has been a subject of research. Although it is risky to draw any definite conclusions at this point [202], we can say this: The more information you have about a situation, the more accurate your judgment will be. More information leads to less "filling in" on your part [133]. A grimace on someone's face can be interpreted in innumerable ways, but if you also see him attempting to lift a 200-pound weight, the meaning becomes clearer for you. Unfortunately, most of the studies on perceptual accuracy have portrayed aspects of persons separated from a total context (such as having the picture of a face flashed on a screen). Not only do we know that we can more accurately recognize emotions in context, but we know that the ability to recognize emotions is mostly developed through social experience. The ability to perceive accurately when someone is kidding you, for example, arises from your experience with kidding behavior in the past. Only the most basic emotional expressions are recognized through innate ability [493]; the rest are recognized as a result of cultural training.

The ability to perceive another's attitudes accurately increases with time. Altman and Taylor [6] specify that as a relationship develops, the participants share more and more central aspects of their orientations. Romantic pairs, for instance, typically go through "periods of adjustment" when one member is learning, often painfully, that the attitude of the partner is not what he or she thought. In experimentally created dyads, initial awareness between partners is very low, although better than chance [497]. With continuing transactions, estimates of the other's attitudes typically improve [74, 497]. It may well be that the most pronounced effect of transacting with another person is a heightened awareness of her attitudes when she is in your presence.

What factors produce an accurate estimate of the other's emotions or attitudes? Allport [4] suggests that personal characteristics such as extent of personal experience, intelligence, cognitive complexity, self-insight, and social skill may be related to the ability to perceive another's emotions and attitudes accurately. On the other hand, accuracy in judgment may simply be a matter of matching judges and subjects who are similar in attributes. For example, if they both have conventional attitudes, the degree of accuracy may be produced by the judge projecting his own attitudes and emotions into the other. It just so happens that they match.

Although the preceding conclusions concerning the accuracy of person perception can be made, their application to our own dyadic relationships is not an easy task. Unlike a rigorously devised experiment, often no standards exist in our dyadic relationships that we can check to determine the accuracy of our perceptions. As with the case in building self-concept, the bases for comparing our person perceptions are social in nature. Our social reality, the judgments of others around us, is our only guide to the "correctness" of our view of someone. All in all, the process of perceiving our dyadic partner is slippery business—not only will our own behavior affect hers, but the only standards for comparison we have are the perceptions others have of her. And their perceptions are subject to the same limitations.

INTERPERSONAL ATTRACTION

The meaning we attach to another's behavior takes many forms, depending on the type of relationship. For romantic pairs the meaning each has for the other's behavior carries sexual connotations; for a teacher–pupil dyad the transaction may be based on mutual respect; and in a doctor and patient dyad, the central meaning in the transaction may revolve around the need for a service. In all types of dyadic pairs, however, the attraction between the two people is a force central to their perceptions of each other. We all experience degrees of attraction toward others—there are some people we enjoy being around and others that, for some reason, we find repelling.

The basic degrees of feeings ranging between liking and disliking another—the degrees of attraction—are produced by a host of factors. Tagiuri [492] and Lindzey and Byrne [83, 84] have cataloged many of the factors that influence the attraction people feel toward others. The present section will highlight propinquity, similarity between participants, and the communication experience as inextricably tied to the attraction one feels toward another.

Propinquity

Propinquity simply means proximity or physical closeness. The physical closeness of two persons has a dramatic impact on the attraction between them. The close geographical placement of two individuals allows a communication transaction to occur and sentiment or attraction to intensify.

Propinquity is one of the initial determiners in the formation of friendships. Close friendships are formed by being geographically close. The classic Festinger, Schachter, and Back [147] study perhaps most clearly demonstrates the pronounced effects of physical proximity on friendship. They studied friendship development in a new hous-

Friendships are more likely to occur between people who live near one another or who share activities that bring them into contact with one another.

ing project. A series of small houses formed a U-shaped court and some houses faced inward to an open grassy area while the end houses faced outward. Friendships were most affected by the distance between houses and the direction the houses faced. As the distance between houses increased, fewer friendships formed. The effects were so marked that it was rare to find friendships forming between individuals separated by more than four or five houses. Furthermore, those individuals who by chance happened to occupy the houses that faced outward had less than half as many friends in the project as those whose houses faced inward.

In order for friendship to result, some activity has to provide a setting for contact to occur. In my former neighborhood, the effects of the seasons significantly altered friendships. During the winter my neighbor across the street kept his car in his garage behind the house. In the summer he kept it out front. So when he used his car in the winter, we could not see one another; as a consequence, the usual chit-chat and the "Hey, come on over for a drink!" atmosphere of the summer disappeared. Likewise my friendship with the person across the alley from me waned in the winter. During the summer we saw each other in our gardens (his was much better than mine!) and talked for long periods of time. But carrot and tomato talk totally disappeared in winter, and we saw each other only about once a month. Your own friendships probably developed because a job, hobby, class in school, or living area placed you in the proximity of the other people. Friendship develops from transacting with others, and conversations are often started between those who share in an activity that places them in close physical proximity.

One interesting sidenote is that men seem to form friendships based on mutual activity, while women more often form friendships based on sharing feelings [88]. If this is the case, then men should especially be aware that the presence or absence of activities will have a significant effect on the friendships that they form.

Not only are friendship pairs affected by propinquity, but the selection of a romantic partner is heavily influenced by it. Many marriages are between people who reside close to each other [59]. Numerous studies have demonstrated that the closer two potential marital partners live, the higher is the probability of a marriage occurring. If the building is designed to promote transactions, the single man and single woman who move into an apartment complex to find a mate are making a wise choice. You have to meet someone before a romantic relationship can form, and physical proximity provides the opportunity. Even extramarital romantic relationships are greatly affected by propinquity. The boss–secretary relationship, for instance, is a classic one. This type of relationship has the opportunity to develop because the participants work in close relation to each other.

Why doesn't proximity also produce intense dislike? Sometimes it does, but it usually produces the opposite. Of course, if people are forced so close together that they hardly have room to breathe, proximity can work against close friendship. When two fur trappers are penned into their small cabin for two months by the winter snow, they get cabin fever, but such cases happen rather infrequently. For most of us, carrying out routine activities in close proximity to another produces some degree of fondness. Newcomb [350] notes that with close contact comes more information, usually favorable, about the other. This mutuality of rewarding each other produces positive sentiment [213, 53].

Seen from another point of view, a transaction with another often give us the feeling of being included. Since inclusion is a basic human need [443], it follows that the satisfaction of a need produces pleasure and therefore liking. In any event, proximity has a tendency to produce liking more than disliking. However, a specific prediction of the effects of proximity on any two dyadic participants would be risky. To predict whether two particular individuals thrown into proximity will form a friendship or romantic pair would require an amazing amount of information. You would have to know their backgrounds, needs, past transactions, meanings they assign to others, and self-concepts— and these are only a few of the crucial elements. We will have to be satisfied at this point with a very general conclusion: Propinquity allows friendships and romances the opportunity to flourish. But making predictive statements about love is a risky business.

Similarity

Interpersonal attraction is not only affected by propinquity; as two individuals begin to interact, a host of other factors influences their mutual attraction. One of these factors, similarity, has been extensively investigated.

Do birds of a feather flock together? Or do opposites attract? A number of studies have shown that if the birds are lovebirds and human, then those flocking together do tend to be of like feather. Byrne's review of literature led him to the conclusion that, "the association between similarity and attraction has consistently been verified in the husband–wife studies" [84]. The similarity was attitudinal; marital partners tended to agree with each other about topics ranging from communism to birth control. Furthermore, friendship pairs show the same type of similarity of attitude patterns [57]. Therefore, for marital and friendship dyads, there is an association between attitude similarity and attraction [84].

Why should similarity and attraction be related? Duck [144] has demonstrated that friends have similar personal constructs and, in addition, they are aware of the similarity. The similarity leads to attraction because "cognitive similarity leads to communication effectiveness, communication effectiveness leads to rewards, and these to interpersonal attraction" [498]. It does seem reasonable that as we communicate effectively with another, our attraction is built because a successful transaction is rewarding, and we like those who reward us [59].

The relationship between similarity and attraction can be seen in reverse by specifying that attraction produces similarity. One of the things that happens is that as individuals interact, each selects objects of common interest that highlight agreement [351]. Of course, it may be that we select people to interact with when we see some potential for agreement. According to balance theory [210], we strive to make sense out of our relationships. If we see ourselves as similar to others, we expect to like them. Furthermore, if we dislike someone we expect to have dissimilar attitudes on important issues.

Dyadic participants often overestimate the similarity between their attitudes. The studies of Levinger and Breedlove [293] and Cavoir et al. [95], for example, showed that husbands and wives tended to be similar in some attitudes, but the assumed similarity was higher than the actual similarity. Spouses typically overestimate their attitudinal agreement [85], yet this overestimation has desirable consequences. When one overrates attitudinal similarity with his or her spouse, and vice versa, rewards are increased [84]. We are rewarded by others when we agree with them, and it is certainly easier to receive those rewards by misperceiving the other's attitude than to change one's own [85].

Interpersonal attraction is closely associated with attitude similarity, but similarity in "social desirability" is slightly more difficult to interpret. A "socially desirable" person is one who is seen as desirable for dating purposes. The early literature on social desirability consistently showed that people were attracted to romantic partners who were the most desirable. For instance, if women were judging a group of men for their suitability as dates, they would pick the most attractive man of the lot. In addition, the studies using men as subjects showed that men almost always preferred the "most attractive date possible" [59]. Attraction (at least initial attraction) was not contingent upon any perceived similarities in desirability between the two people [60]. Attraction in fantasy situations is quite a different story from attraction in a real-life situation, as research has shown. Of course, in the realm of fantasy, most of us would be attracted to the most desirable person. But choosing whom to date is usually a more carefully based choice than first attraction and is related to similarity. In fact, "one's social choices are a compromise between fantasy and reality" [515]. Our enduring attractions are directed to the people who are similar to us in social desirability [60]—because they are the ones who will also be attracted to us.

For romantic dyads, most of us expect people in the same range of social desirability (usually judged by physical attractiveness) to seek

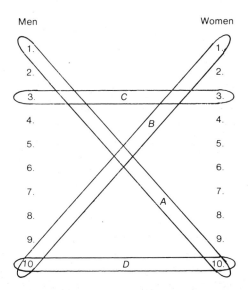

Figure 3-3. Attractiveness ratings and matchings for men and women.

one another. To illustrate, let us assume that ten men are ranked from the most attractive to the least attractive, as in Figure 3-3. Women from the same age grouping are also ranked from the most attractive to the least attractive.

Man number 1 is the most socially desirable, as is the number 1 woman. Number 10s are the least desirable. Now suppose you meet a man and a woman who are dating and the man is a 1 and the woman is a 10 (the grouping *A* in the figure). What would you conclude? What if the most socially desirable woman, number 1, is paired up with the least desirable man, number 9 or number 10 (grouping *B* in figure)? What would you conclude? Usually, most of us would conclude that the least desirable person was offering money, sex, or some other resource to compensate for the lack of physical attractiveness. Or the most attractive person is seen to have a serious flaw—such as an offensive personality. The matches that "make sense" are those within the approximate similar social desirability ratings, such as matches *C* and *D*. Most of us expect persons to match up with others that we see as similar in attractiveness. One word of cheer to those who are not seen as socially desirable, and a word of caution to those who have a date every night: Although perceived physical attractiveness is a prime factor in dating choice, it is not in the selection of marital partners [133].

There are, of course, some limitations to using similarity as a predictor of our successful dyadic relationships. To begin with, simple similarity in attitudes is only one of the many dimensions we can use to compare ourselves with others. We can like people for a variety of reasons, not limited to our similarity of attitudes. For example, you may be attracted to one person because of his ability to liven up a party, to another because of her deep thoughts, and to a third because of his physique. To expect to find some similarity between you and all of them (compared with the things in which you are dissimilar) is asking a bit too much. Hendrick [212] demonstrated, for example, that most people choose extroverts when choosing leaders and those who would be interesting at a party. The demands of each particular social relationship influence which qualities we will perceive as desirable. Few of us would select an exact replica of ourselves as a friend, nor would we choose an opposite with whom we had absolutely nothing in common [382].

Even more important than the diverse types of attractions are the limitations on the attraction research. The traditional examinations of attraction treat the process as if people are passive. We see someone "at a distance" and the researcher tries to see what predicts your attraction to the person. Perceptions are, however, more of an active than a passive process [54]. Even the *anticipation* of interaction with someone predisposes us to collect different information and to react to someone differently from the way we would if we viewed him or her at a distance [130, 54]. Most of the attraction research does not follow the participants to watch the effects of their actual communication and to see how the communication transactions affect their perceptions of the other [490]. Sykes conducted a field experiment where the participants were in a situation of "free choice," where the communication transactions were not manipulated by an experimenter. He found that in such real-life contexts, "demographic and attitudinal similarities have only a small effect" [490]. The communication transaction with another affects our attraction as well as other responses to another.

The Communication Transaction

Attraction between people depends more on their reaction to the communication experience than it does on other factors. To begin with, the other's communication behavior is the core information we use for the basis of our judgments. For instance, people who are apprehensive about oral communication are seen as less attractive than those who are not [321]; similarly, in work situations those who communicate more often are usually seen as more attractive than those who do not [343].

Because communication-based information is derived from our transactions with others, we treat it as important and it often overrides other information we might have about them. A variety of studies by Sunnafrank illustrates this principle. He found that if people are allowed to have a normal conversation with someone, the effects of that communication experience resulted in "attitude similarity" failing to exert influence on attraction [484, 485, 486, 487]. Many of us have had the experience of thinking we dislike someone and then discovering in a discussion something we like about them, whether it be their sense of humor, how they treat us, their hobbies, or a host of other factors. Attitude disagreements can be important, but if we have a communication transaction with the other that is rewarding, the initial disagreements fade in importance.

One of the reasons for this "communication effect" is that as a relationship develops, attitude similarity becomes less important [216]. We gain information from transactions that is not available from simple knowledge of attitude similarity or dissimilarity [460]. As Sillars and Scott note, during the communication transactions, we get information about (1) the way the other sees us, (2) the degree of receptivity the other has to our own perspectives and points of view, and (3) the intentions of the other regarding us [460]. It is far more important for an ongoing relationship to know how someone sees us, whether we can trust them or not, and other interactive factors than it is simply to know about their attitudes.

Not only is the information derived from our communication more central to our perceptions than superficial information, but our *own* communication behavior greatly influences the perception of the other. In one study, the attraction people had for others was a consequence of their own behavior [440]. For example, if you do a favor for another, you tend to like him better [243]. Another experiment found that subjects who read negative evaluations to another (and did not anticipate meeting that person afterward) changed their impressions in a negative way [115]. In a study by Glass, subjects with high self-esteem who acted out some aggressive behavior toward another person came to dislike their victim [172]. In these cases, the evaluation of the other changes in order for it to be consistent with one's behavior. If you voluntarily treat another as if you like him or her, your liking will increase; if you treat another poorly, you will tend to dislike him or her more. Not surprisingly, the other typically will reciprocate and like or dislike you in return. Finally, your communication activity will influence how attractive the other is to you [320, 343]. Persons who are less outgoing and sociable communicate less with others; as a result, the other communicates less with them.

The research by Bell and Daly [44] shows rather dramatically that we choose communication strategies based on a desire to have others like us; they label this process *affinity seeking.* As they demonstrated, people seek to have others like them for a variety of reasons and choose communication strategies to accomplish that goal. Similarly, Schlenker's overview of "impression management," shows that people often select communication behavior in order to impress others [437]. The central point is this: When we know others are perceiving us, we alter our communication to try and create the image we wish them to have. Whatever the particulars, our own communication behaviors directly affects how others see us.

The fact that perception of others is influenced by your own behavior underscores the transactional nature of person perception. Obviously, the process of person perception is "even more complex than one ever dreamt" [493]. It is complex because all the elements of the process are related:

1. Perception leads to evaluation and evaluation leads to perception [210].
2. Similarity leads to interpersonal attraction; interpersonal attraction leads to similarity (see above).
3. Perception of yourself and perception of others are highly related and part of a cyclic process (see Chapter 2).
4. Transactions with another lead to positive sentiment; positive sentiment toward another leads to transactions with him [222].
5. Communication transactions provide the core information for perceptions of others.

The work on person perception has not typically focused on a transactional point of view. Few pieces of research have attempted to look at such perception as a joint process of both the perceiver and the perceived. Furthermore, instead of concurrently looking at *A*'s perception of *B* and *B*'s perception of *A*, most of the studies have focused on only half of the process. As Hastorf, Schneider, and Polefka note, "We need to know more about how people get to know one another; such knowledge would entail the matching of one person's perception of another with the other's perception of himself" [202]. We would obviously be concerned with more aspects than that, but the point is clear. We should look at the process of coordination of meaning between communication participants—at their joint perceptions of each other. When this is done, our understanding of dyadic transactions will be strengthened.

SUMMARY

One of the central parameters of dyadic communication is the process of person perception. When another person is perceived, the perceiver (1) imposes perceptual patterns on the available cues, by using perceptual sets and attributing causality and responsibility, and (2) is subject to numerous biases in the perception process. What we see is a function of the transactional process of available cues, our perceptual sets, and the situation in which we perceive the other. Our attractions and repulsions to others are influenced by propinquity, similarity of attitude, and the communication experience. In ongoing relationships the communication transactions provide us with the core information we use to determine our reactions to others. In addition, because person perception is a transactional process, how *we* behave affects the other, which in turn influences how we see him or her.

Chapter 4

Perception of the Relationship

The initial elements of communication relationships have been sketched by providing an orientation to relationships, examining the maintenance and effects of self-concept, and charting the essential features of perception of others. In addition to perceptions of self and other, we have perceptions of our relationships. All parties to a relationship, whether they be family members, work mates, friends, or romantic partners, have views of the nature of their relationship. This chapter will examine the underlying nature of relationships, illustrate how participants view them, and sketch the connections between communication and the development of relationships.

FORMATION OF A RELATIONSHIP

You are sitting alone in the library and are watching a man who comes in, selects a table 20 feet from yours, and settles down. Then, just as you are beginning to stare at him, he looks back. You are caught, somewhat embarrassed, and try to pretend that you were not really looking at him. You try to deny that a relationship has been formed.

Experiences such as this demonstrate that a relationship between two people is something uniquely different from the act of one person observing another. Dyadic communication does not occur simply because two people are placed near each other. The participants have to recognize that they have formed a *relationship* before a dyadic system is fully operable. A relationship is formed when the following elements are present:

1. You and another are behaving.
2. You are aware of his behavior and, at the same time,
3. He is aware of your behavior.
4. As a result,
   a. you are aware that he is aware of you.
   b. he is aware that you are aware of him.

Persons are aware that they are in a dyadic relationship when each has the *perception of being perceived* [421]. When both persons can say, "I see you seeing me," then an interpersonal bond has been formed because of their reciprocal awareness.

When you enter into a dyadic relationship, the world is no longer exclusively your own. The other person has to be considered. You have to adjust to her presence and she to yours because each transaction you enter entails segments of commitment and adjustment. Each person is a full participant in the transaction; no one is strictly an observer, or strictly the observed. Each person's perceptions influence the relationship because each participant affects and is affected by the other. Put another way, once you have entered into a relationship, a system has been formed in which there is no such thing as isolated behavior.

100

A SYSTEMS VIEW

A dyadic transaction can be described as having the qualities of an open system. Once a relationship is formed the system has been activated, and once in process it has certain qualities. Some of the most important qualities of a dyadic communication system are (1) wholeness, (2) synergy, (3) circularity, and (4) equifinality [519].°

Wholeness occurs whenever all the elements of a system are interrelated. Such is the case with dyadic communication. When a change occurs in one participant, its effects reverberate throughout the system. For example, take the case of the dyadic transactions between a wife and husband. The two of them form a unique system based on their relationship, in this case characterized by the wife raising the children and staying at home. If she undergoes a change in her aspirations and wants to launch a career of her own, the wife–husband relationship will be altered. Their relationship cannot stay the same if one of the partners undergoes change. In any ongoing dyadic transaction, any change in one part of the system affects other parts.

Dyadic communication is also characterized by synergy. Synergy means that the whole is greater than the parts, that $1 + 1 = 3$ [369]. The combined efforts of two people produce a greater effect than the sum of their individual actions. Putting two people together in a dyadic relationship creates a system that is composed of (1) person A, (2) person B, and (3) the ways A and B operate in relation to each other. Obviously, once in a relationship, the two begin mutually influencing each other, thereby creating effects that would not have occurred if the two were separated. Consider two young boys. They enter into a relationship and begin talking about stealing. Pretty soon each boy is daring the other to steal some food from the local grocery store. While they are being escorted home by the store manager, each boy blames the other. Each boy is aware that he would not have gotten into trouble if he had been alone. The combined effects of dares and counterdares produced effects that would not have arisen had the boys not been together.

The effects of synergy also can be positive. In a romantic dyad, for example, the love and warmth generated in the system can reach quite intense levels. As one partner responds with open affection, that response stimulates an openness and warmth in the other—which cycles back and produces more love in the other. Two "starry-eyed" lovers are a pleasant reminder that all dyadic relationships have synergy.

Circularity and feedback also characterize dyadic communication systems. The processes of influence are circular; everything influences everything else. Each participant is engaging in behavior and simulta-

---

°For a more complete discussion, see [478].

neously monitoring the other person. Each person watches the other and responds to the other's response to him. Stated another way each dyadic event is an uninterrupted sequence of interchanges [519].

The usual way of thinking about communication does not encompass the circularity point of view. If a romantic pair is involved in a conflict, each participant tends to assess causes and effects. Mary says, "John just doesn't treat me with respect and that's why we fight." Meanwhile John is analyzing their dyad and saying, "If Mary were not so domineering, we would get along fine." Both Mary and John are "punctuating"—stopping an ongoing circular process and labeling one behavior a cause and another an effect. The truth is probably somewhere in the middle. Mary and John are both right and both wrong. By not realizing that each person's behavior is both a cause and an effect, they will probably not arrive at a successful resolution to their conflict. Mary could change her behavior (or John could) and break the cycle they are caught up in. If Mary would stop acting in a domineering way, then John could respect her. And if John would respect her, Mary could stop acting in a domineering way. The processes of dyadic communication are indeed circular.

One other quality of any open system applies to the description of dyadic communication: equifinality [417]. Equifinality means that in an open system the same state can be reached in different ways and from different beginning conditions. For instance, take a romantic pair who can be described as having a relationship based on self-respect, concern for the other, and open love. This same state can be reached in numerous ways. The pair could have met in Glacier National Park and might have known each other only four weeks before marriage. Or they could have been childhood sweethearts and continued as a dyad until marriage, never having loved anyone else. It doesn't matter. The same state of an excellent romantic relationship can be arrived at from different directions. Similarly, you might have a work situation that is fine in the initial stages but later deteriorates into hostility. Or you might have a difficult relationship with someone from the first moment you see him or her. In both these cases the important point to remember is that the same point can be reached via a number of routes. Communication viewed as an open system is a set of processes that are continually changing and adapting.

Because dyadic communication is a transactional process that has the attributes of an open system, to capture accurately the essence of any dyad, one must *focus on the relationship* between the participants. The productive study of dyadic communication is not limited to a study of each individual's psychology, because each personality comes into existence only in relationship [421]. Individual behavior is only one part of an ongoing communcation system. As Parks and Wilmot note, it is a "shift away from the individual as the unit of analysis to the relationship as the unit of analysis" [381]. The focus is on the properties that the participants have *collectively created* [328]. We look at the exchange as a whole, rather than at a single message, and note the patterns of exchange that occur [376].

The central difference between looking at the individual as the unit of analysis and selecting a relational unit of analysis can be seen in the example of Joan and Tom. If you were to observe Joan when she is in the presence of Tom, you would notice that she stares intently, asks a lot of questions, seeks feedback from him frequently, and is generally highly involved in the interaction. What kinds of conclusions would you draw about her as a communicator? Would you conclude that she is an attentive, open, loving person? What kinds of predictions would you make about her partner? Just knowing what her behaviors are can give you a hint about Tom, but you have no way to know fully what he is like in her presence. In this case, Tom always acts in a rather aloof manner. When he is with Joan, he sits far back from the table, stares over her head, looks around the room, and generally ignores her. If he were as intently interested in the conversation as Joan, then the two of them would look like two intense lovers. But because he is aloof, they make a nice complementary system. What he doesn't do in the transaction, she does.

In order to understand how the communication system of Joan and Tom (or any other relationship!) works, we need to know two major things. First, we must know how the behaviors of each participant form interlocking patterns. In this case, the fact that Tom does not give Joan eye contact causes her to work extra hard at providing the contact in the conversation. And the fact that she works so hard makes it easy for him to "tune out" and put less energy into relating directly to her. These patterns and not "individual actions" [381] become that unit of analysis.

Second, however, when humans are involved, *their* perceptions of the component parts of the relationship become a crucial element in the events. For instance, if Joan sees Tom as "uncaring," she may well see the relationship as heading for destruction. On the other hand, if Tom sees the relationship as "just fine," then he may not be willing to change any of his behaviors. In the remainder of this chapter, the relationship perceptions are treated as an essential element in the communication system. Relationship perceptions are just as important as perceptions of self and other; they are simply the next step and are built from these basic building blocks. Once constructed, the relational perceptions exert forces on the particpants.

RELATIONAL FUNDAMENTALS

The Coorientation Model

The work of Theodore Newcomb [349, 350] provides a starting point for a relational analysis of dyadic communication. His system consists of two individuals, *A* and *B*, and their orientation toward some object

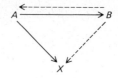

Figure 4-1.   The coordination model.

X. Each individual is cooriented—he has an orientation toward the other person and toward the object. Take *A*, for instance. He will have an orientation toward *B* (his attraction to *B*) and an orientation toward object *X* (his attitude toward object *X*). Communication performs the necessary function of enabling both *A* and *B* to "maintain simultaneous orientation toward one another and toward the object of communication" [349].

A friendship dyad can be used for illustration. *A* is Joe, *B* is Sam, and object *X* is motorcycles. Figure 4-1 outlines the essentials of the system.

The *minimal* components of this (or any) dyadic system for Newcomb's point of view are the following:

1. *A*'s attitude toward object *X*.
2. *A*'s attraction to *B*.
3. *B*'s attitude toward object *X*.
4. *B*'s attraction to *A*.

In this case, Joe dislikes motorcycles and is attracted to Sam. Sam likes to ride motorcycles (he owns a $2,500 machine) and considers himself a close friend of Joe. Each person has a coorientation, an attitude toward object *X* and an attraction toward the other person. With these minimal components, Newcomb postulates what he calls a "strain toward symmetry." If the object is important to us and we are attracted to another person, we expect them also to like the object. Strain develops because of a perceived discrepancy between *A*'s orientations to object *X* and what he perceives *B*'s orientations to be.° From Joe's point of view, if he likes Sam and dislikes motorcycles but Sam loves to drive motorcycles, then there is a strain on the system. Joe is an avid hiker, and when hiking he is bothered by the noise of motorcycles roaring past. Yet he is a close friend of Sam. The system is not balanced, and Joe will have to reconcile the strain by some action. Some of the alternatives he has are to (1) decrease his liking for Sam, (2) reduce the importance or relevance of motorcycles by chang-

---

°This cursory treatment omits many details. The degree of felt strain is a function of the degree of perceived discrepancy, the degree of attraction to the other, and the importance and relevance of the object (motorcycles). For more details, see Newcomb [349].

ing his attitude, or (3) communicate to Sam in order to change Sam's attitude.

Newcomb's analysis sets the building blocks for a relational approach to studying any dyadic pair. Joe, just like people in other dyads, does not function in a vacuum. His actions are dependent on both his own orientations and his perceptions of Sam's orientations. And Joe's orientations are influenced by his perceptions of the other's orientations. When we are in dyadic relationships, we have perceptions of what the other is thinking and the other has perceptions of what we are thinking. We each *make estimates of the other's orientations.* Rather than observing two individuals as separate entities who just happen to communicate, we can begin to examine the relationship itself. At a minimum, therefore, any index of a dyadic relationship should encompass (1) what each person's orientation is (attitude toward the object and attraction toward the other person) and (2) what each person perceives the orientations of the other to be. What we want are the *joint products* of the participants' views of each other.°

Like the coorientation model, any approach that centers on the *interpenetration of perspectives* of particpants would qualify as a relational approach [434]. Drewery's [132] interpersonal perception technique, for example, focuses on how one person "perceives another and expects to be perceived" by him. Drewery analyzed a marital relationship from the standpoint of the mismatched perspectives of the participants, and the method does show some promise for providing insight into dyadic processes. Ichheiser [231] mentions that a model of human relationships would include:

1. What we actually are.
2. What we think we are.
3. What other people think we are.
4. What we assume other people think we are (p. 150).

When one assesses items 3 and 4 for both participants, relational assessments can be made. Whatever technique is chosen, the useful study and understanding of dyadic transactions can occur *at the relationship level.*

The Interpersonal Perception Method

Although Ichheiser mentions the relational approach, Laing, Phillipson, and Lee [274] specifically discuss the interperceptions and interexperience of the participants in a dyad. They take as a fundamental

---

°A rather interesting body of research, coorientation theory, has been developed that does essentially the same thing as the IPM method. For a discussion see [90, 91, 308, 480] and the first edition of this book.

postulate that the "world is peopled by others, and these others are not simply objects in the world: they are centers of reorientation to the objective universe." For each individual two aspects are related, namely, (1) one's own behavior and (2) the other's experience of that behavior. When Peter engages in behavior, Paul can react only in terms of his experience of that behavior. The meaning that Paul attaches to Peter's behavior in turn influences Paul's behavior. *The behavior of each toward the other is mediated by the experience each has of the other.* Clearly, Laing, Phillipson, and Lee see two participants in a transaction mutually affecting each other. In fact, they state, "The failure to see the behavior of one person as a function of the behavior of the other has led to some extraordinary perceptual and conceptual aberrations that are still with us" [274].

The interpersonal perception method is a fine device for you to use to understand your own relationships. For example, if you find yourself unclear about what is happening in a relationship, the method can allow you to "unpack" it to see the locus of the difficulties. It can be used for any relationship you are in, ranging from your patterns at work to those in your more personal relationships. Basically, the interpersonal perception method highlights the three perspectives each participant has in a relationship. In the case of a romantic dyad, for example, they are as follows:

Husband's view of object X	Direct perspective
Husband's view of wife's view of object X	Metaperspective
Husband's view of wife's view of his view of object X	Meta-metaperspective

Similarly, the perspectives assessed from the wife would be:

Wife's view of object X	Direct perspective
Wife's view of husband's view of object X	Metaperspective
Wife's view of husband's view of her view of object X	Meta-metaperspective

Dyads utilize such perspectives, and Laing, Phillipson, and Lee try to heighten our awareness of that process. The following case illustrates the perspectives of a romantic dyad. The woman and man have been seeing a lot of one another, and frequently the man has invited his roommate along on their outings. In this case, the man likes his roommate and the woman does not. Their perspectives are:

He—"I sure do like my roommate."	(his direct perspective)
He—"She likes my roommate."	(his metaperspective)

He—"She thinks I like my roommate."   (his meta-metaperspective)

She—"I don't like his roommate."   (her direct perspective)
She—"He likes his roommate."   (her metaperspective)
She—"He thinks I like his roommate."   (her meta-metaperspective)

It's quite apparent that a relationship based on these perspectives will have some areas of conflict. The degree of overlapping or matching of perspectives is crucial for any dyadic encounter. Laing, Phillipson, and Lee suggest that the following relational aspects are helpful in understanding dyads:

1. Comparison between one person's direct perspective and the other person's direct perspective on the same issue yields *agreement* or *disagreement*.
2. Comparison between one person's metaperspective and the other person's direct perspective on the same issue yields *understanding* or *misunderstanding*.
3. Comparison between one person's meta-metaperspective and his own direct perspective yields the *feeling* of *being understood* or of *being misunderstood*.
4. Comparison between one person's meta-metaperspective and the other person's metaperspective on the same issue yields *realization* or *failure of realization*.

Using the sample case of the romantic pair, we can observe the operation of each of these relational statements. Figure 4-2 outlines the comparison of participant perspectives.

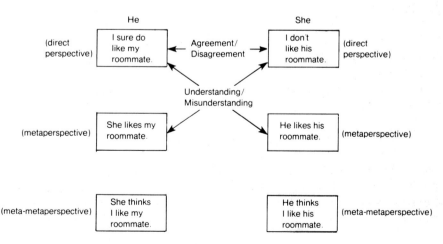

Figure 4-2.   **Degrees of agreement and understanding with the interpersonal perception method.**

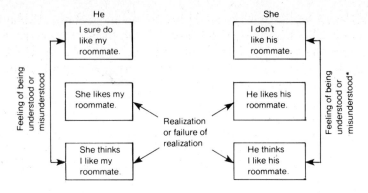

Figure 4-3.   **Degrees of realization and feeling understood with the interpersonal perception method.**

The example demonstrates that the direct perspectives do not agree in this case. She correctly perceives that he likes his rommate, so she understands him on this issue (her metaperspective matches his direct perspective). Note, however, that he does not understand her on the issue (his metaperspective, "She likes my roommate," does not match her direct perspective).

Figure 4-3 completes the analysis. Here the feeling of being understood or misunderstood and the realization or failure of realization are sketched. If you were she, you would feel misunderstood because what you thought (direct perspective) and what you thought he thought you thought (meta-metaperspective) do not match. On the other hand, his direct and meta-metaperspectives match, so he feels understood.[°]

Realization means that a participant realizes the other person understands or misunderstands him. In this case, he realizes that she understands him. Correspondingly, she realizes that he misunderstands her. In each case, realization can be seen as follows: When he becomes aware of her metaperspective ("He likes his roommate"), he can compare that to what he thinks she thought about his recreational tastes ("She thinks I like my roommate"). The comparison of the two allows him to realize that she understands him. The corresponding process can be followed for her, too.

Now that the fundamental elements have been covered, let's see how it applies to a *perception of a relationship*. In the following example, the "object of perception" is the relationship itself—not an unusual event in all types of dyadic relationships.

[°]Note that the "feeling of being understood" is operating within one person's perceptions and isn't strictly relational. But it does illustrate that many of the internal feelings a person has in a relationship arise because of perception of your partner. Therefore, even the feeling of being understood is generated relationally.

Mario and Adelle have been dating for a year and on a Friday night go to a mutual friend's house for a party. A number of Mario's former buddies are there, but Adelle knows no one at the event. During the evening, Mario is with his circle of friends and they are all kidding him about his seriousness with Adelle. One says, "Hey, Mario, we don't see you anymore. All you seem to do is hang around with women these days. Whatever happened to old hell-raising Mario?" Another chides him for stopping his former weightlifting exercises. Then, when Adelle is just in earshot, he is asked, "Mario, how are you and Adelle getting along? Is this thing moving toward marriage or something?" Mario says, "Oh, we're doing OK, but nothing to write home about."

Later that evening, Adelle gives Mario a "what for." She begins by saying, "If this relationship isn't important to you, then you can just get out. I don't care to be associated with someone who takes advantage of others." Here is what is actually happening with their perspectives:

Mario	*Adelle*
"I like our relationship." (DP)	"I like our relationship." (DP)
"She likes our relationship." (MP)	"He doesn't like our relationship." (MP)
"She thinks I don't like our relationship." (MMP)	"He thinks I like our relationship." (MMP)

As the dialogue unfolds, Mario feels hurt and misunderstood by Adelle, and after lashing back at her for not having any faith in him, tells her that he cannot show his buddies how much he really cares for her because they would continue to give him a difficult time. She responds by telling him that she felt foolish—she went to a party with him, didn't know anyone, then was devalued by him when he told his friends she was "not anything to write home about." After a long argument, it finally became clear that Mario *did* care for Adelle; in fact, he loved her very much. And they reached a new agreement about what behavior is acceptable to the two of them in public and what kinds of statements were not.

Notice, by rechecking the preceding dialogue, that the two of them are in agreement—they both think that the relationship is important. However, Adelle misunderstands Mario; she was thrown a curve by the statement he made to his buddies. She also realizes that he understands her—he thinks that she likes the relationship, and she does. And she has the feeling of being understood. But even with all this, she is angry—because she *thinks* they are in disagreement about the relationship. And, of course, Mario feels misunderstood by her and realizes that she misunderstands his intentions.

There is no clue to what combinations of perspectives, metaperspectives, and meta-metaperspectives make for the most productive relationships. The interpersonal perception method highlights the fact that relationships can be maintained on any number of bases. For instance, the participants may agree on an issue, yet one or both misunderstand each other. Or as we saw in Chapter 3, "Perception of the Other," the participants in a marital dyad may overestimate their similarity on issues. They may misunderstand each other and as a result think there is agreement when there is not. The possible combinations of all the relational aspects are numerous. For instance, when there is agreement on an issue, there are four possible configurations of understanding:

1. He understands her; she understands him.
2. He understands her; she misunderstands him.
3. He misunderstands her; she understands him.
4. He misunderstands her; she misunderstands him.

When (1) the feeling of being understood or misunderstood and (2) the realization or failure of realization are added in, the complexity of dyadic relationships becomes apparent. The easiest configuration is obvious—when there is agreement, understanding, the feeling of being understood, and the realization on the part of both participants. It may be, however, that other configurations are are more functional for particular dyads. For instance, in an employer–employee dyad, agreement on direct perspectives may be less important on crucial issues than understanding. The participants may "agree to disagree" on some items as long as they understand each other's position. And there are even cases where misunderstandings may be a positive factor. For one thing, misunderstandings can cause two people, like Mario and Adelle, to work on their relationship and further clarify the nature of their commitment to one another. Many a couple, working pair, or aider-aided dyad has engaged in overt misunderstanding and argument as a prelude to a clearer perception of each other. This "working through" in a relationship can produce excitement, bring needed energy back into a relationship, and provide new impetus for working together to "make it go."

Furthermore, to say that agreement, understanding, realization, and feeling understood are always desirable goals is to overlook the sometimes negative consequences of the "perfect matching" of a pair. It can be argued that matching perfectly with another provides for a relationship that obscures the identity of the participants. For instance, married couples sometimes get to the point of being unable to separate their individual personalities from one another. If you ask the husband, "Would you and Donna like to come over next Monday?" and he says, "Of course, we always like being with you," he has made a decision without checking Donna's preferences. *We* can sometimes be inappropriately substituted for *I*.

The effects of each relational configuration for a pair—whether it be marital dyad, generation pairs, friendship pairs, superior–subordinate pairs, or others, is still unknown. In general, however, relational satisfaction appears to be enhanced by more agreement, understanding, realization, and feeling understood. Laing, Phillipson, and Lee found, for example, that disturbed marriages, when compared with nondisturbed marriages, manifest more disagreement and more misunderstanding. However, recent research by Sillars and his colleagues illustrates that much of the research has confused understanding with agreement. Two spouses, who often have the same attitude on a topic, would appear to "understand one another" when they simply have the same attitude—and their estimate of the other's attitude is based on their own attitude [459]. Furthermore, an understanding [460] between spouses may be due to their nonverbal cues and other factors, so that "understanding (or misunderstanding) of the spouse is not related in a simple causal fashion to marital satisfaction" [459]. Even given these reservations, the researchers conclude that understanding may be important to marital satisfaction when sharing is an important value for the spouses [460]. Whatever the final resolution of the understanding–satisfaction issue, it is very clear that we can study the dyad from a relational point of view. The degree of complexity may vary according to the particular dyad, and it may be that everyone cannot process at the level of meta-metaperspective [476], but matching the perspectives at some level does give us information about the relationship as a whole.

IMPLICIT RELATIONSHIP PERCEPTIONS

One of the most intriguing features of relationships is that even when the participants do not focus directly on the relationship per se, they do so implicitly. Put another way, perceptions of relationships are *embedded* within the content communicated by the participants. For example, when the parent tells the child, "Go to bed," two messages are sent. The content message revolves around being in bed, the relationship message is that the parent has the right or obligation to tell the child what to do. Whenever one person communicates with another, *the relationship is being defined* [192, 519]. *It is impossible to relate to another individual only on a content basis*—relationship and content are inextricably bound together. Each individual has her own definition of the relationship and projects it when she communicates to another. The definition she has is rarely called to her or the other's attention, but is there nevertheless. For instance, when a professor assists a student in finding materials for a project, he doesn't preface each remark with, "I have the right to help you, so read this book that I recommend." And the student doesn't say, "I'm placing myself in the

Each person in a relationship has a view of the relationship and of the other person's view of the relationship. What are some of the factors that may define these co-workers' relationship?

position of needing help in order to borrow some of your books." Relational definitions can be indicated by who talks first, who talks the most, paralinguistic cues (tone of voice, volume, and other vocal qualities you use to say something), the seating arrangment, eye contact, and a host of other factors. Different means are used in different situations, but in all cases each participant defines the relationship.

Each participant has not only a direct perspective on the relationship, but also a metaperspective. Each has a view of how the other person is defining their relationship. In essence, each is taking the role of the other. Each modifies her or his "intended behavior in light of his anticpation of the other's reaction to this behavior" [145]. Each person, therefore, (1) takes the role of herself and (2) takes the role of the other. There is some dispute over whether these direct perspectives and metaperspectives are taken simultaneously or alternately, but the central issue is that one has to assume both points of view [10]. In a dyadic transaction, therefore, this is mutual adjustment to the other [442].

A specific case will illustrate part of the relationship complexity of a transaction. Person A and person B are engaged and about to be married. Person A wants to dominate person B, and B wants to dominate A. As their transaction unfolds over the issue of finances, it is clear that each has a perspective and metaperspective on (1) the content issue

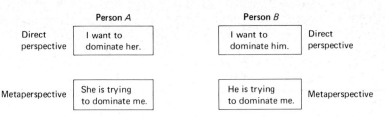

Figure 4-4. Perspectives on a relationship.

and (2) the relationship issue. On the question of finances, person *A* wants two checking accounts, one in each person's name. *B* wants one account, a joint one that both will use. *A* and *B* articulate their views well and understand each other's position. On the content issue there is *disagreement* (direct perspectives differ between *A* and *B*), but there is *understanding* (*A*'s metaperspective matches *B*'s direct perspective; *B*'s metaperspective matches *A*'s direct perspective). On the relationship level, the degrees of agreement–disagreement and understanding–misunderstanding become crucial to the direction the relationship takes. As the argument continues, let's assume that *A* and *B* have the perspectives and metaperspectives shown in Figure 4-4.

A and *B* understand each other because *A*'s and *B*'s metaperspectives are correct. But in this case, there is disagreement over the relationship. *A*'s and *B*'s desires for influence in the relationship clash directly. During the continuing discussion, *A* and *B* will undoubtedly jockey for relational position. As they vie back and forth concerning the relationship, they will probably be centering their arguments around the issue of checking accounts. As the arguments over the content issue come to a standstill, it is likely that someone will open up the relational issue by saying something like, "Well, I don't care about the advantages of that kind of an account—I'm the boss around here and I say we'll have the other kind!" Now the relational conflict is out in the open and the basis of the discussion has shifted from the content to the relationship.

This analysis demonstrates that dyadic transactions can be analyzed on both content and relational lines. For many transactions, the distinctions between the two levels become obscure. For instance, if the partners in a romantic dyad are arguing over which movie to see and the issue is not readily resolved, it will soon escalate into a full-scale relational conflict. The issue of which movie to see becomes secondary and the paramount issue is relational—who has the right to make the decision. The basis for the disagreement has shifted. In addition, it is often the case that (1) a relationship disagreement or misunderstanding will emerge as a conflict over content, and (2) a content disagreement or misunderstanding may emerge as a relational conflict [220]. Of these two cases, by far the most common is a relational disagreement acted out in terms of a particular content issue [220]. Pete had an experience along these lines. When he was growing up as a boy in a small town, a friend of his family (we'll call him Charley) exposed Pete to the fundamentals of training workhorses. Charley would occasionally give assistance to ranchers and farmers who needed to train their horses for work. After Pete left home and moved to western Montana, he developed an interest in quarter horses. Having raised them for a number of years, he became proficient at the entire enterprise, from selecting good horses to exhibiting them in local contests. In fact his horses did quite well in local competitions. When he saw Charley again, they began discussing the techniques of training horses. Charley, who had only worked with rather rough workhorses, began arguing with Pete about the correct way to train quarter horses. The disagreement over the content issue (training horses) was shifting to the relational level, each person trying to be in the role of instructing the other. From Pete's perspective, Charley was saying, "Only I can offer insight into training horses," and Pete found the relationship hard to accept.*

The embedded relationship perceptions are always there, sometimes articulated, sometimes not. Their ever-present nature, in fact, promotes some people to *try* to deny they are defining a relationship. This is done in one of four ways: (1) He may deny he sent a message by labeling himself as someone else, say a messenger of God; (2) he may deny he said something by manifesting amnesia or by claiming the other person continually misunderstands him; (3) he may deny that he is talking to the person by labeling the person as someone else; or (4) he may deny that he is in this situation by pretending he is somewere else [191]. These four techniques are elaborate devices used to demonstrate that, from the one person's perception, he is not defining the relationship. Interestingly enough, whenever a person tries to deny defining a relationship, he is at a different level defining the relationship as one he won't define!

We maintain our transactions with others so long as the content and relational disagreements and misunderstandings do not force termination of the relationship. The relationship hangs on more of a slender thread—mutual definition by participants—than is usually observed. Any relational threat—the spouse who has a lover, the employees who derogate their employer, the Army private who refuses to salute—quickly attunes us to the fragile nature of relationships [123]. A successful transaction depends on the coordination of content and relational meaning for the participants and, at the very least, some overlap of perspectives and metaperspectives.

---

*It would be revealing to know Charley's perception of the event. One could predict that he would make relational statements such as, "Darn kids, give them a quarterhorse and they think they know everything." In other words, Pete wouldn't let Charley be the only one with the expertise on training.

RELATIONAL TRANSLATIONS

Just why is it that people have difficulties over the relational meanings that their behaviors have? Can't we just say, "Try and solve content conflicts on the content level, and don't let it spill over to your relational definition, and things will be fine"? Content and relational issues cannot be segmented, because the two are inextricably tied.

We all *translate into our own relational language.* Each of us makes implicit linkages between content and relational messages. For instance, in one person's case, if the married partner doesn't want to engage in the same social activities, it translates as, "You don't love me," yet for another person, the lack of interest in the same social activities is not even a cause for concern. For one employer, being late to work doesn't matter as long as you get your work done. For the next, punctuality is the essence of goodness. For one college teacher you can "cut class" anytime as long as you get your assignments done and do well on your tests. For another, cutting her class is a "personal slam to her teaching ability." Two people can observe the same behavior and translate it into different relational meanings.

It is clear that we cannot control the content-relational linkages that another has. Take, for instance, the case of the medical doctor. He attends college, goes to medical school, spends a great deal of money on equipment and learning the latest advances, and begins his practice. Then, upon beginning to practice his specialty, he suddenly notices that his patients, on whom he spent hours diagnosing and prescribing medicines, do not take their medicine and their health declines. As Costello [108] notes, from 30 to 50 percent of patients do not comply with doctors' directions. Furthermore, doctors report that their greatest degree of dissatisfaction comes from their "inability to control their relationship with patients." The patients have different relational translations for the doctor's behaviors. Many patients feel that the efficient, analytical, jargonized doctor is not interested in them, so they do not believe his or her pronouncements about what to do to get well. And even if they do believe the doctor, they may want to exercise some control by their defiance of the directives.

The following postulates can be advanced regarding the relational translations that we make in our communication relationships with others:

1. Every content statement has relational meaning.
2. Each participant in the dyad translates the relational messages in a unique way.
3. Successful dyads negotiage and work through their different relational translations of content statements and actions.
4. We develop rituals as ways to assure ourselves that the relational translations are similar.
5. A relationship develops explicitly on the content level, and simultaneously builds implicitly on the relational level.

6. Content competence is not equal to relational competence.
7. Every relational definition has content implications.
8. Relationships cannot be constructed or maintained only by relational talk.

The first postulate is one we have already discussed. If you are a new student at a university and someone says to you, "What do you mean you haven't heard of the 'Stocks'—everyone drinks there," it soon becomes clear to you that the content is being used as a relational sword. Or take the fellow who tries to use the outmoded line, "Want to come up to my apartment for a drink?" (and guess what else!). We cannot communicate on a content level without both ourselves and the other having some relational meaning for the message.

Much of the conflict between a pair results from individual differences in content-relational linkages. As a result of the ever-present difficulties in our linkages (compared with others' linkages), we develop rituals to send consistent relational messages. The family that camps together each summer uses this ritual as a way of reaffirming the family bond. The wedding ritual is meant to provide for a common meeting ground for relational statements. The employer who says, "Judy is retiring and we will present her with a gold watch," is only expressing the wishes of the company by sending its relational message in the form of a ritual.

Finally, we begin and maintain most of our relationships by focusing on the content level. We exchange background information in a beginning relationship, we engage in activities with our friends, and we share feelings and activities with our loved ones. The content is important—precisely because it has relational overtones. And as some people discover to their dismay, the dyadic partner can engage in content behaviors that imply relational messages of "I love you," yet not continue operating competently at the relational level. Woe to the poor person who can find only a few ways to express support, love, and affection. A bouquet of flowers says, "I love you" loud and clear the first time it is given, but when the same gift becomes predictable as clockwork (he sends flowers on every one of my birthdays), the relational implications may not continue to work successfully. Whereas content competence is the ability to carry on conversations, act appropriately, and be a functioning human being, relational competence requires a more finely tuned set of receptors—watching the feelings going between two people and sensing the relational translations that are occurring.

Just as one can examine the relational linkages inherent in any content message, one can also reverse the process. For instance, if you say "I love only you" to someone yet continue to date six other people, you will probably be called on the carpet for lying or being unfaithful. Once we are clear about our relational definitions, there are content obligations that are associated with them. As a result, as the seventh postulate states, every relational definition has content implications. Take the case of two friends who become close in the process of sharing their favorite hobby, hang-gliding. When one of them suddenly becomes unavailable for gliding, the other may begin to wonder about the strength of the friendship. We engage in content talk and behaviors meanwhile implicitly building the relationship. Once we get some notion of the relational definition, it becomes an activating force for content considerations. Friends and lovers are (for most of us) supposed to spend time with us, show us special consideration, and be available. We expect the boss to "look out for our interests"; otherwise we feel devalued. Similarly, once any relational definition gets accepted, it presumes content considerations.

Postulate 8 is a special reminder to all who tend to be very relationally aware:

> Relationships cannot be constructed or maintained only by relational talk.

Many romantic dyads separated by distance discover that to tell someone you love them and not see them for two years makes it difficult to keep the relationship going. Once the partner returns, there is a period of fumbling and bumbling while trying to renegotiate the content and relational translations. The operation on the content level is necessary to continually reinforce the relational definitions. Finally, some relationships flounder on the content level while the participants are very active on the relational level. A couple with a sexual problem needs to talk about it to help correct it, but they also need to take action. We usually cannot just talk a relationship into succeeding. We need to both act *and* deal with the relational implications.

As we communicate with others, content and relational aspects are always present. Each participant translates content into relational terms, and each relational definition brings content implications.

FRAMES FOR RELATIONSHIPS

Relationships are like a "private culture," where the perceptions of the relationship are its reality [154]. The perceived reality of relationships builds over time, and although most research on relationships comes from an "outsider" view, the relationship participants supply an equally valuable "insider" perception of them [288]. Such participant perceptions of their relationships are on a different dimension from their perceptions of the self and the other. There is, to be sure, "relational level reasoning," or "relationship attributions" we discussed when exploring perspectives and metaperspectives of the Interpersonal Perception Method above [394]. Or as Bateson puts it, the interaction adds an extra "dimension" to seeing that transcends the individual elements [38].

Relationship participants need to "make sense" of their relationships, because, as we noted earlier, relationships are more than the sum of the individual parts. The "third party" in a dyad is the relationship itself—with a life of its own. This synergistic creation is built by the participants yet goes beyond them. As Hymphreys says, "There is no such thing as two, for no two things can be conceived without their relationship, and this makes three . . . " [229].

Rudimentary forms of relationship definitions are supplied by the participants' culture [341]. Whether the dyad is teacher–student, mother–son, friend–friend, or doctor–patient, some rough approximations for relationship definitions are learned in all cultures as children grow up and absorb the labels and categories of the adults around them. In addition, however, the participants have their own conception of the relationship, their own "relational culture" that encompasses what they do and who they are to one another [549]. These creative "relational cultures" are more important to the dyad than the general labels we all learn [394]. The dyadic partners develop a label, or metaphor for their relationship, replete with its own system of obligations and rights [342, 87, 216].

People's metaphors and myths about relationships supply meaning for those relationships [62]. For example, if your friend is a "fishing buddy," that label tells both you and the other that you spend time together fishing, and probably you do not engage in lots of other activities or much intimate talk together. If the relationship is broadly based, you might say he or she is your "best friend" rather than simply a fishing buddy. If a marriage is described as a "battleground," it conveys a clear image of what is occurring.

When an ongoing relationship does *not* have an agreed-upon definition, it is a sign of a less than healthy nature. Jackson says that "in a pathologic relationship we see . . . a constant sabotaging or refusing of the other's attempts to define the relationship" [235]. And Weick notes the same effect in organizations: "One of the major causes of failure in organizations is a shortage of images concerning what they are up to, a shortage of time devoted to producing these images, and a shortage of diverse actions to deal with changed circumstance" [521]. Cohesive views of the relationship are necessary for the participants to have coordinated action, a sense of common purpose, and agreement about "who they are."

The choice of metaphor or image for a relationship evokes a feel for the dynamics of a relationship. If a man described his marriage as an "endangered species," it conveys the fragile, close-to-extinction nature of the relationship. Themes that emerge in ongoing relationships have been explored by Owen. He notes that thematic interpretations become a way to understand relational life"; for instance, "A male and female meet as 'friends,' become 'daters,' then 'lovers,' perhaps finally becoming a 'married couple' making transitions to the different relationship states or definitions primarily through communication" [371]. In his study composed of married couples, romantic dating partners, sets of relatives, sets of live-in friends, and groups of friends not living together, Owen identified some central determinants that participants use to make interpretative sense of relationships [371]. The participants saw their relationships illustrating

1. *Commitment*—dedication to this particular relationship in spite of difficult times.
2. *Involvement*—some relationships, such as marriage and family relationships, demand more involvement than others.
3. *Work*—relationships require "work" to keep them functioning in a healthy manner.
4. *Unique Special*—this bolsters the belief that the participants have "beat the odds" and survived a "breakup."
5. *Fragile*—for dating couples, the fragile nature of the relationship is paramount, whereas for married couples it helps them feel they have "held it together."
6. *Consideration-Respect*–married couples primarily saw respect as an important gauge of the relationship, whereas others did not.
7. *Manipulation*—women who were dating especially noted that the person might be "playing games" or "using others" in dates [371].

Owen notes that relationships vary according to these themes—they are the dimensions the participants use to make "sense" out of the relational experience.

Now that we have charted the basic elements of relational meaning-making, it is time to extend the analysis. Thus far we have discussed (1) when relationships are formed; (2) a systems view of the inner dynamics of relationships; (3) the "fundamentals" of relationship perspectives, metaperspectives, and meta-metaperspectives; (4) the "implicit" relationship meanings and relational translations we all connect with content events; and (5) how participant images of their relationships "frame" or make sense of their communication experiences with the other. We now turn to a more detailed discussion of relationships and communication—how the two are inextricably tied and how relationship perceptions and communication behavior are inextricably related.

COMMUNICATION AND RELATIONAL SCHEMATA

Communication occurs at a different level from relationship definitions [384, 543, 544, 545]. This section sets forth some principles about the connections between communication events and relationship definitions, specifying how relationships are perceived and how communication and relationships are mutually influencing aspects of dyadic pairings.

Principle 1: Relational definitions emerge from recurring episodic
  enactments

An "episode" is a communication event—a short discussion in the student union, a "Hi, how's it going" on the street, or an extended evening spent with another. Relationships and episodes are at different levels, and episodes tend to have a "building block" effect on the relationship; they are part of a chain of events [383]. Episodes are used to build relationship definitions intermittently, over time, in spurts and with cumulative effects [318]. Although one individual episode [150] does not predetermine the entire course of a relationship [208], the recurring episodes implicitly build a relational definition over time. For example, negative interactions early in a relationship appear to influence relationship satisfaction several years later [309]. The "Relational Translations" from the content provides an implicit relationship definition as you have repeated experiences with someone. Figure 4-5 illustrates this process. Each episode is pinpointed with a small *e*, from episode 1 to infinity.

When you have your first experience with someone it gives you some indication of what the relationship will be. The first time I went to Vicki for a haircut, for example, we had a fine time joking around and laughing a lot. But it isn't until you have *repeated* episodes with someone that the relationship begins to have some resilience and form. Now that Vicki and I have spent numerous times together, it is well established that we have a fun-loving, jovial relationship. Similarly, the first kiss does not mean the romantic relationship will blossom; it has to grow past one episode for the relationship definition to gain strength. By the time you get to the one-thousandth episode with someone, the relationship definition begins to have some overarching power to define the two of you. Most young people experience the difficulty with altering these relationship definitions once they are

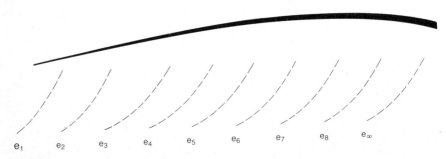

Figure 4-5. Episodes accumulating into a relationship definition.

formed when they see themselves as grown, but their parents persist in seeing them as "kids" because of the numerous experiences in the past. The subprinciple operating here is that *the more frequently a relational definition is reinforced by episodic enactments, the more potent it becomes.* Finally, not each episode has a demonstrable effect on the relationship definition—many episodes simply follow the usual pattern, which reinforces the relationship definition without anyone noticing [38].

Although communication and relationships are at two different levels, they are obviously linked [91, 154]. Gottman notes that the communication patterns of disssatisfied couples are characterized by more "cross-complaining" than those of satisfied couples [181]. In sum, the first principle specifies that relationship definitions are constructed via the meanings we have for the episodic enactments.*

Principle 2: Relationship definitions "frame" or contextualize communication behavior [540, 543].

Communication events cannot be properly interpreted outside their relational context. If you see two men, one forty years old and the other twenty, and they are standing with their arms around one another, you will intepret their communication behavior quite differently if you discover they are father and son rather than gay males. Similarly, the refusal of a good-night kiss for a man and woman on a date means something totally different if it occurs on the first date instead of six months into the relationship. As Hinde states it, "The significance of interactions to the participants may depend on the content of the relationship in which they are embedded . . . " [216].

Not only do relationship labels "frame" our interactions so that they make sense to us, but certain relationship types are associated with consistent patterns of communication within given cultures. The labels we learn to use for relationships have some commonality across people. For example, Knapp, Ellis, and Williams presented different relationship terms to large groups of people to see what they associated with the labels. They found, for example, that more intimate relationships (such as lovers or best friends) were associated with more

---

*The "levels" of relationships and communication can be charted a number of ways. Pearce and others [385] specify multilevels, whereas Wilmot and Baxter [545] discuss three levels. Although I prefer the three-level approach, it is a bit complicated for presentation here, and the straightforward levels of (1) relationships and (2) communication are retained in this discussion. For more detailed treatment of all these issues, see Hinde [216]; Baxter and Wilmot [38]; Bochner [62]; Bateson [25]; Wilmot and Baxter [545]; Pearce et al. [384]; Wilder [385]; Knapp, Ellis, and Williams [261]; Wilmot and Baxter [544]; Hecht [208]; Bateson [25]; Bochner [62]; King and Sereno [258]; Capella [91]; Pawlby [383]; McClintock [318]; Fisher and Drecksel [150].

synchronized and personalized communication activities. Although these perceptions may be the result of our cultural stereotypes about what makes a "good" intimate relationship and may not actually happen in relationships, it is significant that some overall patterns did emerge [261]. In all cultures, there are certain qualities linked to particular relational definitions, since the relational definitions arise from repeated communication experiences. Most people know this intuitively and sometimes use it to their own advantage. Take the case of a young woman and man, involved in a romantic relationship, living together. They might choose to introduce the other as "my roommate" or "my friend" rather than "my romantic partner." The use of labels sets the stage for expectations for the participants and outsiders, and this linkage between relationship definitions and assumed communication behavior follows some regular patterns. For, after all, the communication is interpreted and associated with given relational definitions.

Principle 3: Relationship types are not necessarily mutually exclusive—
their boundaries are often "fuzzy."

When most people talk about their relationships, they treat them as if they were totally discrete from different types. For instance, a "friendship" is talked about differently from a romantic relationship or family relationship. However, as Wilmot and Baxter note, "Social relations in real life are rarely so stable and nonchanging . . . " [544, 289]. Relationships are more a process than a static state. And because of the process nature of relationships, many relationships are not "sharply and completely distinct" [245].

The "fuzzy" boundaries between types of relationship was illustrated in the work of Wilmot and Baxter [545]. They specified that we have relationship prototypes—our ideal image of what a relationship should be. For example, romantic relationships, when compared with friendships, are generally seen as (1) more mystical or inexplicable, (2) more intimate and sexual, (3) more inclined to involve relationship, and (4) more likely to require additional effort. These distinctions between the prototypes, however, are not all the story. In addition, both friendships and romantic relationships are characterized by trust, respect, caring, ease in communicating, general comfort and security in the other's presence, and openness. The prototypes, then, are "fuzzy," with some overlapping qualities and some distinct features.

The issue is further complicated by the fact that many relationships move from one category to another. A friendship may evolve into a romantic relationship, and a romantic interlude that is unsuccessful may result in the participants redefining themselves as "friends." Some married people, for example, refer to themselves as each other's best friend, and two sisters may well be each other's best friend. While the prototypes may seem distinct on the surface, the qualities of each may overlap with another. Such "fuzzy" boundaries, of course, may bring confusion to the participants, when one person thinks close physical contact is a sign of developing a "romantic" relationship, whereas the other interprets the physical affection as "friendly."

Principle 4: Relationship definitions and communication episodes reciprocally frame one another.

We noted earlier that participants' interpretations of communication episodes set the forces in motion for arriving at a relationship definition. When the communication behavior is seen as fitting a prototype, such as helping the other being associated with friendship, the participants begin to see the relationship as forming [396].

But relationship definitions *do change.* Friendships deteriorate, romantic relations fall apart, family members become estranged, and work associates move closer and farther apart. The "frames" (relationship definitions) we use to interpret communication behavior are in process and do undergo alterations [545]. Although the relationship frame supplies the context for understanding the communication behavior, it only remains unchallenged while it works. For example, if you see a friendship as based on keeping confidences between the two of you, when Sarah "tells all" about you to a third person, it challenges the existence of the friendship. One man, upon learning that his friend, now living elsewhere, was "bad-mouthing" him to others, wrote to him, saying, "Friends of mine don't go around getting social points by misusing the friendship. Consider yourself an ex-friend!" When the prototypes for the relationship have linkages to communication behavior, and when they are not fulfilled, the definition of the friendship is challenged. Put another way, communication is interpreted against the backdrop of the relationship, and the obverse is also true—relationships are judged according to the episodic events that unfold [258]. There is a reciprocal influence between the two.

One goes about changing a relationship by enacting episodes that do not "fit" the prototype for that relationship [544, 545, 301]. If you are in a committed relationship and begin staying out all night without the other, such actions erode the assumed definition of the relationship. Negative episodes, where the two people are constantly in unproductive conflict, is like an acid on the relationship definition—it slowly "eats away" at the definition. Similarly, of course, if you are in a relationship that is not going well, *altering the communication patterns* is the fastest way to begin bringing back a healthy relationship. Often when people "fall out of love" or have a waning friendship, they try to alter the global nature of the definition, when what is most effective is changing the episodes. Over time, the change in behavior influences the relationship to come back into consistency with it, and the couple may actually have their love "rekindled." Put simply, the interpersonal communication patterns in a relationship influence the feelings that emerge, and each exerts an influence on the other [251, 301].

METACOMMUNICATION

We noted earlier that communication occurs within a "frame" or context, and the frame gives us information about how to interpret the communication cues. Anything that frames or contextualizes our communication serves the metacommunication function—providing communication about communications. Basically, metacommunication provides information about the relationship between the parties; the content is always interpreted within the relationship parameters expressed metacommunicatively. If Kathy says to Bryan, "Darn it, Bryan, quit interrupting me," she is metacommunicating—commenting on their evolving relationship and letting him know that she expects to be treated as an equal.

The metacommuncation function can be enacted in a variety of forms. It can occur on either the (1) episodic level or (2) relationship level [543]. Whenever you make some comment about the ongoing transaction, you are engaging in episodic metacommunication. Episodic metacommunication can be directed to the other's acts, yourself, or the transactions between the two of you [58]. Saying, "You interrupt me a lot," or, "I'm sorry, I guess I wasn't clear," or, "That was an interesting talk—I enjoyed our give and take" is episodic metacommunication. Satir [432] provides a more detailed listing of samples of episodic metacommunciation. It occurs when someone:

- Labels what kind of message he sends and how serious he is.
- Says why he sent the message.
- Says why he sent the message by referring to the other's wishes.
- Says why he sent the message by referring to a request of the other.
- Says why he sent the message by referring to the kind of response he was trying to elicit.
- Says what he was trying to get the other to do.

These episodic metacommuncation expressions perform the "contexting" functions mentioned earlier. They are overt cues to signal the other how to interpret the communcation messages, whether you say, "I was only kidding," or, "You are not giving me eye contact." The episodic metacommunication can, however, be conveyed *implicitly*, without verbally labeling what is occurring. All the available nonverbal cues of our interaction—leaning close to another, talking in a hushed

**Episodic metacommunication may be implicit
or explicit.**

voice, making intense eye contact—provide information about the
"framing" you intend for the episode. If you meet a good friend on
campus and he winks and calls you a nasty name, you both know it is
not really an insult, but a form of play. Dogs often get into mock fights
with their owners, and the metacommunciation cues sent by both the
dog and the owner make it clear to all that the snarling and bared teeth
are not really to be feared. These implicit metacommunicative cues are
sent in almost all our communicative exchanges—we cue the other
how to interpret what we are doing, even it we do not explicitly label
it. All our "content" messages carry the implicit message, "This is how
I see you in reference to me." Of course, many people send implicit
metacommunication cues they are unaware of—being unfriendly or
acting superior, for example—and then wonder why other people do
not approach them [332].

Before we discuss the other types of metacommunication, an over-

	Implicit	Explicit
Episodic Level	1	2
Relationship Level	3	4

Figure 4-6.   Types of metacommunication.

all look at them might be helpful. Figure 4-6 illustrates the types of metacommunication.

Relationship metacommuncation arises from our recurring episodes with another [543]. As we have noted, individual episodes are clustered by the participants to provide an overall relational meaning or definition. Just as with episodic metacommunicative exchanges, relational-level metacommunication is exchanged both implicitly and explicitly.

The implicit relationship definitions or frames are built over time by having repetitive episodic events. For example, if one person always interrupts, controls the topic flow, and generally "runs over" the other, this says that the first person has the right to control the interaction with the other. As illustrated in Figure 4-5, these repeated episodes build a relationship definition for the participants, and the more frequent the episodes, the more potent the relational frame. The content of discussions and actions serves as the vehicle by which the relationship is constructed, defined, and maintained—while the content is expressed, the relationship is defined implicitly [543]. Many times, these implicit relationship definitions are never shared or verbalized. Two people just "know" what their relationship is, and it is all done implicitly. Newman gives yet another example of how people implicitly define their relationships. She notes that talk about a past relationship partner can serve to clue the other about how you see the current relationship. As she says, "Talking about a past partner can be a means of implicitly communicating what is, or what would be, satisfying, dissatifying, desirable, or undesirable, in the current relationship" [352]. If the person complains that their previous romantic partner was "stubborn," it might well be an implicit clue that he does not want you to act in a stubborn manner in this relationship.

Often, however, a change occurs in a relationship, where the frame or relationship definition is expressed verbally. When you say, "We are friends," you have provided an *explicit* metacommunication. Calling someone your "bridge partner" or "best friend" or "live-in lover" tells the participants and others how to interpret the communication that is exchanged between the two of you. Any statement that overtly pertains to "this is how I see you and me in relation to one another" performs a contextualizing function for the communication acts [543].

Obviously, a relationship-level definition arises from the recurring episodes, but once formed it exerts an interpretive function on all subsequent transactions. Owen [372] examined one of the most common forms of relationship metacommunication, the phrase "I love you." He found that it served as a "bid for the relationship," where the person who utters it is essentially asking "Are we in love with one another?" After it is expressed, it exerts a pull on the other to reciprocate, and saying it too early in a relationship might frighten the partner into terminating the relationship. The relationship definition does bring with it obligations and assumptions about how the two of you will operate. As a result, many times there is a struggle over the overt definition. John says, "We are just friends," whereas Joyce says, "We are beginning to move toward romance." They then get into an argument about whether they are devloping a romantic relationship.

To what degree do people share their perceptions of their episodes and overall relationships with one another? If you are being treated badly by a waiter, it is unlikely you will say, "I find you expressing a lot of negative nonverbal cues. Have I done something to offend you?" Similarly, many people resist explicitly talking to an important other about the status of the relationship. As one young man said, "Talking about a carefree relationship would ruin it" [40]. The exact conditions under which explicit metacommunication can serve to help rather than harm a relationship are not yet known, but we do know that people often actively *avoid* explicit metacommunication [40, 220]. Baxter and Wilmot, for example, interviewed ninety people, asking them what topics were "taboo" in their relationships. All but three people stated that there were taboo topics; the four most frequent types involved explicit metacommunication. For example, people said it was a taboo to discuss (1) the state of the current relationship, (2) extrarelationship activity (other relationships such as other friends or romantic partners), (3) relationship norms (the "rules" for the relationship), and (4) prior relationships [40]. Other studies demonstrate that explicit metacommunication does occur, yet it may also be seen as threatening or conflict inducing [220]. The key may lie in *how* one metacommunicates and the effect it has on the other and the relationship rather than in whether one should metacommunicate explicitly or not. This issue is discussed in full in the final chapter, "Communication Competence," but for now it is clear that (1) messages are sent to others that serve to "frame" or contextualize the communication, (2) these metamessages can focus on the episode level or relational level, and (3) the metacommunication can be expressed implicitly or explicitly.

DIMENSIONS OF RELATIONSHIPS

Participants' perceptions of their relationships have been overviewed, but as valuable as these perceptions are, they do not tell the entire story of either communication or relationships. A more microapproach, observations of the actual communication behavior, can also yield information about how communication behavior and relationships are perceived. Researchers exploring from these vantage points have tried to specify the underlying *dimensions* of relationships. A dimension would be a fundamental property, along which relationships would vary. For example, if you specify that dominance–submission is a fundamental dimension, all relationships could be classified according to degrees of dominance or submissiveness shown by the participants.

The underlying dimensions of relationships have been viewed from many vantage points. Fitzpatrick's work on marital types suggests that there are three basic types of marriages—independents, separates, and traditionalists [155]. Burgoon and Hale argue for twelve conceptually distinct dimensions underlying interpersonal relations [80]. Braiker and Kelley suggest four fundamental dimensions of relationships—love, conflict, ambivalence, and maintenance—whereas Kurth sees voluntariness, uniqueness, intimacy, and obligations of participants at the heart of all communicative transactions [72, 267]. Even more alternative schemas have been formulated by Yablonsky [556], McCall [515[, Ruesch [479], Jackson [235], and Goffman [178]. Schutz has a well-known theory that relies on three interpersonal needs—control, inclusion, and affection [443]. Finally, White has proposed that across cultures there are two underlying dimensions to how personalities are perceived and around which we interpret the communication behavior of others: conflict–solidarity and dominance–submission [533]. A detailed review and critique of these dimensions for personal relationships would be more confusing than enlightening, but Carson [94] has synthesized some of the earlier research into meaningful patterns. His review suggests that:

> On the whole, the conclusion seems justified that major portions of the domain of interpersonal behavior can profitably and reasonably accurately be conceived as involving variations on two independent bipolar dimensions. One of these may be called a *dominance/submission* dimension; it includes dominant, assertive, ascendant, leading, controlling (etc.) behavior on one hand, and submissive, retiring, obsequious, unassertive, following (etc.) behavior on the other. The poles of the second principal dimensions are perhaps best approximated by the terms *hate* versus *love;* the former includes hateful, aggressive, rejecting, punishing, attacking, disaffiliative (etc.) behavior, while the latter includes accepting, loving, affectionate, affiliative, friendly (etc.) social actions [94].

Therefore, any dyadic relationship can be characterized as having two components: (1) dominance–submission and (2) love–hate. In other words, in terms of the relational component of any dyadic transaction, the participants relate to each other by expressive behavior centered around control of each other (or lack of it) and affection (positive or negative).

Timothy Leary's [280] work on the dimensions of relationships illustrates how one can use these two dimensions of relationships to characterize communication styles. A person who is competitive, for instance, is manifesting both a desire to control the other person (dominance) and some hostility (hate). A person's cooperative behavior is best characterized as somewhere between dominance and submission, while at the same time demonstrating positive affection (love). Figure 4-7 is a reproduction of Leary's behavioral classifications. Leary specifies that "interpersonal reflexes" are prominent in our transactions with others. A reflex is a probable response that one almost "automatically" makes. For instance, when someone says to you, "I hate you," your reflex action is probably one of like nature (a dislike for the other person). Dominating or bossing someone provokes its opposite, obedience. Leary's circumplex, the circular arrangement of behaviors around the dimensions of dominance–submission and love–hate, can be summarized as follows:

1. Behavior on the love–hate dimension provokes similar behavior. Love provokes love; hostility provokes hostility.
2. Behavior on the dominance–submission dimension provokes its complement. Being submissive provokes leadership behavior in the other; managing and directing provoke obedience.

In order to discuss fully the implications the two dimensions have for dyadic relationships, they will be treated separately. Note, however, that both dimensions are always present in dyadic transactions.

Dominance–Submission

If two communication participants implicitly agree on the control aspects of their relationship, struggles over dominance–submission are likely to be minimal. For example, in a friendship dyad, if each participant expects to exercise some dominance and some submissive behavior, and each does, there will be few difficulties encountered on the dominance–submission dimension. On the other hand, if both participants wish to control the relationship, definite struggles over dominance will occur. For instance, in a romantic dyad, if both individuals try to dominante the other, a conflict will ensue. The difficulty comes about because there is a tendency for different roles to develop; the

Each of the 16 interpersonal variables is illustrated by sample behaviors. The inner circle names adaptive reflexes, such as *manage*. Proceeding outward, the next ring indicates the type of behavior that this interpersonal reflex tends to 'pull' from the other one; thus the person who uses the reflex A tends to call up in others *obedience*. These findings involve two-way interpersonal phenomena—what the subject does and what the other does in return—and are therefore less reliable than the other interpersonal categories presented in the inner and outer rings. The next circle illustrates extreme or rigid reflexes, such as *dominates*. The perimeter of the circle is divided into eight general categories employed in interpersonal diagnosis. Each of these general categories has a moderate (adaptive) and an extreme (pathological) intensity, such as *managerial-autocratic*.

Figure 4-7.   Leary's circumplex—classification of interpersonal behavior into 16 mechanisms or reflexes. *From Timothy Leary, "The Theory and Measurement Methodology of Interpersonal Communication,"* Psychiatry 18 *(May 1955): 147–161. By permission.*

individuals are expected to accommodate each other. In Leary's terms, if an instructor is trying to direct a student to read a good book on communication, the student is expected to jot down the title and heed the advice, namely, to give the proper reflex behavior. However, if every time a book title is mentioned he suggests one for the instructor to read, the instructor's expectation has been violated. Most of us expect the other to respond to our attempts at authority by accepting such attempts (by being submissive).

The dominace–submission aspect of relationships can be characterized by labeling relationships as *complementary, symmetrical,* or *parallel.* In a complementary relationship, each person's behavior complements the other's. The relationship is based on differences; one person primarily is dominant. A mother and young child are in a complementary relationship—the mother is superior, the child inferior (until the baby cries in the middle of the night). A boss–employee relationship is usually complementary, as are those between teacher–student, doctor–patient, policeman–automobile driver, president–secretary, and other relationships based on inequality of control. "One partner occupies what has been variously described as the superior, primary, or 'one-up' position and the other the corresponding inferior, secondary, or 'one-down' position" [519]. One person initiates action and the other follows it [235]. In such a relationship both individuals need each other because the "dissimilar but fitted behaviors evoke each other" [519]. A woman needs a child in order to be a mother; a boss without any employees is no boss; a doctor cannot treat anyone unless he has a patient. Likewise, the person in the less dominant position needs the other person. Both participants are fulfilled by the actions of the other [271]. A complementary message exchange can occur with (1) one-down message followed by a one-up message or (2) a one-up message followed by a one-down message from the other participant [408]. When studying a dyadic pair's complementary definitions, the patterns of dominance and submission unfolding over time are extremely important. For instance, if a young man and his sister are in a pattern of one-up, one-down, the pattern would proceed as follows: he says, "Sarah, you sure don't know how to wash a car," and Sarah says, "You're right, I'm terrible at it." This pattern is distinct from one where someone says, "I don't know how to do anything right," and the partner replies, "You're right." The statement "You're right" is a one-down response in the first pattern and a one-up response in the second pattern, which illustrates that the two types of complementarity are distinct. Although both are forms of complementarity, the first sequence ends with the initiator as "one up," whereas the respondent is "one-up" in the second sequence.

Relationships based on complementary needs for dominance are not necessarily dysfunctional or harmful. In fact, complementary relationships enable us as dyadic participants to share in the expertise of the other. While you are in the submissive position, you can absorb what others have to offer. A student, for instance, can gain insight by letting a professor be dominant over the relationship; she can "pick the professor's brain." And it is probably wise for the professor to engage in transactions with a student where the student is the dominant one. One could argue that people who are accustomed to dominant role positions can learn the most by engaging in communciation interchanges where the two participants engage in periodic role reversals. The doctor should be a patient, the teacher a student, and the social worker a client. Similarly, it probably would be wise to assign the dominant position to individuals who usually cannot define the relationship. When, for example, student–teacher roles are reversed, the student will likely discover the teacher may not be as dominant as he first thought. Role reversals in dyads can illuminate the dominant dimension of the relationship, and if someone refuses to reverse roles, he is simply affirming that he likes the way his role is presently defined.

We are always defining the dominant–submissive dimension of our relationships by the way we communicate. If the other person attempts to exercise dominance over you, you do not have to accept her definition. You always have the option of refusing the other's definition of the relationship and supplying your own [464]. But any definition you advance has its consequences. If you give the expected reflex behavior by being submissive, the transaction may proceed smoothly, but you could be frustrated by the lack of control. If you attempt to redefine the relationship by exercising dominance over the other, a struggle over the relationship will likely develop. If the two of you establish equality over dominance, a *symmetrical* relationship has developed [519].

In symmetric relationships, the participants behave as if they have equal status. Close friendships, for instance, are often dyads based on equality. Both individuals are free to exercise control; they have the same options available. "Each person exhibits the right to initiate action, criticize the other, offer advice and so on" [235].

At first glance, symmetric relationships may appear to be the most desirable ones. After all, if the participants treat each other as equals, then struggles over dominance should disappear. Usually, however, the dominance issue is more unsettled than in a complementary relationship. When people treat each other as equals, they are not ignoring dominance, they are in competition for it [235]. Whereas in a complementary relationship the rights of dominance are clearly defined, in symmetric relationships rights of dominance are constantly being redefined. For instance, "If one person mentions that he has succeeded in some endeavor the other person mentions that he has succeeded in an equally important endeavor" [235].

Rogers and Farace [408] and Parks [375] have expanded the usual views of symmetry by further specifying differing types of symmetry. They identified three types of symmetry: (1) competitive symmetry, where both participants are trying to get into a one-up position; (2) submissive symmetry, where the participants are trying to both be one-down and not dominate the other; and (3) neutralized symmetry, where clear one-up and one-down messages are not identifiable and the issue of relationship definition is not pertinent to either participant. The first two types are the most useful for our purposes here. Competitive symmetry is the type we have already illustrated where two people are overtly struggling for control in the relationship. Submissive symmetry situations are also common. Take the case of a man and woman who are going out on their first date together. When the man arrives, he says, "What would you like to do tonight?" and the young lady replies, "Oh, I don't know, what would you like to do?" He says, "Anything that you want to do is fine with me," and she counters with, "I just don't have a preference—you decide." His final offer is, "I like to please the girl. You decide where we should go." The struggle is over trying not to take control of the conversation and submissive symmetry results. Paradoxically, "trying not to control" is an attempt to limit the other—by getting him or her to take the responsibility.

The resulting effects from symmetric and complementary relational definitions are not yet clearly known because so little research has been done. One of the more interesting studies, however, was done by Millar [327]. He found that marital couples who had greater rigidity in their use of control, that is, who used consistent symmetrical exchanges, had more agreement and satisfaction about their marital relationship. The predictability concerning relational messages was associated with greater knowledge of the other partner. Undoubtedly, in the future we will be able to specify which types of complementarity and symmetry are more appropriate for given relationships. One tantalizing finding by Rogers [407] was that couples whose role expectations of the other were not met engaged in more competitive symmetry than did more satisfied couples. As the relationally based approaches to measuring dominance and other relational characteristics flourish, we will be more able to (1) describe the types of relational control that people use, (2) specify the changes in those patterns over time, and (3) study the overall configurations of the patterns over time [408].

Distinguishing between sending a domineering statement and being dominant is necessary. A domineering statement is a one-up message whose purpose is conversational control. Only when it is responded to with a subsequent one-down response by the other does dominance result [330]. We can only dominate when the other cooperates, however implicitly, with our definition of the relationship at that particular time. One day on campus I was having coffee and overheard a drama professor and a beginning student in a discussion. The professor was a director, and in response to the student's question about his acting, he said, "Of course, what you did as an actor was fine. But until you are in the craft for twenty years, you will not be a seasoned actor. Only when you have many years' experience will you understand what I am talking about." If the student had gotten up and said, "Thanks for your advice, but that kind I don't need. I want to know if I'm good enough for professional theater and you just tell me I have to be your age before I understand," the transaction would have been greatly different. As it was, the student accepted the domineering statements and said, "Yes, I can see that I don't understand."

When we accept the one-down position, it allows the other to be one-up and to be dominant in the conversation.

Before leaving our discussion of dominance, we must examine how it is related to *power*. One of the more exciting trends in the study of communication is viewing interpersonal power in relational terms. You do not *have* power—it is given to you by the others with whom you transact. As Hocker and Wilmot [220] note, "All power in interpersonal relationships is a property of the social relationship rather than a quality of the individual." Millar and Millar [330] and Parks [375] identify power as central to an understanding of how a relational view of our dyadic linkages will unfold. Power is a central concept to the understanding of how two individuals work out their relationship between themselves. While power is vitally important in dyadic relationships, *it is not synonymous with dominance.* Because of the ease of measuring domineering behaviors, many researchers mistakenly imply that one has power only when one dominates. However, exercising *conversational control* by interrupting, or making other one-up moves, *is not the same as relational control.* Conversational control or dominance is any communicative "device or strategy (e.g., speaking at length, speaking frequently, or interrupting one's partner) which lessens the communciative role of another" [277]. But one can exercise relational control without dominating individual conversations. We all know of the couple where the "silent partner" is the one who really makes the decisions, while the person who does all the talking, interrupting, and other forms of conversational domination is just a spokesperson for the dyad. Similarly, sometimes the person who exercises the most relational control is the one who sulks, goes silent, or plays the martyr role. If you are submissive and the dyadic partner responds to your submission, then you have relational power without exercising conversational dominance.

People seem to be intuitively aware that they can gain even more control in a realtionship by avoiding behaviors that are easily classified as dominating. As Bochner, Kaminski, and Fitzpatrick say, "It is likely that individuals attempt to camouflage their use of these interpersonal behaviors to make sure that others like them" [64]. In fact, they found that when other people demonstrated overt attempts at control, they were less well liked than if they didn't demonstrate as much control [64]. It may well be that when we perceive the other person to be higher in dominance than we are, we often castigate their power use and make counter moves to equalize it more fully. The entire dimension of dominance and submission is central to understanding the relational impact that our messages have. Dominance and submission define the amount of conversational control that one exercises and have an influence on the type of relationship that is constructed. Whatever your own view of the wisdom of using dominating behaviors, they are like power—they occur in some form in every message and in every dyadic relationship.

One cannot *not* define the relationship. Put another way, each individual will act upon his direct perspective, metaperspective, and meta-metaperspective concerning control of the relationship. Furthermore, the definition of the relationship by the participants will often change.

When conversation shifts from topic to topic, so may the dominance. In fact, in informal dyadic transactions, each person has areas he defines. When this is the case, as it often is, the relationship is *parallel* [235]. In parallel relationships there are frequent "crossovers" between complementary and symmetric relationships [235]. There is some evidence to indicate that if a relationship is parallel, namely, that if both complementary and symmetric definitions occur, the transactions are less rigid and less inclined to be pathological [283, 327, 464, 519]. The implications of parallel transactions and of transactions that are exclusively symmetrical or complementary are just being explored [373].

The relational control dimension we have discussed has potential significance for understanding what makes a relationship function well. *How* decisions are made is probably more important for a dyad than what the particular decisions might be [266]. The control of interaction is on the relational level and governs the overall interactive patterns in a relationship [341]. The central notion is that the patterns of message exchange define the relationship, and with outcomes for satisfactions for the participants [409, 22]. Rogers and Millar, for example, found that in marriages in which the husband is conversationally dominant, there is more satisfaction than in marriages where the wife is conversationally dominant [409]. This may be due to the finding that when the husband is dominant, the wife gives supporting responses, but when the wife is dominant, the husband does not give as many supporting responses. In subsequent studies, it was again found that the more domineering the wife, the less the marital and communication satisfaction [110].

Although some have argued that complmentarity and symmetricality are properties of overall relationship patterns and note individual interactions [216], the degree of correspondence between individual interactions and overall relationship satisfaction is yet unknown.

Love–Hate

The other major dimension that emerges in communicative exchanges is affection and hostility, or love–hate. As noted in the opening chapter, it is in dyads that the most intense emotions come to the surface. Romantic dyads range from pairs in which each would give his life in order to save his partner's to those in which one takes the life of the partner—clear expressions of love and hate. Most dyadic transactions, however, have degrees of hostility or affection that are between the two extremes, but they can be characterized as possessing predominately affection or hostility at specific times.

Dyadic transactions that are characterized by hostility can take many forms. In the more extreme case, an antipair can be formed. In such a dyad, the participants heap abuse and malice on each other and the dyad functions because petty nagging and scolding, threats and counterthreats become behaviors that the partners cannot do without [513]. The dyad is woven together by the hostility because they have not learned how to express the positive feelings they possess. The person who is always compelled to make snide remarks, who continuously plays one-upmanship, or who is always trying to impress others with his intellect is doing one thing—he is rejecting others so they will accept him. If he truly loves someone yet constantly "puts the other down" in public, he is simply disguising positive affection in the clothing of hostility. The person receiving the put-downs, however, may find it increasingly hard always to interpret the negative remarks as positive.

The hostility felt between two individuals is often not openly expressed. When the secretary really hates the boss, or the student dislikes the teacher, the feelings are often not shared. Instead of openly expressing the hostility, it is covered up and related to someone else. The student swapping tales of "Isn't that teacher terrible," the wives having coffee and complaining about their husbands, or the husbands discussing how they dislike their wives are all attempts to deal with hostility. It is gossip that is an "unhealthy way of creating one relationship by betraying another" [17].

Close dyads thrive on affection. Showing positive regard for someone is acceptance, thereby increasing the chances of reciprocal acceptance. As a dyadic relationship becomes more positive, the participants tend to disclose more positive emotions. Until certain upper limits are reached, positive affect provokes positive affect [112, 141, 553].

The differences between types of dyads can be at least partially explained by the expected level of expressing positive feelings. It might be somewhat awkward if employees continually tell their employer, "I love you." And if a marital dyad has no more intimacy and positive affection than a casual friendship dyad has, it may be a "surface marriage," showing all the outward signs of a strongly committed marital dyad, but with the crucial element of a strong bond of affection missing. On the other hand, by expecting too much positive affection, similar relational difficulties can arise. As anyone who has tried to snuggle up to a romantic partner who wants only friendship can attest, there are differences in expected affection.

The expression of positive affection does not have to be dramatic. You do not have to run up and kiss someone in order to show positive affection. In all types of dyads, it is often sufficient to pay attention to someone, give them a smile, or just be responsive to their existence. The individual who fails to become fully involved with another is called a "cold fish" or "wet blanket" [178], both of which say, "You are not giving me positive affection; you do not respond to my existence."

Messages of positive or negative emotion are more often sent non-verbally to the other dyadic participant. Unfortunately, even given the recent popularity of books about nonverbal communication, there are no perfect predictors of exactly what a given nonverbal cue means in a given situation. First of all, as Burgoon and Saine attest, we do not express a single, pure emotion when we act. We more often express a combination of emotions, such as emitting anxiety or fear cues when we are angry [94]. Further, there is not a one-to-one correspondence between given sets of cues and an emotion. And there is even disagreement about what the number of primary emotional states is that humans are capable of deciphering and using in their communicative transactions. It is the *combination* of expression of dominance–submission and love–hate that gives a message its relational force, as Leary notes for us in Figure 4.7. For instance, if you show domineering behavior to the other with hate, others would classify you as domineering, bossy, or autocratic. However, the same amount of domineering expressed positively—by taking control and having the other's best interest at heart—makes for the world's best nurturing behavior and is something most of us prize highly. Millar and Millar [330] made an interesting finding regarding the combination of these two dimensions. They found that when wives manifested domineering attempts, they offered few accompanying support statements, but when husbands acted in a domineering manner, they also gave supportive statements to their wives. As a result, when the wives dominated conversations, the couple expressed less satisfaction with the communication pattern than when the husband dominated conversations. Clearly, the affective, love–hate component of our dyadic messages interlock with dominance and submission and create their effects due to the unique combination of the two.

Shostrom and Kavanaugh [453] explain some differing relational types based on how the messages the partners send fall on the love–hate and dominant–submissive dimensions. They label the dimensions as weakness–strength and anger–love, but they are essentially the same as the ones we have been discussing. Two examples will suffice here. One relationship is composed of a man who shows weakness and love (a "nice guy") and a woman who shows weakness and love (a "doll"). This is a case of submissive symmetry mentioned earlier. A second relationship is composed of the same "nice guy" and a woman who shows strength and anger (a "bitch"). Their relationship is based on exaggerated hostility from the woman and suppressed anger on the part of the man. These two examples (although labeled in a sexist manner) should make the point—it is the combination of the two dimensions that makes for the essential force in the dyadic system. Shostrom and Kavanaugh do point out that their couples are in immature stages of growth and rely on messages that are destructive to one or more of the parties. A close examination of the relational types they set for this reveals some inconsistencies and mislabelings, but the point is the same as Leary's: When we send messages to our dyadic partner and get a response in turn, we have begun to set the system in motion. And each act reflects some degree of dominance–submission and some degree of love–hate. These two dimensions, therefore, are central to all dyadic processes.

SUMMARY

Just as individuals have perceptions of themselves and others, they also have perceptions of their dyadic relationships. This chapter has examined when a relationship is formed, sketched the major tenets of systems theory, and provided a view of relational fundamentals—what the perceptions, metaperceptions, and meta-metaperceptions are in relationships. In addition, the process of implicitly building relationships was discussed, as well as how people "translate" content messages into relational terms. It was argued that the relationship definition becomes the organizing frame for interpreting the communciation behavior that occurs and that communciation and relationship definitions exercise mutual influence. The important area of metacommunication—communication about episodes or overall relationship—was set forth. Finally, the major dimensions of interactions that occur in relationships were summarized, with examples given for how dominance–submission and hate–love operate in our dyadic relationships.

Chapter 5

Relational Intricacies

Up to now, we have dealt with the fundamentals of dyadic relationships by providing an overview and examining perceptions of self, other, and the relationship. This chapter takes the relationship analysis one step further by probing some of the intricate events that occur in dyadic relationships. The foregoing material hinted that every relationship has the potential to be quite complex; this chapter will deal with those complexities. Specifically, self-fulfilling prophecies, communication spirals, paradoxes, double binds, and dyadic dialectics will be treated.

SELF-FULFILLING PROPHECIES

If men define situations as real, they are real in their consequences.
—W. I. THOMAS

A tremendous number of things we believe in, because we see them done, are done for no other reason except that we believe in them.
—WENDELL JOHNSON

Each person defines her own world and acts on the basis of those definitions. The perspectives we have of ourselves and others determine our actions, and, in turn, our actions determine our perspectives. "Man lives by propositions whose validity is a function of his belief in them" [424]. When we are in a communicative relationship with another person, the mutual definitions of self and other determine the character of the relationship.

A self-fulfilling prophecy is one of the more dramatic examples of the impact one's definition of a situation can have on behavior. It was originally formulated by Merton as a *"false* definition of the situation, evoking a new behavior which makes the originally false conception come true" [325]. The prophecy leads to its own fulfillment! For instance, if a bank is financially sound, but a rumor of its insolvency becomes believed by enough depositors, the subsequent run on the bank will result in insolvency. *The human definition of a situation becomes an integral part of the situation and therefore affects the situation.*

Merton's analysis of self-fulfilling prophecies is a valuable contribution to social theory and has direct application to interpersonal communication. Moving from "prophecies" about banks to beliefs about people and relationships is a large step. One can observe a bank before the belief is activated and determine if it is solvent or not. But in applications to interpersonal relations *how do you determine whether the original definition is false?* Your beliefs about the other and the relationship cannot be put "on hold" to determine if they are "true" or not. We cannot objectively observe others or our relationships; we have expectations about the outcome that influence the outcome. For instance, if you think that another person cannot be trusted and you act distrustful, he or she will likely respond appropriately. Your definition of the other will often create the behavior you thought was there. Whether the person was initially untrustworthy is a moot issue. You cannot know if your original definition was true or false, because whatever your definition initially was, it is always part of the situation.

Self-fulfilling prophecies occur because an original definition of a situation by one participant is acted upon by a second participant responding appropriately. Sequentially, the process goes like this:

1. Person A makes an inference about person B.
2. A acts toward B in terms of this inference.
3. B makes inferences about A in terms of this action.
4. B tends to react toward A in terms of this inference.
5. Thus A's inferences tend to be confirmed by B's actions [193].

When we are caught in an interpersonal self-fulfilling prophecy, we do not know it. We act on the basis of our definition because we treat it as an accurate understanding of the situation. Once the system begins operating, however, each individual typically does not see her own behavior as part of the system, though it necessarily is. "A and B claim to be reacting to the partner's behavior without realizing that they in turn influence the partner by their reaction" [519]. In a triadic situation, when two people form a coalition and reject person C, C's response to the rejection typically validates the coalition's actions. After all, A and B had to form a pair because C was hostile to them. The effect of the action became a justification for it.

Instances of self-fulfilling prophecies are numerous. A mother's anxiety about a child affects her behavior such that the child, responding to her anxious state, becomes difficult and worrisome to care for. The child's behavior becomes the cause as well as effect of the mother's anxiety [483]. Once an individual is classified as mentally ill, others will often respond to that definition by reinforcing "sick" behavior [166]. Let's assume for a moment that you are sitting home watching television when there is a knock at the door. Three large men in white uniforms burst into the room shouting, "There he is, get him!" As they wrestle you to the floor, you scream violent protest (in between biting and kicking). At the point where they have you under control, they show you a court order committing you to a mental institution because of your aggressive and violent behavior against your relatives, though you know your relatives are committing you unjustly. Once in the institution you are released from the restraint. You demand to see the director, pleading that it is all some horrible mistake. When she comes to your ward, you explain the circumstances. She says, "There now, it's all right. A lot of us think we are something we are not." The more you protest, the less convinced she becomes, so you protest more vigorously. As you scream, "I am not violent," the attendants slap a straightjacket on you. The prophecy is fulfilled.

Examples of self-fulfilling prophecies not only are numerous, but arise in diverse situations. For many years we have known that the way you classify a person can determine your general reaction to him. If one classifies a black person as being a meager performer, the black in a job interview will be treated to nonverbal cues so he perceives the interviewer as cold. Then as a result, he performs less adequately [552].

One of the newest forms of treatment for drug addicts is helping the addict's family members to change their definition of the person. Alexander and Dibb [3] found that the "social perception in addict families serves to perpetuate opiate addiction by undermining the addict's self-esteem." Similarly, the behavior of a person diagnosed as having a psychological problem is likely being reinforced by the behavior of other family members. Henry, a man in his early sixties, suffered from mental depression three times. As a result, one of his daughters became convinced that Henry was mentally ill and could not return to normal. Her behavior toward him—treating him as a non-person, ignoring what he said, and generally "tuning him out"—enhanced the chances that he would enter another stage of depression.

Teacher's expectations of students can have a significant influence on a student's performance.

More often than not, when an individual has a problem, someone in his immediate group reinforces that problem by keeping a self-fulfilling prophecy in operation.

Laing also provided examples of how individuals keep the other locked in by their perceptions of them. The following two examples from *Knots* [272] demonstrate how one's perceptions can override the attempts of the other to refute the definition. They are classically self-fulfilling.

JILL: You put me in the wrong
JACK: I am not putting you in the wrong
JILL: You put me in the wrong for thinking you put me in the wrong

....

There must be something the matter with him
because he would not be acting as he does
unless there was
therefore he is acting as he is
because there is something the matter with him

He does not think there is anything the matter with him
because
one of the things that is
the matter with him
is that he does not think that there is anything
the matter with him

Therefore
we have to help him realize that,
the fact that he does not think there is anything
the matter with him
is one of the things that is
the matter with him

Self-fulfilling prophecies operate full-blown in our educational institutions. Rosenthal's work has shown that a teacher's expectation of a student can lead to its own fulfillment. One of the studies is typical [416]. The researchers selected an elementary school in a lower-class neighborhood and administered an IQ test to all the children. The test was disguised as one that would predict "intellectual blooming." Twenty percent of the children in each room were randomly selected as "bloomers," and the teachers were told that these children would make remarkable gains in test scores during the next year. The only differences between the children were in the teacher's minds. Eight months later, when the students were retested, the children that teachers had been led to believe were going to bloom did. They showed an average additional gain of four IQ points over the children whom teachers did not expect to bloom [415, 416]. The teachers' expectations benefited students. Although there have been some ethical objections to Rosenthal's work, the data at this point lend fairly strong credence to the notion that self-fulfilling prophecies exist in classrooms [444].°

Of course, the prophecy need not be a positive one. Garfield, Weiss, and Pollack [164] used a procedure similar to Rosenthal's, but this time with school counselors. The counselors were divided into two groups and given identical descriptions of a boy with behavior problems typical of the type the counselors often handled. One group was given information that the boy came from the upper-middle social class, and the other group was given information clearly indicating that the boy was from a lower-class background. The social class descriptions had a significant impact on the counselor's projected reactions. The counselors were more willing to "become ego-involved in the management of the child who is seen as 'more important' and worthier of attention" than the youngster who comes from the lower class. "By passively accepting the expectancy of unfavorable outcome, the counselor all too frequently contributes to the 'inevitability' of events" [164].

Knowing how self-fulfilling prophecies operate, we can put them to work for us. The example cited in the second chapter about the woman graduate student who had her self-concept raised is an excellent case in point. The suitors, other graduate students, redefined her as desirable, and she became more so. If the participant responds to your definition of him, you can remake him to be more what you describe him to be [126].

Constructive ways of handling self-fulfilling prophecies exist. For instance, many schools are not passing on negative information from teacher to teacher in hopes of arresting the rigid perceptions that have worked to a student's disadvantage in the past. A principal of a Job Corps Center has a lot of young people who have had some difficulties with previous school systems or the law. He adamantly refuses to read the prior record of any student and gives each one a "new start" upon entering his school.

But what can you do if others have a self-fulfilling prophecy about you? One of the most dramatic examples of countering a self-fulfilling prophecy comes from the study by Rosenhan [414]. He was interested in seeing if doctors and nurses in mental hospitals could spot normal persons within a context where everyone was considered to have some mental difficulties. He and some of his co-workers, eight in all, got themselves voluntarily admitted to twelve mental health hospitals by alleging symptoms of hearing voices that said "empty," "hollow," and

---

°Rosenthal calls it the "pygmalion effect," based on Ovid and on George Bernard Shaw's play of how Henry Higgins transformed Eliza Doolittle from an illiterate peasant girl to a proper lady based on his expectations of her.

"thud." But other than feigning these symptoms and disguising their true identities, all their other reactions were "normal." They tried to act sane in an insane place. Immediately upon admission, they claimed to no longer hear the voices or have any other symptoms. They even took notes publicly, with the staff members seeing this behavior as consistent with what an insane person might do.

Once in the hospitals their objective was to get out—and it was harder than they expected. While the real patients saw through the deception, the staff continued to see the "new patients" as insane. When one of the bogus patients would ask, "When will I be released? I don't have anything wrong with me anymore," the staff members would give very curt answers. Even when doing everything they could to get out, the averge stay for each of the "patients" was nineteen days. As Rosenhan says, "A psychiatric label has a life and an influence of its own" [414]. Once labeled, the people were kept in that category even after they were eventually released. In all but one case, upon release the persons were diagnosed as "schizophrenic in remission," giving the clear impression that the malady could spring back into force at any time. Especially in educational institutions, in workplaces, and in prisons, perceptions of others tend to be self-sealing, self-prophesying, and self-justifying. Watzlawick et al. suggest how to get out of a hospital after being diagnosed as "insane":

1. Develop a flamboyant symptom that has considerable nuisance value for the whole ward.
2. Attach yourself to a young doctor in need of his first success.
3. Let the doctor cure you rapidly of your "symptom."
4. Make the doctor the most fervent advocate of your regained sanity [520].

Until now in our discussion interpersonal self-fulfilling prophecies have centered on our prophecies of others. *Relationship self-fullfilling prophecies* also exist. The same dynamics are in force—the original definition of the situation is acted upon, thereby validating it. The impacts on relationship prophecies are numerous. For example, if you get married believing that, "All marriages are only good for the first ten years," this belief may create its own fulfillment. At the end of ten years, you expect the relationship to wane, so you put less effort into it (after all, who wants to throw away effort on something that will die anyway?), and because you put less effort into the relationship, it does fail. One person I know says quite clearly, "All relationships become dysfunctional after about five years," and is now in a third marriage. One wonders what would happen if the prophecy had been, "Committed couples can rekindle their love after years of stability, and find even greater happinesss than in the early years."

One final point. Prophecies are not always fulfilled. If you have a definition of the other (or he of you), unless that definition is responded to appropriately, the prophecy will not be fulfilled. For instance, you may think someone is angry and hostile and your responses to her may trigger hostility. But if the other, seeing your aloof and uncaring behavior, says, "Hey, it seems to me like you are upset at me. Can we talk about it?" the definition will probably not be fulfilled. Similarly, if you believe that all romantic relationships can last only six months, and the other person acts differently from what you expected, it may break the cycle of expectations and stop the fulfillment of the prophecy. Prophecies are not fulfilled whenever (1) *B* does not interpret *A*'s behavior as *A* intended, (2) *B* counters with a different definition of himself or herself, or (3) there are institutional controls that constrain the participants from responding fully to each other's definitions [325].

Each person in a communication situation is part of that situation and contributes to its nature. Self-fulfilling prophecies are one of the intricate events that dyadic relationships experience because of the mutuality of influence in a communication system. Self-fulfilling prophecies can be utilized to your and others' advantages. If you search for and reward constructive elements in dyadic relationships, those relationships can become more and more positive. What you look for is what you see, and what you see is what you get.

SPIRALS

Self-fulfilling prophecies do not fully describe the dynamism of transactions. In most communicative interchanges, both people add energy to the system. If the definitions of the two add to each other, a spiral occurs. In a self-fulfilling prophecy, *A*'s original definition is validated. In a relationship spiral, *A*'s definition is *intensified* by *B*'s reaction.

A nondyadic illustration should clarify the essential nature of spirals. My son Jason at age three saw a sleek, shiny cat. With the reckless abandonment of a child his age, he rushed at the cat to pet it. The wise cat, seeing potential death, moved out of Jason's reach. Not to be outdone, Jason tried harder. The cat moved farther away. Jason started running after the cat. The cat, no dummy about life, ran too. In a short ten seconds from the initial lunge at the cat, Jason and the cat were running at full tilt. Luckily, the cat was faster and survived to run another day.

Dyadic participants frequently find themselves in spirals [264]. The two people find themselves advancing through threat and counterthreat so far that they reach a point of no return. The I-wish-I-had-not-said-that feeling after an argument gives testimony to the spiraling effects that build in relationships. Such a building of responses produces a lock-step effect in relationships [280]. On the positive side,

"Friendship is like a fishhook; the farther it goes in, the harder it is to pull out [280]. Communication spirals, whether they head in positive or negative directions, are characterized by these elements:

1. The participant's meanings intertwine in such a way that each person's behavior accelerates the dynamism of the relationship. The relational synergy builds upon itself in a continuously accelerating manner.
2. In any given period of time, a dyadic spiral is building in either a progressive or regressive direction. Progressive spirals promote positive feelings about the relationship; regressive spirals induce negative feelings about the relationship.
3. Unless progressive and regressive spirals are checked by the limits of the participants' toleration, either they become dysfunctional or the dyadic relationship is dissolved.
4. Any spiral can be changed, its pace quickened or slowed or its direction reversed by the participants' actions.

Progressive Spirals

When participants serve each other's needs such that *A*'s acts reinforce *B*, and *B*'s act reinforce *A*, the synergy of the system makes the relationship progressively better. Positive or progressive spirals occur such that each participant feels more and more positive toward the other. For instance, the teacher who can be open and accepting of students can often experience such spirals. Searching for the positive in a student and rewarding it appropriately can open a student up for teacher influence. The more genuinely the teacher relates to the student, the better the student performs; the higher the quality of his performance, the more positive the teacher can become.

Positive spirals are obviously not limited to teacher–student dyads. In all dyadic transactions, as *A* responds to *B* in a manner *B* regards as appropriate, *B*'s behaviors are reinforced. His sense of identity is strengthened and his ability to relate to *A* improves [452]. Jourard [242] titles the acceleration of the system as the "dyadic effect." Each person's actions feed more energy into a system of relations that, like fusion, continues to build the reinforcing patterns. The case of the highly motivated worker illustrates the same ever-widening nature of spirals. As one strives to improve working conditions, the improved working conditions increase the worker's motivation, which cycles back and makes for an even better climate, which increases. . . .

In progressive spirals, the perceptions of the partners become more accurate and their mutual adjustments continue to build [74, 497]. In romantic dyads, "Love generates more love, growth more growth, and knowledge more knowledge [369]. The favorableness builds upon itself. Trust and understanding cycle back to create more trust and understanding. The relationship is precisely like a spiral—

Figure 5-1.   A progressive (or regressive) spiral.

ever-widening. In abstract terms, Figure 5-1 is a diagram of the ever-increasing positive aspect of progressive spirals. As the transaction continues, the positive effects keep accelerating.

We all experience progressive spirals. The student who begins doing work of a high caliber, earns better grades, and becomes self-motivated enters a progressive spiral. Each piece of work brings a reward (good grades or praise) that further encourages her to feats of excellence. And if conditions are favorable, the spiral can continue to progress. A teacher who retrains and becomes more knowledgeable discovers that he has more to offer students. The excited students, in turn, reinforce his desire to work hard so he can feel even better about his profession. In progressive spirals, the actions of the individual supply a multiplier effect in reinforcement. The better you do, the more worthwhile you feel; the more worthwhile you feel, the better you do. The effects of a simple action reverberate throughout the system. An unexpected tenderness from your loved one, for instance, will not stop there. It will recycle back to you, and probably come from you again in increased dosage.

Regressive Spirals

Regressive spirals are mirror images of progressive spirals; the process is identical but the results are opposite. In a regressive spiral misunderstanding and discord create more and more relationship damage. As with progressive spirals, regressive spirals take many forms.

The inability to reach out and develop meaningful relationships can often compound itself. The person who has reduced interest in others and does not form effective relationships suffers a lower self-esteem (because self-esteem is socially derived), which in turn cycles back and produces less interest in others. "The process is cyclical and degenerative" [561]. Or if one is afraid to love others, he shuns people, which in turn makes it more difficult to love. Also, such regressive spirals often happen to people with regard to their sense of worth concerning work. The person who has not established herself in her profession but has been in the profession for a number of years may get caught in a spiral. She may spend time trying to appear busy, talking about others, or using various techniques to establish some sense of worth. Behavior that can change the spiral—working hard or

When a relationship is in a regressive cycle, conflicts between partners may become intense and destructive.

retraining—are those least likely to occur. It is a self-fulfilling proph-ecy with a boost—it gets worse and worse. With each new gamut or ploy perfected (acquiring a new hobby, joining numerous social gath-erings, etc.), the relational issues become further submerged.

Regressive cycles are readily apparent when a relationship begins disintegrating. When distrust feeds distrust, defensiveness soars and the relationship worsens, and such "runaway relationships" become destructive for all concerned [17]. In a "gruesome twosome," for instance, the two participants maintain a close, negative relationship. Each person receives fewer gratifications from the relationship, yet they maintain the attachment by mutual exploitation [435]. Gruesome twosomes can occur in almost any dyadic pairing. When the relation-ship prevents one or both partners from gratifying normal needs but the relationship is maintained, the twosome is caught in a regressive spiral.

Regressive spirals can be observed in romantic, friendship, and generation dyads. Conflicts in intimate relationships seem to take on an intensity that is not found as often in more role-structured situa-tions. A typical case involves the breakup of a significant relationship such as marriage. During a quarreling session one evening the husband says to the wife, "If you had not gone and gotten involved in an outside relationship with another man, our marriage could have made it. You just drained too much energy from us for our marriage to work." The wife responds by saying, "Yes, and had you given me the attention and care I longed for, I wouldn't have had an outside relationship." The infinite regress continues, each of them finding fault with why the other caused the termination of the marriage. The spiraling nature is clear. The more the wife retreats to an outside relationship, the less chance she has of her needs being met in the marriage. And the more the husband avoids giving her what she wants in the relationship, the more she will be influenced to seek outside relationships.

Leary also was aware of regressive spirals caused by the "interpersonal reflex" mentioned in the previous chapter. He notes that parents and children often get caught up in a spiral of dependence and nurturance until it gets to the point that the system is dysfunctional. The more dependent the child is on the parent, the more nurturing the parent is. And the more nurturing the parent is, the more this promotes dependence on the part of the child. As he says, "One's actions toward other people generally effect a mirror duplication or a countermeasure from the other. This in turn tends to strengthen one's original action" [280].

There are many everyday examples of regressive spirals. Take Jackie and John as examples. They started dating and went together for about two months, then the progressive spiral reversed direction. John notes that Jackie is "emotional" and not "logical" in making her decisons about work time. Jackie, in turn, sees John as "controlling" and "cold and aloof," and as the days pass, they each see the other as more extreme. As John becomes more "logical," pointing out to Jackie how "anyone" would make a better decision about work times, she accuses him of "not understanding people." The spiral continues until the two of them stop seeing one another, with John telling his friends, "She is quite an airhead," and Jackie letting her friends know that John is an "automaton—not a real person." One student of mine, Arlene Baltz, gave the following example of a regressive spiral between two romantic partners. The spiral in Figure 5-2 shows how perceptions and communication of the two people can accelerate over time. What begins as a descriptive statement of each about the other's communication becomes more evaluative and negative. Concommitantly, of course, each person will be acting in a more negative way because of his or her perception of the other's behavior.

Regressive spirals come in many shades and hues; examples are literally endless. One thing is apparent. Unless regressive spirals are modified or limited, they can continue until they lead to the dissolution of the relationship—quitting the job, beating the prisoner, getting a divorce, or in the case of the little prince, nowhere:

"I am drinking," replied the tippler, with a lugubrious air.

"Why are you drinking?" demanded the little prince.

"So that I may forget," replied the tippler.

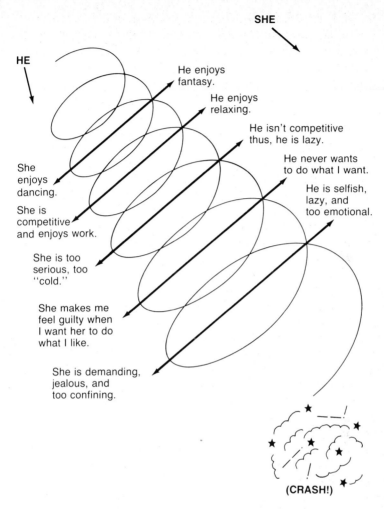

Figure 5-2.   A regressive spiral.

"Forget what?" inquired the little prince, who already was sorry for him.

"Forget that I am ashamed," the tippler confessed, hanging his head.

"Ashamed of what?" insisted the little prince, who wanted to help him.

"Ashamed of drinking!" The tippler brought his speech to an end, and shut himself up in an impregnable silence.

And the little prince went away, puzzled [125].

Fluctuating Spirals

Figure 5.1, although it accurately portrays the ever-increasing nature of both progressive and regressive spirals, has one major weakness. It gives the impression that a spiral, once begun, has no limits and continues unabated. All communication spirals, however, have boundaries. An individual's high self-concept promotes positive responses from others, which in turn enhances his self-concept. Such a progressive spiral, however, has limiting boundaries. If the person's self-concept continues to be encouraged, he will eventually reach the stage at which he considers himself superior to others. At that point, negative responses from others will go to work on him to lower his self-concept. Without such limiting actions, the person's high self-concept will soon become dysfunctional in his relationships. Either a progressive spiral will whirl away unchecked and break a relationship or short regressive phases will occasionally slow it down. In either event, it is clear that progressive spirals cannot continue unabated.

Regressive spirals also have limits. A dyadic conflict, if unchecked or without redeeming features, will lead to the dissolution of the relationship. A person with a low self-concept can suffer only so much continuing maladjustment with others. A romantic pair caught in a regressive spiral will eventually move back to less destructive behaviors or else dissolve the relationship. Even the special case of the "gruesome twosome" is similar. In this case the constant bickering and quarreling are still done within limits; it is only that on the average the transactions are tolerated on a more destructive level than is usual.

Dyadic relationships, if they are maintained, fluctuate between progressive and regressive spirals. In addition to fluctuating between progressive and regressive stages, relationships can be typified over points in time as being primarily progressive or regressive. Take the case of a marital dyad. The relationship begins as a progressive spiral. The two are in love, and the mutually rewarding behaviors of both participants keep the system healthy. But because of more and more separation, for instance, regressive spirals, rather than being an occasional event, become the norm. In Figure 5-3 the fluctuation of the relationship can be seen.

The relationship continues to disintegrate into ever-regressive stages until the critical limit of the regressive spiral is reached. As the relationship begins passing the critical limit, the patterns of regressiveness become more and more difficult to arrest. Finally, after the relationship is on the verge of total collapse, the participants manage

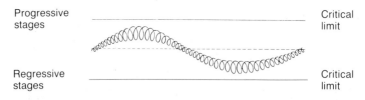

Progressive stages — Critical limit

Regressive stages — Critical limit

Figure 5-3. **Progressive and regressive spiral phases of a marital dyad.**

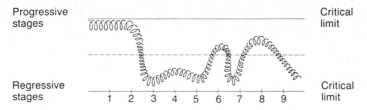

Figure 5-4.   Spiral phases of another marital dyad.

to reverse the direction of the relationship patterns. Through active participation in marriage enrichment programs, self-examination, and a job change, the couple is able to begin building progressive spirals. And because they recognize some of the techniques for altering spirals, they can help other couples in their counseling programs to check the ever-damaging course of regressive relationships.

The particular patterns of fluctuation between the progressive and regressive stages of dyadic relationships vary across relationships. Figure 5-4 illustrates a case where another couple experienced many changes in the relationship over a nine-year span of time. This relationship was characterized by an initial progressive spiral for the first two and a half years, then a dramatic downturn followed by an up-and-down pattern until the final crash just before the termination of the relationship.

In another case an employee was not valued by her superior, yet she managed to build up a slow, ever-improving situation over an eight-year period. The progress of their work relationship is demonstrated visually in Figure 5-5.

This relationship demonstrates that a dyad does not necessarily always wildly fluctuate between the extremes. It can move along with a predominant overall pattern that slowly changes over time. And, of course, a relationship can take on a predominant form for many years and then take a dramatic and unexpected turn. One of the common experiences of parents is that when all the children leave home there is a drop in satisfaction and a series of "rough times" while they work to redefine their living situation. After this transitional period, they often enter a period of very positive relations—they develop new hob-

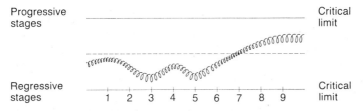

Figure 5-5.   Spirals in a work relationship.

bies, begin to spend more and more time together, and rekindle the flame that got started so many years ago.

These short descriptions illustrate a number of points concerning all dyadic relationships. To begin with, dyadic relationships fluctuate between varying stages of progressive and regressive spirals. The actions of each participant either accelerate a spiral in progress or provide pressure so that the direction of the spiral will change. Second, all spirals have limits, and once the critical limit is reached and the spiral is not reversed, the relationship will suffer so much strain that it will dissolve. Third, relationships can never stand still; they are constantly changing. Woody Allen captured the essence of relational change when he said, "relationships are like a shark. They either move forward or they die." Particpants *can* alter a regressive spiral if they are committed to one another and are willing to undergo significant personal change to improve the relationship.

Regressive spirals serve many functions in relationships, such as testing the commitment of the partners. But most of us want to know how to *change* our regressive spirals into more positive transactions. There are some things you can do if you are in a regressive spiral, even though at the time it may feel like the relationship is "out of control" or in a "runaway mode."

The Changing of Regressive Spirals

The first way to change a regressive spiral is to stop using "interpersonal reflex responses." Whether you are responding to your partner with a symmetrical response (yelling and screaming back at a hostile partner) or a complementary response (assuming a one-down response to escalation), altering your characteristic response can begin to change the system. If you have a roommate who is not very talkative and over the past two months you have tried to draw him out, you soon discover that the more you talk the less he does. Doing "more of the same" does not work, so do "less of the same." Change the natural inclination to talk more when he is silent. Talk less and outwait him. Similarly, if your partner is hostile, you might work at problem clarification. Clarify what the issues are, where you and the other can expect some change, and move to some resolution of the difficulties. Teger [500] observes that a conflict "begins typically with a hostile act, and that the response of the other party has an important bearing on the future course of the conflict." Change your behavior, and you might just change the spiral.

Second, you often can use third parties constructively. Friends, professional counselors, therapists, and relatives can sometimes provide just the right amount of a different perspective for you to begin to open up the regressive system for change. Third parties can often make specific suggestions that will break the pattern of interlocking, mutually destructive behaviors that keep adding fuel to the regression. In one case, a man and wife went to a marriage counselor because they had come to a standoff. He was tired of her demands to always talk to her and pay attention. She was tired of his demands for more frequent sexual activity. As a result, they each withdrew even more—he talked less and she avoided situations of physical intimacy. Upon seeing the counselor, they both realized that they were getting nowhere fast. Each was trying to change the other without changing within. With the counselor's help, they renegotiated their relationship and each began giving just a little bit. Over a period of a few days they found themselves coming out of the regressive phases of the spiral.

Third, you can reaffirm your relational goals. If you really are in a downward spiral, whether with your parents, lover, or boss, the reaffirmation of what each of you has to gain from the relationship can promote efforts to get it back. The previously decribed couple realized that their most important goal was to stay together—for if either one had "won" the fight and lost the relationship, neither would have been pleased. The reaffirmation of the relationship can promote you to think of all the things you can do to help get the relationship back to a more positive phase. Good relationships take energy to sustain; similarly, energy expended will often pull them out of the doldrums.

Fourth, you can often alter a spiral by metacommunicating. When you comment on what you see happening, it can open up the nature of the spiral itself for discussion. One can say, "Our relationship seems to be slipping—I find myself criticizing you and you seem to be avoiding me, and it looks like it is getting worse. What can we do to turn it around?" Such metacommunication, whether pointed to the episodes or the overall relationship patterns, can set the stage for productive conflict management and give the participants more of a sense of control of the relationship dynamics [220]. Metacommunication, especially when coupled with a reaffirmation of your relational goals ("I don't want us to be unhappy, I want us to both like being together, but we seem to. . . .") can alter the destructive regressive forces in a relationship.

Fifth, try to spend either more or less time with the person. If you are on the "outs" with your co-workers, seek them out and begin sharing more of yourself with them. It is amazing what kinds of large changes can be purchased with just a small amount of time. Likewise, relationships often suffer because the people spend more time together than they can productively handle. Getting more distance and independence can bring you back refreshed and ready to relate again.

Finally, we all recognize that changing an external situation can alter a regressive spiral. One parent has a son who got into an ongoing battle with the principal of the junior high school. The fued went on for months, with the principal (according to the mother) tormenting her boy and the boy retaliating by being mischievous. The mutually destructive actions were arrested only when the boy switched schools. He had a chance to start over. Another tactic is to stay in the presence of the person but move to a new environment. Many a married couple has gone on an extended vacation in order to give themselves time to work out new solutions for themselves. If the relationship is important to you and you want to preserve it, effort expended to help the relationship to reach productive periods is time well spent. For once a regressive stage is reached, the behaviors of the dyadic partners tend to be mutually reinforcing. Each person can blame the other and claim his own innocence, but that will not alter the regression. It takes long, hard work to alter the regressive stage of the relationship, and it may be successful if both participants invest time and energy. But as every counselor knows from experience, one person alone can almost never change the relationship.

Our dyadic relationships are dynamic, always moving and changing either toward or away from improvement. When the participants' behavior interlocks such that each one's behavior and definition of the other are intensified, they are in a spiral. Spirals, of course, can be seen in short- or long-range terms. A relationship may not look any different today than it did yesterday, but over a year's time, you can see either overall improvement or disintegration. The long-term spirals are more difficult to identify until you compare the relationship to a much earlier state. The two friends who used to share everything eighteen months ago and who now just say "hi" on the street both know the relationship has regressed over time. But in any given day or week they might not be able to point to noticeable changes in the relationship. Nevertheless, most relationships are in spirals over time—often fluctuating through phases.

PARADOXES

Paradoxes occur when a communication is self-contradictory. For example, a friend looks you right in the eye and says, "I hate you!" Then, just when you are trying to recover, he adds, "But you must remember I always lie." Your friend has placed you in a paradoxical situation; he has made a statement that is simultaneously a statement that contradicts itself [424]. The difficulty arises because (1) the statement asserts something, (2) the statement asserts something about its own assertion, and (3) the two assertions are mutually exclusive [519].°

°This presentation focuses on the essential features of paradox and double bind. For readers interested in the complex conceptual issues, of which there are many, see references 111, 464, 20, 518, 221, and 21.

Paradoxes are prevalent. Once their basic form is understood, their existence is easily recognized. For instance, study the statement within the box in Figure 5-6.

> Every statement in
> this box is false.

Figure 5-6.   A paradoxical statement.

Is the statement true or false? "If the assertion is true, then by its own evidence it is not true; and if the assertion is false, then that tells us that what is being said must be true" [75]. Such classic paradoxes are often used in logic classes to demonstrate the theory of types, that statements occur at many levels. A statement and a statement about a statement are obviously at different levels; they are of a different logical type [25]. Even if you never attend a logic class, you may encounter variations of the classic paradoxes. You might be driving down the street, look at the bumper of the car in front of you, and see a sticker proclaiming

> THIS IS NOT A BUMPER STICKER

Then, just as you are trying to restore some mental equilibrium, you encounter a road sign proclaiming the following:

> IGNORE THIS SIGN

Having read the sign you are supposed to ignore (so you can be sure to ignore it), you turn a corner and find this local ordinance:

> IT IS UNLAWFUL TO READ THIS SIGN
> LOCAL ORDINANCE 86-32

Paradoxes occur in everyday communication as well. Dan Greenburg supplies the following as a sampling of the fare a stereotypical Jewish mother has to offer.

Florence, what have you done to your hair. It looks like you're wearing a wig?

I am—all my hair fell out!

Oh, listen, it looks so natural I'd never have known [187].

Greenburg also offers this advice to the woman who wants to be a successful Jewish mother. When you talk to your son, "Don't let him know you fainted twice in the supermarket from fatigue (but make sure he knows you're not letting him know)" [187]. And for people interested in military life the novelist Joseph Heller popularized one particular paradox in his novel *Catch 22*. Yossarian, the central figure in the story, is flying combat missions and wants to stop. He approaches the doctor, Doc Daneeka, knowing that if Doc declares a man insane, the man will be released from flying. Doc can ground anyone who is crazy and all the man has to do is ask. But there is a catch— Catch-22: "Anyone who wants to get out of combat duty isn't really crazy." All you have to do is ask, but if you ask that is proof that you are not crazy. As Yossarian observed, "That is some catch, that Catch-22."

Paradoxes can appear in unexpected places and times. One investment company sends out a detailed report on their investments, and the second page appears like that in Figure 5.7.

Of course, by telling you the page is blank, it isn't any longer blank. I once received an envelope from Dave in the Bookstore. When I opened the envelope, there on letterhead stationery was this: THIS IS NOT A LETTER. After some reflection, I sent the following to Dave, again

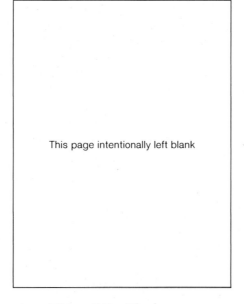

This page intentionally left blank

Figure 5-7. Blank page.

on letterhead: Dear Dave, THIS IS NOT A RESPONSE! One of the funniest paradoxes I observed came from listening to Jason and Carina, brother and sister, having a spirited discussion. Carina was saying that she was going to be the "boss" and get to decide where to eat out that evening. Jason said, "Nobody is boss—*so listen up*," while he proceeded to tell her what to do.

Other variations of paradoxes crop up in conversations from time to time. The wife who says to her meek husband, "Damn it, dominate me!" is placing him in a paradox. If he obeys and dominates her, it is because he responded to her domination of him. Or consider a man and woman who are involved in a struggle over their relationship; the man feels that the woman is too rigid and doesn't have any fun. If the man says, "Be more spontaneous," he has placed the woman in a classic paradox. In order to be spontaneous, she would have to follow the command—but following the command is not a spontaneous act.

Some more common forms of paradoxical statements occur within romantic dyads. The essence of the contemporary American ideal is a romantic relationship where each partner shows love and concern for the other. And that love and concern are freely given. Therefore, if one partner pleads to the other, "Love me," that very command negates the essence of love—freely given attachment. In some cases, partners of many years get caught up in complaining at one another in paradoxical forms that, at first, do not look so paradoxical. A wife who is angry at her husband because he doesn't do special things for her says, "I wish you would bring me flowers" [518]. If his response is to send flowers to her the next day, the act doesn't fulfill the basic requirement that they be sent spontaneously and of free will. One cannot command another to do something that has free choice at its core and expect it to have the desired impact. Haley is aware of the paradoxical nature of some forms of the helping relationship and he notes, "The more help the therapist offers, the more he is defining the person as needing help" [193]. If a person says any of the following to his or her dyadic partner, the other is placed in a paradoxical situation:

"Don't think about me." (parting lovers)

"I always lie." (your friend, the philosophy major)

"I want you to disagree with everything I say." (professor to student)

"Tell me what to do so I can be independent." (client to therapist)

"Don't ever listen to me." (your mother)

"I can't tell you that I love you because then you'll leave me." (your anxious lover)

"I think you should quit school, but it's not my place to say so." (your friend)

"Do things for yourself" (parent to child)

Although paradoxes are readily spotted in other's behavior once the basic form is recognized, a few people are able to recognize them in their own behavior. Golas [179] says, "I am playing the game of refusing pointless games, which may be the most pointless of all." An astute Harlem resident also demonstrated his understanding of paradoxes. "You can't be free if someone else lets you be free" [410]. The next time you attend a party, try this on one of your friends who is not initiated into the intricacies of paradoxes:

> In a small village there is a barber who shaves all the men who do not shave themselves. When he gets down to the last man, the barber, does he shave him? [519]

Paradoxes can be fun or they can cause problems, depending on their applications. Paradoxes appear on both organizational and personal levels [197], and in organizations professional women are often caught in paradoxes. For example, as Wood and Conrad [550] demonstrate, when *professional* or *executive* or *manager* are defined in terms of qualities traditionally seen as masculine (rationality, power, decisiveness, activity, objectivity, and toughness), women are excluded from consideration. A professional woman, then, cannot meet these criteria without the corresponding negative view of her, since *professional* excludes the precise feminine qualities ascribed to her [550].

Regardless of their effects, paradoxes make a serious point about human communication. Communication can occur on more than one level. The first two levels are (1) communication and (2) metacommunication (communication about communication). When these two levels agree, such as someone saying, "I always tell the truth," there is no paradox. But when one's metacommunication denies the communication, a paradox exists.*

DOUBLE BINDS

The habitual use of paradoxes can sometimes be a sign of a communication pathology. We all attempt to control relationships, but if we control them while sending the metacommunication denying that we are controlling, we might be setting up a double bind [192]. The "dou-

---

*For your friends who replied to the case of the barber in the village that it was impossible, a paradox, give them this problem that does have a solution. You are a prisoner held by two guards, one who always lies and one who always tells the truth, but you cannot distinguish between them. You have one chance to gain your freedom. You have to identify which one of the two doors leading to your cell is unlocked and which one is locked. You can only ask one question of one guard. If you don't ask the question, or ask it and then guess incorrectly which door is unlocked, you will be killed. If you guess correctly, you will be set free. You can't guess the correct door by any other method than asking a question. (For example, you can't go try the doors or see which one the guards use.) What is your one question?

ble bind" hypothesis deals specifically with these special forms of communicative paradoxes. The necessary conditions producing the double bind are:

1. Two persons, one of whom is the victim.
2. Repeated experience so that the double bind becomes a habitual expectation.
3. A primary negative injunction.
4. A secondary injunction conflicting with the first injunction, but at a more abstract level. Like the primary injunction, the second threatens punishment.
5. A tertiary negative injunction prohibiting the victim from escaping from the field.
6. A victim who begins to see the entire universe in double-bind patterns [24].

A double bind, therefore, is a special type of paradox. Double binds are often created when the verbal message is contradicted by the nonverbal message [436]. When the mother says, "Go son, be independent of me and make your own life," and then reels backward because of her "heart attack," she has put the boy in a double bind. The mother affirms the son's right to leave and be independent but signals nonverbally her sense of desertion. Similar situations arise when parents tell children to be independent yet send them continual signals that they don't think the child is capable of independence. As the young girl is departing for college, the father says, "We know you will do well. But if things should happen to go wrong, as they do for a lot of people who are their own for the first time, remember that you can come home any time and be our little girl." Sluzki and Vernon [466] also relate the case of parents who send the following messages: "Learn to live up to our expectations that we have for you, but do that independently from what we tell you." Finally, the case of the distraught mother whose son is flunking out of school deserves mention. She makes it plain (after some months of arguing over the merits of school) that, "I want you to *want* to study." "This requires that the child not only do the right thing (i.e., study), but do the right thing for the reason (i.e., study because he *wants* to), which (a) makes it punishable to do the right thing for the wrong reason (i.e., study because he has been told to and might otherwise be punished), and (b) requires that he perform a weird piece of mental acrobatics by making himself want what he does not want and, by implicaiton, also want what is being done to him" [520].

Theoretically, repeated exposure to double binds produces schizophrenia and some early research supports the notion [24]. Berger [50] conducted an inquiry into the double binds that adults saw themselves placed in as children. He constructed lists of double-bind statements and asked schizophrenics, mental patients who were not schizophrenics, ward attendants, and college students the extent to which their mothers typically made such statements. The schizophrenics attributed more double-bind statements to their mothers than did those in any of the other groups. Although there were problems in recalling events because of the selectivity of remembering [441], the data are certainly interesting. While it has been demonstrated that schizophrenics engage in unusual communicative behaviors, the contributing causes to these behaviors are not yet clearly isolated.

In fact, research on the double bind and its production of schizophrenia is not very compelling [111]. There are many unresolved questions relating to the double-bind hypothesis, such as how many types there are [429] or the extent to which they occur in normal transactions. Furthermore, although the original formulation of the hypothesis specified that disturbed individuals could not effectively deal with the metacommunication level, Loeff [302] found they were more influenced by the metacommunicative level of messages. Finally, the original formulation of the double bind specified that "repeated exposure" to the double bind is necessary and that you might not be able to identify a double bind in an individual episode of communication. Taken literally, of course, this means that one might not be able either to prove or to disprove the double bind if it isn't manifested communicatively.

Because double binds are a form of paradox, they can be put to productive use. For example, the Zen master uses them for instructing pupils. One form is when the Zen master holds a stick over the head of the pupil and says, "If you say this stick is real I will strike you with it. If you say this stick is not real I will strike you with it. If you don't say anything, I will strike you with it" [26, p8]. What would you do if you were the pupil? Few of us could react soon enough to avoid being struck. The rapid-thinking pupil must grab the stick, thereby breaking out of the confining conditions set by the Zen master.

Double binds have been used for therapeutic purposes. One of the more provocative views of psychotherapy is that it is designed to "challenge the patient's false and neurotic assumptions so that the more he holds to them, the more he finds himself in a double bind" [510]. Haley [192] advanced the view that all the schools of psychotherapy have one central commonality, that of placing the patient in a paradoxical situation. For instance, when a patient requests the therapist to tell him what to do, he is defining the relationship as one in which he is not in control [192]. The therapist, therefore, can alter the client's behavior by reversing the situation, by placing the patient in paradoxes. As an example, the client knows the relationship is voluntary, yet the therapist makes regular attendance necessary. The client is also blamed and not blamed at the same time. The client is given the message that whatever the matter is, it is not his fault. Yet psychotherapy is based on the premise that the patient can control his behavior because that's why he is there for treatment.

One of the clearest examples of therapeutic double binds comes from Bandler and Grinder, elaborated on by Watzalawick [20]. A woman came into therapy because she found it difficult to say no to people. As a child, she once said no when her father wanted her to stay home with him. When she returned she found him dead. The therapist imposed a double bind by asking her to say no about something in front of a group. She refused, saying "No! It's impossible for me to say no to people!" [20]. Here is the structure of the interaction:

1. Symptom: "I cannot say no."
2. Symptom prescription: "Say no to everyone present!"
3. Double bind: Two alternatives (either to say no to everybody or to say no to the therapist), which both lead to the desired outcome [518 p.105].

Some therapists call these double binds *positive double binds* [305]; others simply say the therapist is *prescribing the symptom* [518, 540]. Whatever your favorite label, such double binds have many positive applications for people who are "stuck" in behavior that they have difficulty changing. For example, one way to deal with temper tantrums, which seem to be examples of out-of-control behavior, is to prescribe them—setting aside a time and place for temper tantrums [195]. When one invokes a tantrum on cue, it is obviously under control and can then be regulated later. Another example of a positive double bind is one use by Fritz Perls [305]. While treating a patient who had problems asserting himself, Perls would continually fall asleep. "The individual then had to either wake Fritz up, which required considerable assertion, or he had to face the fact that he was deliberately choosing to allow himself to be invalidated in that way . . ." [305]. The individual is placed into a situation where they have to assert themselves through anger, a desire to escape, or rebellion. The paradoxical nature of the communication forces one to respond—which is the goal.

Sometimes the person herself will generate a double bind that has desirable consequences. The often quoted Groucho Marx line, "I would never join a club that would have me as a member," sets forth the basic form. For instance, take the case of a woman who is married and makes the following statements:

"I would cheat on my husband only with a man I considered worthy."
"I would never consider a man worthy who was the type that would run around with a married woman."

Such a self-generated double bind can have positive effects on one's relationships by setting limits on behavior.

Watzlawick, Weakland, and Fisch [520] offer several suggestions for coping with paradoxes and double binds. For example, one can do *less of the same* when caught in a paradoxical situation. Watzlawick relates the story of a married couple who had a very close relationship with one set of parents and wanted to change the situation. The "concerned parents" spent all of their vacations with them (flying across the country to do it), bought the house for the couple, and when visiting, spent all their time cleaning up the place and just generally taking over. The couple got into the situation of trying to have everything spic and span before the parents arrived, yet that only motivated the parents to do a more thorough job of recleaning everything in the house. The solution was to do less of the same. During the parents' next visit, the couple left things in a real mess. The parents worked harder than usual, even at times not being able to keep up with the messy couple. And when the parents sent money, the couple did not thank them. You can guess the outcome. The concerned parents realized that the "children" needed to be on their own and develop a sense of responsibility. The money stopped flowing and the visits no longer lasted three weeks. The couple did "less of the same" in order to break out of the paradox.*

The second suggestion for getting out of paradoxical situations is *to make the covert overt.* For instance, if you are afraid you will cry in a conflict, simply say, "I may cry. Sometimes I do when I'm angry. But I don't want anything from you if I do." This is the same technique as "paradoxical intention" mentioned earlier. You try to do the very thing that you were frightened of.

Sometimes the most effective technique for dealing with a paradoxical demand from the other is to *refuse to choose.* If the other person places you in a paradoxical situation, you can sometimes find a way out by simply refusing to choose. If you recognize the existence of the paradox you can refuse to be trapped by it. For instance, you may say, "If I make Sue leave our apartment she will be angry. If I don't, you will hate me. I'm not going to make that choice—we'll have to figure out something else."

Chesbro suggests that if you are faced with paradox, [98] you have three major options—accepting, avoiding, or rejecting the other's views of you and the world. Acceptance of another's double binding or paradoxical structure on you can lead to some of the harmful results mentioned earlier, such as complying with all the injunctions of the other. However, you can avoid the other's communicational structure by spending less time with the other so the double bind can't be invoked, shifting the responsibility to others, or even "block the chan-

---

*This technique is also very useful for altering the course of regressive spirals. When shouting produces more shouting and alienation begets more unhappiness, to do the "unnatural" thing is often the best. Some couples break regressive spirals by just agreeing, "We are not getting anywhere with all this fighting. Why don't we stop." This is a productive stopgap that clears the way for a more creative problem-solving session.

nels of communication" [98]. Finally, if you reject their worldview, you have the option of totally withdrawing or of confronting the other in such a way as to alter the communication structure.

In summary, paradoxes occur when a statement asserts something about its own assertion and when these two assertions are mutually exclusive. In dyadic transactions, paradoxes often occur in the form of double binds. Bateson's double-bind hypothesis states that prolonged exposure to them without the opportunity to withdraw can produce communicative disturbances in the victim. Recently, however, some of the more productive uses of double binds are beginning to be explored, and a more systematic understanding of their role in human relations will continue to emerge. Whatever the outcome of future research and speculation, communicative paradoxes remain one of the most maddening and challenging patterns of relational intricacies.

DYADIC DIALECTICS

At almost any level of human experience, contradictory and opposite elements occur. American society, for instance, supports dichotomous values. On one hand, materialism is valued; on the other, moral behavior is stressed [151,428]. On the individual level, our minds support contradictory abilities. The left hemisphere of our brain gives us the ability to think logically and methodically in a step-by-step fashion, and the right hemisphere lets us perceive totalities, the Gestalt, in metaphoric and analogic terms [518].

The dialectical approach stresses that phenomena that appear to be opposites are bound together and that there is a dynamic *interplay* between such opposites [67, 31, 36]. It presumes that polarities that appear unconnected in nature mutually presuppose one another [269]. Heraclitus taught that there is a "dynamic and cyclic interplay of opposites" and that there is a unity of opposites [93]. An example of recognition of connectedness and similarity where one previously perceived opposites comes from Jim, the son of one of my colleagues. When he was seven he was asked, "What is the similarity between the first and the last?" He replied, "They are opposites but they are related. Because if you push on the first kid in the line, the last one also has to move back."

Those of us raised in Western cultures are often less sensitized to thinking in terms of the dialectic of opposites. As Smith and Williamson note, "Where Western languages tend to use polarities in a categorical 'either/or' fashion, Eastern languages use them in a 'both/and' fashion [486, p.170]. Perceiving the unity of opposites allows one to see that, "Each person is both male and female possessing qualities of both maleness and femaleness; an event is both good and bad; food is both sweet and sour; a person is both weak and strong [468, p.170].

As Watts notes, we pay for the exactitude of our factual language with the price of being able to speak from only one point of view at a time [61]. We often deal with the world in a dualistic way, which sets us apart. Even "dealing with the world" presumes we can be separated from it [122]. Our cultural "frame" promotes the view that elements are opposite and not connected, rather than seeing the dialectical interrelation of opposites.

The dialectical viewpoint brings fresh insight into how personal relationships operate. While the full range of opposites has yet to be cast, some initial work illuminates the basic approach [36, 67, 40, 204, 272, 397, 148, 398, 253, 205, 93]. Baxter [31, 34, 148, 427, 36] has identified some of the opposites in personal relations, and they will be used for purposes of illustration, though as more work focuses on dialectic theory, new lists of "the opposites" may be derived.

The most frequently cited set of opposites in personal relationships is that of *autonomy–interdependence,* or stated another way, the tension between separateness and connectedness, or between *me* and *we*. They are dialectically bound together, because as one of them is stressed in a culture, the other is "always hauntingly there in the background." [151]. For example, each person in a close relationship wants (1) interdependence mutuality with the other, and (2) separate "breathing space" for the self independent of the other. Pat's personal choices reflect this well. She is in a committed romantic relationship with Sol; while they were living together she found herself always "wanting to get away"—to get more separateness. When she moved into her own apartment, she had the "breathing space" to allow herself then to be closer to Sol, or as she said, "Now that I know who I am, I can deal better with the two of us!" Such opposites between me and we also occur on the organizational level. As Peters and Waterman wrote, we seek self-determination and, simultaneously, security with others [387]. People often have ongoing struggles in their jobs over whether to "adopt the organization as your identity" or "develop your own identity." Both of these reflect the classic me–we dichotomy.

The dialectical tension between autonomy and interdependence is manifested in numerous ways. In the 1970s, for example, the emphasis was on *me,* with many writers arguing for "looking out for number one." People were encouraged not to let their relationships bind them, to discover themselves, assert themselves, and downplay their dependence on others. We were in an age of narcissism, with enhancement of the self being the goal for many. Of course, this came on the wake of a previous social emphasis on the interdependence of people, downplaying the individual for the good of the relationship group.

The tension between autonomy and interdependence is also present within each relationship. In families, for instance, one of the main ongoing struggles is between the growing child becoming an individual and being loyal to the needs of the family [68]. In romantic relationship, "Everyone feels an intense conflict between the desire to be free and independent versus the desire to merge with others" [203]. This "dynamic tension" is present and tends to have an ever-present influence on the relationship. The friend who drops out of sight for a few days and the romantic partner who professes close, enduring love but then suddenly retreats both illustrate attempts to deal with the opposites. As we get closer to the other, it can trigger a fear of being "swallowed," which causes a need for more autonomy. Some of the "craziness" and unpredictability in close, intimate relations comes from the oscillations between autonomy and interdependence. As we get farther away, we miss the other, and when we feel at "one" with the other, we sense a loss of the self. These alternating patterns of close–far respond to the dialectical nature of opposing needs in a relationship for autonomy and interdependence [159]. Of course, the issue is made sharper by the fact that the two people probably feel the polarities at different times and with different intensity. Just as your romantic partner is trying to "get some space," you may feel the need for more closeness and intimacy, or vice versa. Robin, one of my students, said it this way: "He wants to be closer, I back off. He tries harder, I move farther. He gives up, I move closer. He responds, I back up, and on, and on it goes." Such contradictory needs, felt at disparate times by the partners, fuel the inherent difficulty in close personal relations. Both ends of the dichotomy are true—we need to be independent from others and we need to have a connection with them in order to be fully human.

A second dialectic identified in personal relations is that of *expressiveness–protectiveness*, between openness and closedness [26]. In all our relations, we have needs to share information with the other and to withhold information from the other. Our dyadic relationships can be characterized as differing in terms of openness and closedness, and openness is taken as the single most important quality in intimate relationships. Most of our dyadic relationships are, in fact, not close and intimate, and even among those we withhold some information [378, 63]. On the other hand, intimacy and closeness are built by disclosure of important information. The tension between candor and restraint underlies our relationships, just as did the dialectic of autonomy and interdependence. Rawlins, in an intensive study of friendships, highlighted the expressiveness–protectiveness dimension well [397]. He found the contradictions implicit in all friendships because the person faces the contradictory tendency to protect the self by restricting disclosure *and* to strive to be open by confiding in the other [397]. The friends in this sample did not engage in unrestrained openness because of the possible negative consequences, yet they also worked for more openness while placing boundaries on the areas they allowed for being vulnerable to the other [397]. Family members, friends, work associates, and romantic partners cope with the contradictory poles by a variety of means—emphasizing one pole over the other or oscillating between poles to balance out over time. When someone says, "You have to always be open and honest in all relationships," and another says, "You can't trust anyone with private information about yourself," each is stressing one pole of the dichotomy. Some people construct entire lives based on their feeling that one pole of the expressiveness–protectiveness dichotomy is preferable. For example, in many close relationships partners try to find out information by using "secret tests," a clear preference for using a closed strategy to try to get information [39]. Rather than choosing one pole or the other, some people engage in an oscillation between the poles. A person who gets a divorce at age thirty often becomes totally disclosive with a brother, sister, or parent for a period of time. Once equilibrium is established, however, he or she then retreats from the openness and returns to not sharing much information. And as with the first dichotomy, each peron's preferences for how to deal with the opposites can run counter to the timing or desires of the other. While one person wants to share all, the other feels like retreating and being less open.

The third type of dialectical opposites in personal relationships is that of *predictability–novelty*, or between stability and change. Some writers on interpersonal relations stress that we want to "reduce uncertainty" [53]; the opposite is also true—too much certainty is often avoided. We want relationships that have some stability—for continual flux is unsettling, but a boring relationsip also is to be avoided. Many relationships, once they are defined, go on "automatic pilot," with little change occurring in them. In attempts to bring some predictability to our personal world, many of us define the relationship as a way to get some certainty. Saying, "We are friends," or "We are married," are just two examples, for without some stability, you never know "where you are" with the other. However, without some risk and change, a relationship can become so predictable as to be boring. As with the other dialectical dichotomies, individuals have different solutions to the opposing needs. For given relationships, Lorraine may opt for complete stability and sacrifice excitement, change, and risk. Or Shelley may choose to have a series of relationships, each "risky" and full of change, and sacrifice the stability for the excitement. In romantic relationships, people sometimes try to do both, but do it in separate relations. The person who stays married and has outside romantic involvements is often pursuing stability at home and change somewhere else. Of course, another option is to oscillate between stability and change in the same relationship. As the friendship becomes predictable, you throw some change and alteration into it. When the romantic relationship becomes too unpredictable, you get married in order to provide stability.

The three dialectics of autonomy–interdependence, expressiveness–protectiveness, and predictabilty–novelty underly all our fundamental dyadic relationships. It may be there are other central dialectical forces yet to be identified that operate in the same fashion. Regardless of the particular dialectic, however, the participants in a relationship have some choices for dealing with them. We cannot "solve" the dialectical opposites, but we do have some options for dealing with them [93]. Some even argue that the index of our adulthood is the ability to deal with the "contradictory demands" of relationships [448]. Some of the generic ways to face dialectic tensions in relationships have been charted by Fisher, Frentz and Rushing, and Rushing [151, 159, 427]. As applied to dyadic relationships, they might be *dialectic emphasis, pseudo-synthesis,* or *reaffirmation* of the dialectical opposites. When one engages in dialectical emphasis, one of the poles is stressed over the other, ignoring that the opposite also exists in the background [427]. For example, when one emphasizes his or her autonomy, argues for complete openness in relationships, or is totally predictable, one pole of each of the three dichotomies has been emphasized. Such choices, from a dialectical point of view, will lead to the emergence of the opposite later. The person who prides himself or herself on complete autonomy, for example, later discovers that friends or close relations with family members do not exist and then must deal with loneliness—the opposite side of the coin. Similarly, if you are totally predictable, introducing no change into your most important relationship, the net result will be boredom with the relationship.

Pseudo-synthesis occurs when the two disparate elements are "brought together effortlessly, glossing over their inherently contradictory nature [427]. Someone who says, "Well, I can be independent, and so can you, and we still can be close to one another all the time," is engaging in pseudosynthesis. Refusal to see the power of the opposing forces can, of course, seem like a viable alternative, but from a dialectical point of view, the opposites are still operable. The net result will be an unclear accommodation—neither will the individual needs be met nor will the need for interdependence or community be satisfied.

Finally, reaffirmation of the contradictory nature of relationships is one method for dealing with the three dialectics. In using reaffirmation, one recognizes the opposites and believes that they are truly contradictory and cannot be easily explained away [427]. In reaffirmation you expect the relationship to oscillate between the two poles on each of the three dimensions, and you see that as a natural process. You might, for instance, say, "Well, when times are stressful at school, you can't expect to be close and helpful—but once vacation comes, we can get back together again." You see the relationship in a state of dynamic tension between the poles and see continual fluctuation as bringing the balance [93]. Put another way, you see that relationships are not "fixed," that they do vacillate between contradictory poles, whether those be autonomy–interdependence, expressiveness–protectiveness, or predictability–novelty. If in your judgment the relationship is moving too far toward one of the poles for a period of time, you take effort to move it in the other direction [159]. Out of this new balance of forces, you have essentially created a new "synthesis," which then sets up forces for the next fluctuation. As Capra says, a relationship arises from the opposites, and the conflict between them "can never result in the total victory of one side, but will always be a manifestation of the interplay between the two sides" [93, p.131].

One of the prime advantages of viewing relationships from a dialectical framework is that the natural fluctuations can be seen as normal, useful, and temporary processes and that each individual has a stake in (1) his or her interests, (2) the other's interests, and (3) the relationship as the interplay between the two [122]. Furthermore, seemingly impossible, contradictory views can be held to be true. For example, which of the following do you believe?

1. "Get yourself together first, then get into a relationship with someone."
2. "You improve yourself through your important relationships."

Is one of these more true than the other, or are they contradictory yet equally provocative beliefs, both of which can be true?

One final note. It may be that the entire notion of dialectic is dependent upon a Western mind set that tends to divide things. For example, young children first developing language in the United States often say *mine* among their first few words. Such views imply we are separated from others and that our interests are not the same as those of others. In some cultures, the forces at work may be different. Eiji, a student in one of my classes, expressed it this way:

> I believe I have been culturally trained not to aggravate any existing relationship one has. The Japanese society, it seems to me, emphasizes among others, the following two things: (1) There is no such thing as dichotomy, and (2) anyone you see suffer today can be the image of yourself tomorrow. The result is that people in a relationship behave in a certain way: They intuitively pay attention to the dynamics of the relationship and are ready to put themselves in the shoe of anyone they are dealing with at any moment.

Our understanding of dyadic dialectics is in its infancy, and further work on the fundamental forces of relationships will clarify their nature. Until then, dialectical tensions can be recognized as one form of relational intricacy that helps explain the complexities of dyadic relationships.

SUMMARY

Our dyadic relationships are complex; as a result, some intricate events occur. Self-fulfilling prophecies exist when a person responds to another's definition of him or her in such a way as to validate it. Communication spirals happen when each person's behavior feeds energy into an ongoing system that further increases its basic nature, whether progressive or regressive. Paradoxes exist because of the unique abilities humans have to communicate at different levels. When the levels contradict, a paradox is present. And when one meets special conditions, paradoxes can be double binds. Finally, there are dialectical tensions inherent in all relationships that are contradictory but that nevertheless occur together. The tensions revolve around how separate or connected you will be with the other, how open or closed, and how predictable or novel your relationship will be. Dyadic relationships *are* complex, and the relationship intricacies illustrate the complexity.*

---

*Are you still caught in prison from the example given earlier? Here is how you could get out. You simply ask one guard, "If I asked the other guard if the door on the right was unlocked, what would he say?" Regardless of which guard you asked, the liar or the truth teller, if he says, "No," the answer is yes; if he says, "Yes," the answer is no. The liar will lie about the true answer and the truthful guard will tell the truth about the lie.

Chapter 6

Relationship Development and Dissolution

RELATIONAL TURNOVER

One of the realities of life is that every significant relationship we have with another person will dissolve, either through the drifting apart of the participants, through a decision to part, or through death. The very relationships that are our mainstays of security and support change and disappear. Think for a moment of your life five years ago. Who was your best friend? Is he or she your best friend today? How about your work associates or fellow students of five years ago? Are they still sitting beside you on a daily basis? And how about your romantic partner who aided and sustained you? Is that person still central to your life today? For most of us in this mobile society, each new change of life pattern, each new job, each new decade of life brings different relationships.

Relational turnover is one of the most common yet least acknowledged experiences of contemporary people. We act toward our most intimate friends and lovers as if they will be with us always, yet there is a good chance they will not. We are taught in our early years how to make social ties, but the process of dissolving them is shrouded in mystery, hurt, and misunderstanding. A study by Bell and Hadas [43] of first- and third-grade children showed that the young people knew how to make friends—offer some candy, go to the person's house after school, or meet at recess. But when asked how they would dissolve a friendship with someone, the children assumed that it would "just happen" and that the process was beyond their control. One youngster said, "You just wait until the end of school." Another suggested that, "You could just punch him out." Many adults view dissolution in a similar way, believing the process is always harmful. A more complete understanding of the dynamics of developing and dissolving relationships will provide new options for dealing with the experiences.

The rate of relational turnover one can expect depends on a number of factors. The single most important determinant is the type of dyadic relationship. The following relationships are listed in order of the amount of change a person can expect, with the first relationship subject to the most change and the fourth subject to the least.

1. Work relationships.
2. Neighbor relationships.
3. Friendships.
4. Family relationships (both with family of origin and with family you create) [505].

Because the majority of our dyadic contacts are nonintimate, they are more subject to turnover and replacement than more intimate relationships.

The consequences of relational turnover are difficult to specify: we

176

do not know what the optimum rate for replacement is. Nor do we know what rate of relational change will be harmful. Nor is it known how many of our relationships can be productively managed on a short-term, high-turnover basis. Our mobile society prompts people to move and continually reestablish their residences. As a result, a large proportion of our behavior is search behavior—searching to find new friends or romantic partners to replace the ones we left behind or who departed from us. Relational turnover is a reality of both modern life and the maturing process. As we grow and change, our relationships also change.

Even though there is more turnover in nonintimate relationships, little systematic research regarding their dissolution has been conducted [287, 30, 32, 33, 36]. Most of the available information comes from studies of persons who were married and dissolved their relationships through separation and divorce [525]. As a result, this chapter will focus primarily on the development and dissolution of intimate relationships. The closest relationships—friendships and romantic attachments—also produce the most pain upon their dissolution. If we can understand the most troubling processes, the development and dissolution of other dyadic pairings will also be grasped.

Marriages typically endure longer than do friendships, yet we are all aware that the divorce rate in the United States is one of the highest in the world. Think of the person who sits on your right in the classroom, the person who sits on your left, and yourself. The chances are, given current rates, that one of you will be divorced in your lifetime. Only a few years ago, divorce to most people was a scandalous, immoral act. But as more and more individuals seek divorces, it is not uncommon to know someone who is divorced or whose parents are divorced. In fact, any sizable group of people will include many who are divorced or have parents who are divorced. In a typical college class I taught, of the twenty-two people there were four previously married people and four people whose parents were divorced. The divorce rate fluctuates rather markedly, so predictions for the future are difficult to make with any accuracy. But, if the divorce rate of 1965 is the rate of the future, then about 30 percent of newly formed marriages can be expected to end in divorce, and if the divorce rate of 1971 carried forth, then we can expect fully 40 percent of newly formed marriage to end in divorce [525]. Probably somewhere between a third and a half of all first marriages formed this year will end in divorce.

What are the elements of a successful marriage? For some people, as long as the marriage continues they will be satisfied. When asked, "Are you happy in your marriage?" they will reply, "I must be. I have been married for thirty-five years." For others, however, the enduringness of their marriages is not necessarily related to their happiness. Hicks and Platt [213] report that persons who say they are happy in their marriages tend to stress the "relationship sources of happiness," while persons who express dissatisfaction tend to concentrate on the situational aspects of marriage—home, children, and social life. Furthermore, Navran [347] found that happily married couples (1) talk extensively to each other, (2) convey the feelings that they understand what is being said to them, (3) have a wide range of subjects available to them, (4) preserve communication channels and keep them open, (5) show sensitivity to each other's feelings, (6) personalize their language symbols (by saying "I," for instance), and (7) make use of supplementary nonverbal techniques of communication. In short, the more happily married couples tend to focus on the elements of the relationship per se as central to the definition of the marriage. They require more than the maintenance of the marriage; they experience close communication with their partner.

Marriage partners serve a variety of functions for each other. At one end of the spectrum are the expressive functions—exemplified by those listed earlier. These are direct person-to-person expressions. At the other end are the instrumental functions—making money, keeping house, and performing the tasks necessary to keep the unit in pace with demands made on it. Hicks and Platt [213] report that the husband's instrumental functions are correlated with overall reported happiness—the monetary situation and place in the society. Similarly, the higher the socioeconomic level of the partners, the more likely they are to be happy in their marriage. Paradoxically, more and more marriages are being dissolved precisely because people want so much from marriage. The most fulfilling marriages (as reported by the participants) are those where the companionship, sexual, recreational, and compatibility needs are being met by the partner. But these complex functions are so demanding that the impossibility of meeting them contributes to divorce [328]. Persons divorce because at least one of the partners is dissatisfied—yet often they still believe in marriage. Norton and Glick [348] express this dilemma well:

> Viewed in this manner, the high rate of divorce can be interpreted as an understandable pursuit of happiness. This does not necessarily mean that people are marrying and subsequently divorcing without care or concern, but rather that there exists a new awareness that a marriage which is subjectively viewed as not viable can be dissolved and—hopefully—replaced by a more nearly viable one.

The high divorce rate is a fact, but this does not mean marriage is declining in importance.

A Roper Poll of some years ago demonstrated that nine out of ten people still believe in marriage, with 96 percent of the women and 92 percent of the men wanting to be married. The trend toward equal work opportunity for women does not replace women's desire for marriage. Fully three out of five women under the age of thirty want to combine marriage with a career [295]. Furthermore, if a young woman is married and divorced at the age of twenty she has a 97 percent chance of being remarried, with the percentage dropping with age. At forty years of age her chance for remarriage is still 50 percent [281].

Cohabitation is viewed by many as a sign that marriage is a thing of the past. Even with a high cohabitation rate (one-fourth of university students), cohabitants are as likely as noncohabitants to wish to marry eventually [69]. While the consequences of living together impact on choice of romantic partners, the arrangement has not yet replaced the institution of marriage. Marriage, although more easily dissolved than in the past, is still important. Because people seem to want marriages to work well, they dissolve ones that do not work [295]. So far, divorce and remarriage seem to have been rather effective mechanisms for replacing poor marriages with good ones and for keeping the mean level of marital happiness fairly high [175].

In summary, even the more enduring relationships—marriages and friendships—are subject to change. Yet these processes of turnover do *not* necessarily mean that people do not want secure, longlasting relationships. Rather, especially in the case of marriage, the relational turnover often arises precisely because one of the partners wants more intimacy, sharing, and close communication. Relational turnover brings with it both opportunity and danger, both excitement and trauma.

The perspective of this chapter is one of *change* within and across relationships. As indicated earlier, relationships are "seldom static"; they grow, reach some forms of equilibrium, and sometimes fade away[216]. Even within a relationship that appears stable, there are elements of fluctuation—a dynamism underlying the overall stability. Relationships are in continual change, evolving, fluctuating, and dissolving. The rest of this chapter will present the processes of forming, maintaining, dissolving, and replacing relationships and examine the costs and benefits of such movements.

DEVELOPMENTAL MOVEMENT

Initiation

The General Process

Our dyadic relationships with others progress through initiation, maintenance, and dissolution. For instance, if you know a cashier at the local coffee shop and over a period of time talk to her about the weather and how she is feeling, your relationship can stabilize at a very superficial stage of development—and you are both satisfied with that level. Similarly, if you meet someone while doing your long-distance running and later become friends, you may want the relationship to continue toward becoming best friends. One of the most universal experiences that people have is beginning a relationship with someone and then finding out that the other person wants more, or less, of an intimate relationship than they do. If you are a college student and discover that your professor is very friendly, you may later be dissatisfied that he or she wants to be "only friendly" and does not appear to want a close friendship with you. Whether the participants in a given relationship develop their relationship to the point of commitment to one another or limit the relationship to a more restricted level, the progression of the relationship can be analyzed according to stages. Our relationships develop during the course of many separate encounters with the other, and it is this overall pattern of relational growth that we will be concerned with here.

The development of dyadic relationships, whether with co-workers, with friends, with romantic partners, or within families, does not just magically "happen." Relationships follow a somewhat orderly sequence over time. The growth of a love relationship demonstrates the wide range of stages that partners can experience in a dyadic relationship. When you first meet the other there is an initial degree of attraction. As noted in Chapter 3, "Perception of the Other," we tend to be attracted to persons we see as approximately at our same "social worth" [515]. During our communicative exchanges with the other, we "construct a picture" of the other, to which we orient ourself [515]. While this attribution to the other is continually subject to change, our image of the other organizes our communicative behavior. For instance, if upon meeting the other you discover that you have many hobbies in common, you become even more interested in continuing the relationship. And, certainly, the estimated attractiveness of the other is a central force in continuing the relationship. If you meet at a social function you might offer to meet the other at a subsequent party, suggest going to a movie together, or in some other way make an overture to continue the relationship past the initial meeting. If the other is responsive to you, this responsiveness is a key determiner to subsequent moves you might make to develop the relationship [8]. Upon returning home that evening, you might exclaim to your roommate, "I met the neatest woman this evening. She's really super and seems to like me." Privately, you will probably estimate the chances for a more in-depth relationship. If, however, when you meet her she said, "I'm married and do not spend time alone with anyone of the opposite sex except my husband," your estimated relationship potential for a love relationship would be rated at zero (unless you're the type who doesn't give up easily!).

As the relationship continues, you will revise your notions of the other, yourself, and the relationship many times, depending on the events that take place. Relationships are not predetermined; none of them are "made in heaven" or "made in hell." Rather, relationships develop based on what the participants are willing to expend and do with and for one another. We selectively filter out people on the road to intimacy. For instance, not everyone you meet will become an acquaintance; many names and faces will be lost in the shuffle. A small number of your acquaintances will become friends. Similarly, not every person of the opposite sex will become your romantic partner, and fewer yet will become your spouse.

Kerckhoff and Davis [255] have proposed the notion of "selective filtering": At different stages of our relationships we utilize different criteria for continuing the relationship. If the cashier is nice to us and doesn't violate social norms, she meets the criteria for that relationship. But if one wants a romantic partner, other criteria are important besides the ability to make small talk. As Duck [134] notes, our filters act as gates to different stages of relational development. In order to carry on a casual conversation in public, ones does not need to know the other's religious preferences or values, but for developing a close friendship or romantic relationship over an extended period of time, these elements often become important.

Figure 6.1 illustrates one person's filters and the number of people that might be "filtered" at every step along the road to intimacy.

Figure 6.1 is constructed as one hypothetical view of Abraham's filters. The chart shows the categories he uses for "friends" and the number of people he processes at each step along the way. His "filters" might be as follows:

Filter 1: Anyone who is not obnoxious, yet lively in social settings.

Filter 2: Males who spend some time with me and who seek me out for activities such as skiing.

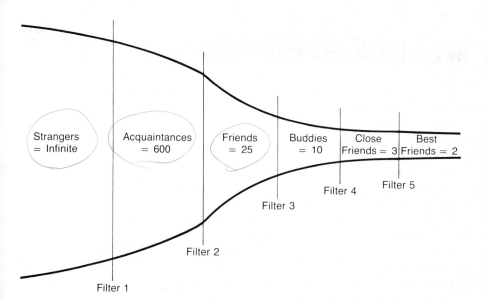

Figure 6-1.   Relationship filters.

Filter 3: Friends who have had some intense experience with me, such as being lost in the woods, become "buddies." Buddies are closer than friends; buddies are people who can share interesting stories with you about some joint adventure the two of you experienced together.

Filter 4: You have to be a buddy for over two years to become a "close friend," and have argued for me when others in a group didn't like me. In addition, I tell close friends about my romantic partner and some of the difficulties I have with her. Finally, close friends are people I can call anytime day or night when something is really bothering me, and they can do the same with me.

Filter 5: Best friends are those who went through school with me, and remained in contact for a number of years regardless of where we have moved and lived. They have been like close friends for a long period of time and we all know that we will be friends no matter what happens or where we go.

Abraham's filters, of course, would be different from yours or mine. For example, you probably have different categories and filters others must meet before becoming a "best friend." You might not use the category of "friends" as loosely as does Abraham, and the number of people at each stage would be vastly different. Some people, for instance, have a small number of friends and only one best friend. Others see themselves as having literally innumerable "friends" and use the category in a very nonrestrictive way. And one's categories for romantic partners would follow a similar path of moving from many people down to a few, but the categories and labels would be distinct from those used for friends.

Regardless of your specific categories and filters, however, a couple of general conclusions can be made about filters. First, we all use sets or clusters of criteria that others must meet before we will let them come close to us. Second, the more intimate categories contain fewer people than the less intimate ones. Third, as the categories become more intimate, the criteria for each filter become more stringent and difficult for others to meet. (Rose, a student in one of my classes, completed a "filters" assignment for the categories and filters she uses for romantic partners. For the last filter, leading to marriage, she had a list of requirements two and one-half pages long!) Finally, as we have experience with relationships, the filters undergo change. The filters you might use in junior high school are quite different from those you use as a twenty-five-year-old adult.

One final point about filters. The notion is useful to highlight the choices we all exercise in allowing others to form relationships with us, but they imply that relationship choices are mechanistic—that the filters are used no matter what. They give the impression that, "Each person brings to a relationship a preexisting bundle of characteristics that, if they can only find a proper match with someone else's bundle, will lead to a properly compatible pairing . . ."[290]. For most of us, our filters are preferences we have for an ideal, and our actual relationship partners differ from the filter criteria. When we meet someone, he or she may have characteristics we like and are attracted to, yet the characteristics would not appear in our list of filters. Furthermore, he or she may be so good at some dimension (such as talking to you when you are in need of support) that it overrides our preferences in other areas. Put bluntly, our filters are a starting point for choices about others and shouldn't be taken as the final word for what will actually happen in our relationships.

Relationship Stages

Numerous writers have specified the stages through which they see relationships going in the process of development. Of course, not all relationships move to an intimate level, so many of the stages only apply to the more intimate relationships that we experience. Most writers place relationships on a continuum of intimacy: strangers, acquaintances, friends, and lovers, with the earlier levels representing less intimate relationships [116, 334, 391]. Miller and Steinberg see relationships as developing from noninterpersonal relationships to interpersonal relationships [334]. Noninterpersonal relationships are those that are based on role demands—those in which we use data about cultural or group norms to make predictions about the other. For instance, if you go into a professor's office for the first time and say, "Dr. Payne, I'd like to talk to you about the assignment for our final paper," you behave according to your expectations of most professors in this circumstance. The rules for transacting with the other are socially derived rules that you apply regardless of the specific person. The relationship is more formal than your closer relationships. However, if you become acquainted with the professor and learn that he would rather be called Tom than Dr. Payne, you are now using psychological data about him to predict his reactions. Miller and Steinberg feel that the more idiosyncratic, informal, and individually formed the rules for transacting are, the more interpersonal the relationship is for the participants. Certainly, our closest friends make predictions based on more unique data than do persons who encounter us in our formal, prescribed roles.

Proponents of exchange theory speculate that participants pass through the following relational stages: (1) sampling—searching out others who fit our needs and who reward us, (2) bargaining—working with one other to develop a relationship that is mutually satisfying to both, (3) commitment—forming bonds between each other, and (4) institutionalization—publicly affirming that the relationship has an ongoing status [489, 502, 446]. Some forms of institutionalization are marriage, business partnerships, adoption and in some cultures, friendship.

Lewis [298] has clearly specified the stages dyads go through in the process of building a bonded unit. He labels the processes as follows:

1. The process of *perceiving similarities*. The participants find out about each other's background, values, interests, and personality and find areas of overlap that they can share with one another.
2. The process of achieving *pair rapport*. The rapport is evidenced by the pair's ease of communication, positive evaluations of each other, satisfaction with the pair relationship, and validation of the self by the other.
3. The process of inducing *self-disclosure*. The members share more deeply with one another by displaying openness through mutual self-disclosure.
4. The process of *role-taking*. The participants achieve interpersonal role-fit by achieving role complementarity and need complementarity with one another, and they display an observed similarity of personalities.
5. The process of achieving *dyadic crystallization*. The pair will manifest progressive development of the relationship, function as a complete unit, establish boundaries around the relationship, show identity as a couple, and show commitment to each other.

Lewis conceived this model based on his study of dating pairs. It develops notions similar to the filtering hypothesis of Kerckhoff and Davis [255]. Lewis's model stresses that at different times in a relationship, the participants put their energy into disparate tasks.

Altman and Taylor [6] have presented one of the most influential pictures of relational development, which they call "social penetration." According to their view, perceived rewards and costs govern the development of relationships. Our interpersonal ties develop incrementally, much like peeling off the layers of an onion. As a relationship begins, the dyadic participants expose more and more information about the central aspects of their personalities. The items of information that people disclose can be characterized by (1) the *topics* that the participants choose for sharing, (2) the *breadth* dimension of the topics, and (3) the *depth* dimension of the topics. For instance, asking someone, "What is your major?" is a topic with little depth—it isn't usually seen as being central to someone's self-concept. However, if someone comes up to you and says, "Hi, my name is Sam, I'm from Cutbank, and I'm a homosexual," the last bit of information is more central to his self-concept. In Figure 6.2, category A and category B are the topics that two participants might discuss. Of course, the number of topics is not limited to only two. If two individuals have a relationship characterized by discussing a large number of topics at a superficial level, they would have a high-breadth–low-depth relationship. Few central elements of each person's personality would be revealed in their discussion.

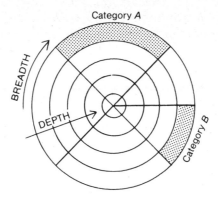

**Figure 6-2. Breadth and depth
elements of personality structure.**

Whereas the breadth is the number of topics you open up for discussion with another, the depth is the centrality or connection of each topic to your self-concept. As illustrated in Figure 6-2, as a topic moves to the center, it has more depth and is more connected to the core of the personality.

The depth dimension is related to several key dimensions of personality. The peripheral areas have to do with biographical characteristics: age, sex, personal history, home town, college major, and so forth. The more central or core areas contain the fears, self-concept, and basic values of the person. These areas have a greater impact on peripheral areas than vice versa. For instance, knowing an individual's basic outlook on life, such as trust in others, will allow you to predict his or her particular beliefs about a given topic, such as welfare. As you proceed inward, the personality items move from common to unique and from high visibility to low visibility. While your biographical characteristics are known to many, your inner values and the items central to your self-concept are known to fewer people—they are less visible. The more "socially desirable" characteristics reside in peripheral areas, and the more vulnerable aspects of the personality reside in the central, or core areas. [6].

These elements are acted out in the process of social penetration in our social transactions. Altman and Taylor state that "social interaction is generally predicted to proceed only gradually and systematically from superficial to intimate topics" [6]. As we continue to experience someone in a social relationship, we seek a balance of personal rewards and costs. The greater the rewards and the less the costs, the more satisfying the relationship. Furthermore, we project into the future interactions and have "forecast rewards and costs"—estimates of what the future will bring. And as our transactions with another continue to occur over and over, we build a cumulative balance of rewards and costs [6]. Our relationships develop systematically and incrementally.

> Thus there are norms about invasions of privacy, rules of decorum, implicit guides to avoid noticing foibles in others, extended courtship concepts, socially approved modes of response which protect the individual from exposure, and sanctions against those who violate the norm of gradual interpersonal exploration. All these may be designed to pace the process of interpersonal exchange. Were there no such controls, interpersonal relationships would be unpredictable and volatile [5].

The stages of relationships, therefore, follow patterns influenced by these considerations. Altman and Taylor [6] specify these stages in the development of relationships over time: (1) orientation, (2) exploratory affective exchange, (3) affective exchange, and (4) stable exchange. The process begins in the public areas of the personality where individuals convey a favorable image and do not evaluate one another negatively. Exploratory affective exchange is found in relationships between casual acquaintances or friendly neighbors. The communication patterns of the participants become more synchronized as the participants adjust to one another. Interaction is still limited to the superficial or intermediate areas of the personality, with little or no interaction on the core items. Affective exchange occurs when the participants reach the state of being close friends or intimates in the courtship phase. The individuals are more able to engage in conflict over the peripheral areas without disrupting their relationship. This stage is also characterized by a definite increase in revealing private areas of the self to the other as the communication becomes more unique. The difficulties of blending two distinct personalities at this stage become clear, with the individuals opening up the more fragile areas of the self to the other. During stable exchange, the spontaneity and richness of exchange continues to improve. While few dyadic pairs achieve this level of intimacy, committed couples and friends experience the central, private areas of each other. Usually at this stage the participants feel a "we-ness," feel that the other can be told most secrets, and the communication flows smoothly.

The social penetration model also applies to "instant relationships." Individuals sometimes form relationships of apparent intimacy with surprising speed. Today, many couples progress through the courtship phase more rapidly than in earlier decades [292]. Few mourn the passing of such bygone customs as bundling boards, chaperones, protracted dinners with the partner's family, five-year engagements, and expansive correspondence while the man was away "preparing a home" for his bride-to-be. Some people advocate the opposite—"getting to the core" of the other, doing away with small talk, and skipping general social norms regulating how to interact and build relationships. However, small talk and other forms of incremental development serve the function of building confidence in each other and building a reservoir of good feelings and common experiences upon which to draw [260]. Altman and Taylor feel that although the penetration process may be more rapid than in the past, it is still the same:

> What may be different nowadays is nothing more than what is considered to be intimate, personal, or central core characteristics of personality. The difference between generations may be in what is defined as superficial and intimate, with the developmental process following the same systematic course described here. Or, to put it in another way, the game and rules are the same, the only difference may be the words [6].

Relationships that proceed too rapidly to the central and core areas are fragile and susceptible to disruption. While exploration of the central areas of the personality can produce extensive rewards, it can also have enormous costs. The experience commonly labeled the "one-night stand," in which sexual intimacy is achieved rapidly, is often without the accompanying transactions that build up trust and understanding. As a consequence, when interpersonal conflict erupts, the relationship shatters. The words of a popular song express it well— "Hello, love, goodbye."

Similarly, the "stranger on the train" phenomenon also illustrates the importance of the sequential development of relationships. This occurs when someone takes a train (or more likely, plane) ride and during the trip starts a conversation with the person nearby. In the course of the trip, the two people discuss very private and vulnerable information—often negative—about themselves. This experience often works precisely because the individuals know that they will not see each other again—thus the general norms for developing interaction can be suspended. Woe to the person who confesses an affair with the boss's spouse to the individual in the adjacent seat on the plane, only to discover later that the individual is the boss's cousin. Rapid social exchange is disruptive if the participants expect to interact again in the near future. As Carly Simon sings, "Sometimes I wish, often I wish, that I never knew some of those secrets of yours."

The Altman and Taylor model of the penetration process seems essentially correct—we develop our relationships incrementally from the superficial to intimate areas so that the relationship has the ability to survive negative information and continue to build and grow.

Knapp [260] has formed a model of relational stages that is even more precise than Altman and Taylor's. Knapp outlines the following stages for developing a relationship.

1. *Initiating.* This stage includes small talk, opening lines, and initial reactions to the other (such as attractiveness as a romantic partner, utility as a business associate, and the like). The stage is dominated by the conventional modes of address: Greg says, "Hi, how are you?" and Brooks says, "Fine, and you?"

2. *Experimenting.* At this stage we begin to try to discover the unknown and engage in a lot of small talk in order to uncover topics and areas about the other that we can relate to effectively. Knapp says that small talk serves these functions:
    a. It is a useful process for uncovering integrating topics and openings for more penetrating conversation.
    b. It can be an audition for a future friendship or a way of increasing the scope of a current relationship.
    c. It provides a safe procedure for indicating who we are and how another can come to know us better (reduction of uncertainty).
    d. It allows us to maintain a sense of community with our fellow human beings [250].

    Most of our social relationships do not progress past this point; we exchange basic information, maintaining the relationship at the experimenting level.

3. *Intensifying.* Just as the word suggests, during this stage the participants begin to delve into the deeper areas of each other's personality. Each person begins to expose more of his or her vulnerable areas to the other. The disclosure that one's father is an alcoholic, for instance, usually occurs in a more intense relationship than during social chitchat. Often intensification is so slow that we do not even recognize the deepening relationship. But sometimes deeper information is revealed that calls for a response at its level. In a class dealing with communication skills the class members were engaging in small talk when one person turned to the instructor and said, "I tried to kill myself a year ago and was committed to the state hospital." The move to intensification was apparent to all. The dyadic participants at this level begin to use their special language, which is more informal, and begin to communicate in ways that are more coordinated to the presence of the other [260].

4. *Integrating.* When a dyadic pair, whether a romantic pair, a friendship pair, or a generation pair such as brothers and sisters, achieve a sense of "coupling," they have integrated. Integration is evidenced by a "we-ness," where the two act as a unit, develop a shared history, and merge their social circles. Part of each person is blended into the relationship. Once a pair has integrated, others will also treat them as a unit. If your college roommate is also your best friend, when one gets invited to a party, the other will probably also be invited. Integrating is easily seen in the case of a romantic dyad, where the two become a "couple." More decisions are made jointly because the two persons have an identity as a single unit.

5. *Bonding.* This final stage in development occurs when the couple undergoes a public ritual and formally contracts their relationship. Marriage is the most common form of bonding, yet in other cultures there are also public ceremonies that link friends in a committed

relationship much like the friendship oath in ancient Greece. Other public acknowledgments of bonding are christenings in which godparents are named, adoptions, business partnerships, and ceremonies of unity for homosexual couples. Bonding is an important step, and much is made of it in Western cultures. For instance, if a young man announces that he is getting married, others react with congratulations and talk about how the person is "taking the big plunge." Making a public commitment to share your future with another person is no small step. Many contemporary people (especially college students) resist the bonding stage longer in their romantic relationships than used to be the case. Some feel that the process of bonding will mean death to the relationship and that if bonding occurs, each individual will "suffocate." Others delay bonding because they want to make a commitment that has the best chance of success. Still other people totally avoid bonding with another. Whether one engages in, delays, or avoids bonding, it is a significant stage in the development of a relationship.

Knapp's [260] contribution to the understanding of stages of relational development can best be seen by summarizing how he thinks participants move in and out of the stages. First of all, *movement is generally systematic and sequential.* When a relationship develops and dissolves, participants usually experience each stage in sequence. Knapp, however, says that the process is not linear and fixed, but that there are trends in this direction. As Altman and Taylor wrote, we can sometimes skip steps, but that makes the relationship more fragile at the core areas. For instance, if a man and woman meet, engage in close physical contact, "fall head and heels into love," and get married fourteen days later, after the bonding experience they will probably have to recycle through the early stages in order for the relationship to survive the natural strains of living together. Similarly, committing oneself to a business partnership quickly will probably necessitate some effort to get to know the partner better.

Not only can people skip steps, but they can go through the steps in a very rapid fashion, an idea advanced earlier in this chapter. Many conditions lead to such developments. Summer romances are legendary because the processes of moving to integration and bonding are speeded up. Facing the end of their time together, a couple will speed up the process of getting to know one another and act like a unit. Also, any external threat, such as the feuding parents in the classical Romeo and Juliet story, will often speed up the process of development through the stages.

Second, *movement may be forward or backward.* Movements forward are toward greater intimacy, those backward are toward less intimacy. As specified by Altman and Taylor [6], we become more intimate and close by building on our past experiences together. And, of course, if a dyadic pair moves toward dissolution, they are moving "backward" toward less intimacy (even though the move may not be "backward" for the individuals).

Third, movement occurs within stages. As Knapp says, "There will always be a certain degree of instability associated with any stable relationship" [260 p.2]. As a result, being at one stage is not necessarily a sign that the next stage will follow automatically. Many relationships will encounter considerable variation within one stage. It is common, for example, for married couples to go through what Davis [116] calls "reintegration ceremonies" as a way to supply some of the energy spent on accomplishing the original bonding. Similarly, work associates, friends, or any other set of participants can move in and out of these stages more than once. A counselor and client may move to integration each time they meet. Friends who reestablish contact also recycle through the early stages. There are even cases in which the entire sequence from development to dissolution is repeated more than once. One couple was married for six years, went through a divorce, and eighteen months later remarried. Their experiences would, of course, not be the same the second time, but the stages are. Quite an experience in relational stages!

Finally, Knapp specifies that *movement is always to a new place.* Our experiences with others are not repeatable—we cannot totally erase our previous interactions with them. A man and woman who begin as friends, become romantic partners, and then attempt to move back into friendship discover that it takes considerable effort to "move back" to where their relationship was initially. Even at that, the friendship can never be identical to what it was before. As time changes, so do our relationships.

Dyadic pairs are configured through many paths, and although some relationships follow sets of stages in their development, many show much more variation than suggested here. Knapp says that "movement occurs within stages," meaning that development is not a step-by-step process leading to a predetermined goal. In fact, there are many "paths" to the development of a relationship, and probably most of them have some circular loops in them. One researcher, Bolton, studied twenty couples and found the development process involved "advances and retreats along the paths of available alternatives [290]. The work on stages does, however, give us some general notions of possible sequences of stages that might be followed, allowing for many twistings and turnings along the way.

Stabilized Definitions

Reaching Definitional Agreement
As participants progress in a relationship, they work toward agreement on the nature of their relationship. For instance, if you ask Shelly, "What is your relationship with Pam like?" she might answer, "It's

okay, she's a friend, but not my best friend." Shelly and Pam each have a view of what their relationship is. For most of us, at a given time, see the relationship as stabilized, though it may be subject to later change. Either both parties will agree (for a time at least) on what their relationship is like or they will continue to struggle until the relationship is defined or dissolved. Once there is some minimal agreement, the two people will act *as if* the relationship is stable. As noted in Chapter 4, there are two levels of events occurring: (1) the actual communication events and (2) the relationship label the participants use to characterize their relationship. When some accommodation is reached on the relationship label (e.g., "We are friends"), then the two people act as if the relationship is stable. The key to "stable" relationships is that the two people reach some agreement, either explicitly or implicitly, on the nature of the relationship.

There are three important aspects to "stabilized" relationships: (1) Relationships are seen as stable because the participants reach minimal agreement about the relationship, (2) relationships can "stabilize" at differing levels of intimacy, and (3) a "stabilized" relationship still has considerable change occurring in it.

First, relationships can be relatively stable in almost any form, depending on what the participants want. Some business relationships become defined as "competition," while others become defined as "friendly cooperation." A counselor may in one case work to define his role as giving intellectual insights, yet in another case the client may want him primarily to give emotional support. One romantic dyad may serve a wide variety of functions, whereas another may be based primarily on the financial advantage of living together. As long as the participants can agree on the definition of their relationship, they can stabilize it to serve particular functions. It is often difficult to understand the relationships of others that stabilize in ways that we would not like for our own relationships. Jerry is a professional man, married, with three children, who has had a long-term relationship with a woman in another city for thirteen years. He maintains that the lifestyle is very favorable for all concerned and that when his children are out of high school, he and his wife will probably get divorced. His wife also has an outside relationship, and it has been going on for two years. This relational definition is a dramatic example of one that has been stabilized for a long time. Similarly, the relationship between parents and children often stabilizes while the children are young. Then, with the turbulent late-teen years, new definitions are forged. When the children reach maturity, new relationship definitions are often agreed to, with the parents and children treating one another more as equals than before. At each phase in the long-term relationship, each time there is agreement by the participants about the nature of the relationship, they have reached a "stabilized" relationship for a period of time.

One of the studies dealing with the communication differences in relational stabilizations of married couples was conducted by Fitzpatrick [152]. She discovered three major types of relational definitions used by married couples. *Independents* are committed to an ideology of uncertainty and change in their relationship, and they exhibit a high degree of autonomy in their relationship. Their bonding is less intense than most, and they engage in a moderate amount of disclosure to one another and rate themselves as "less socially restrained" in their communication than others. Their relationship is opposed to the traditional value system, and each person sees himself or herself as relatively autonomous. They, as compared with other couples, are simply more independent. The *separates* are characterized by very little sharing with one another and a high degree of conflict avoidance. Although they do see themselves as connected to one another, they have many separate activities from the other. Neither are they "independent" from one another nor do they see themselves as traditionalists. *Traditionals* follow a fairly customary belief in the marital relationship. They prefer little autonomy from one another and impose few limitations on the other's use of physical and emotional space. They have a high degree of sharing with one another and tend to engage in rather than avoid conflict, at least in this sample. They are highly interdependent and are opposed to the ideology of uncertainty and change. These three relational types illustrate that married pairs do reach agreement on the major aspects of their relationship and stabilize around their given choices. Stabilization types for other dyadic pairs will undoubtedly emerge as more research is conducted, and their relational definitions will be reflected in their communication patterns.

The second aspect of stabilization is that relationships can stabilize at any degree of intimacy. For instance, your relationships with teachers, employers, and acquaintances are initiated, defined, and eventually terminated, but do not necessarily become intimate, bonded, or close. Most relationships do not progress to the bonding stage; rather, they become beneficial to both parties at a certain level and then stay at that level until they terminate. The process of attempting to stabilize a relationship at a given level is one that we all experience. You meet someone in your class, engage in a short work project together, stabilize at that point, and part at the end of the semester. The rewards that each wanted were fulfilled in the stabilized relationship. When you go to see your physician, the service functions she performs are what you want. Neither of you is distressed that the relationship does not progress toward further intimacy or bonding.

It is important to remember that *most of our relationships do not move to intimacy* [118]. But any relationship can be satisfying if the two people reach some level of accommodation on their needs. For instance, with someone you see each Sunday in a large church, it may be sufficient to limit the relationship to a "Hi, how are you?" basis. The difficulty comes when the two participants want different rewards from the relationship. If one person wants to move the friendship to a romantic relationship, the waters can get a little rocky for both parties. Similarly, if one person wants to move an acquaintanceship to a friendship but the other does not want to be so accessible, then they will implicitly struggle over the relational definitions, often incurring some unhappiness in the process. Roger and his instructor experienced an inordinate amount of difficulty in reaching an agreement on what their relationship should be. Early in their association, the instructor was very friendly to him and became his mentor. Then, over the course of several quarters, Roger made it clear that he wanted primarily to be a friend and did not want to be in the "student role." The instructor, on the other hand, wished to remain "friendly" and to serve as a source of academic inspiration for him. They struggled over their relational definition for many months and finally both adopted a stance of being friendly—but not friends and not academic partners. Neither could get everything he wanted, so they stabilized their relationship at a mutually compromised level.

Even though a relationship can be "stabilized" at the level of the label, the communication episodes within that relationship can show wide variations. Two business associates can become partners, yet at times during the partnership, they may not treat each other as equals. Most relationships spiral progressively and regressively within limits set by the participants. In a counseling relationship, business or work association, friendship, or any dyadic relationship, conflict occurs and has an impact on the ebb and flow of the relationship. Best friends and bonded lovers can "be on the outs" yet not dissolve their basic relational definition. The consistent communication patterns that have been built can be disrupted for multitudes of reasons, yet the pair sees the disruptions as only temporary deviations.

Variations in the communication patterns may be central to the preservation of "stable" relationships. Research by Fisher and Drecksel, for example, demonstrated that a "steady state" is not the absence of change, but "continuous and cyclic change" [150]. Ayers notes, "Stability . . . does not mean that no aspect of the relationship changes. Rather it means that the basic patterns of exchange in the relationship are established and accepted" [15]. Within a "stable" relationship there are many ongoing changes in communication and episodes, yet the basic definitional label for the relationship—best friends, romantic partner, colleague—remains unchanged. It may simply be as Baxter and Wilmot note, that in stabilized relationships the parties go on "automatic pilot" and pay less attention to the swings and sways of the episodes as they occur [38].

Reasons to Maintain a Dyad

Many relationships can be stabilized within limits that serve the functions of the participants, and there is no need to dissolve them. Lifelong marriages still occur, sometimes with more frequency than many

**Work relationships and friendships, like other relationships, may be very
stable in spite of temporary conflict.**

young people believe. It is possible to maintain a valuable committed
relationship with another person over a number of years.

The most prominent reason to maintain a dyad is because it serves
its functions well. Your close friend who serves as your companion can
provide you a continuing basis of support and friendship for years. The
marriage relationship that continues for a number of years *can* do so
precisely because the people are happy with what they can do for one
another and therefore have no reason to dissolve the relationship. Your
business partner or associate can serve your interests well, and you can
serve hers.

A long-term committed relationship also can provide a feeling of
security in a changing world. The old friend whom you can telephone
fifteen years after attending school together serves as a source of continuity with your past. Similarly, your committed romantic partner can
help make your life meaningful through difficult times. Many a spouse
has been helped by the other when terminated from a job, losing a
loved family member, or experiencing some other traumatic life shock.
The two of you can help each other during your respective difficult
times so that you can each "bounce back" and be stronger once again.
Carla was a person who had a rather unhappy teen era; when she got
married at twenty-three, no one knew of the difficulties she was going
to face. At the age of twenty-eight, she experienced a severe case of
manic-depression. She would be "wound up tight" for a few days, then

totally collapse and be depressed a few days later. When she was admitted to a state mental hospital for treatment, her husband Warren stayed by her side day and night. It is now twelve years later, and Carla and Warren have a continuing love that serves them both well. Because Warren prized security and commitment, as well as loving Carla, he was able to stay with her and help her through the difficult times. His unwavering devotion had a sizable impact on her desire to return home. And now Warren knows that if he would be unlucky enough to experience a very difficult shock—such as losing his job or losing his sister to whom he is close—Carla will be standing ready to help him through it. There is a great deal to be said for a commitment in which the other person will stand by you and not desert you in your time of need.

Finally, there is a lot of pride in being a unit that can be positive in spite of contemporary trends toward easier dissolution. Even couples who are not initially "matched" well (they may have different religions, different social backgrounds, or different goals for their relationship) can remain together in a relationship that is satisfying. There is a "pair survival ability," the working together to adapt to one another, putting energy into the relationship, and continuing to relate to each other as significant people [345]. Expending the effort to make a relationship work can be a source of satisfaction for the pair. They can develop the "you and I made it when others did not" attitude that helps them celebrate their willingness to work on their relationship when others might not. They can even take pride in the willingness to be faithful to their wedding vows [525].

A lot of dyads are maintained not because of the rewards, but because the costs of termination are too high. The loss of one's children through divorce, the reestablishment in another town or profession, the paying of child support or maintenance, the fear of being alone, or just the emotional trauma of dissolution can all motivate individuals to maintain their dyadic unit. Sometimes a relationship maintained simply because of the high cost of termination can later become fulfilling for the participants. Many couples survive difficult early years of childraising, then find themselves growing closer again later. Each passage into a new stage of life can bring possibilities for an altered relationship. By maintaining a relationship, one can have a chance to work on it actively again under different conditions.

One of the most crucial issues facing people today is how to maintain a personal relationship over a long period of time. Attempts to enhance or rejuvenate a relationship are often necessary to counteract all the forces that tend to "wear down" even the best of relationships. With marriages it might be lack of time to spend together, money, children, and jobs, whereas in other close relationships there are other erosive factors. Regardless of the causes, there *are* things you can do to enhance a relationship that is slowly declining. Those are discussed in detail in the next chapter. First, however, let us sketch the dissolution process.

Dissolution

"The breaking up of a relationship is a phenomenon known to most and dreaded by all. It accounts for some of our most intense and painful social experiences" [34]. The process of dissolving a relationship is clouded by fear, intrigue, mystery, and pain. Many songs chronicle the sad, intuitively understood process of breaking up ("You've Lost That Loving Feeling," "Home Ain't Home Anymore"). We often intuitively understand that a breakup is coming even when we cannot articulate how or why.

The trauma of one's own relationship loss, however, should not obscure some of the regularities that occur across all dissolutions. Whether the relationship is a work association, a counseling relationship, or your most important romantic love, the process of dissolution can be charted and understood. Levinger, who gave us the notion of "pair relatedness" (see Chapter 1), specifies that a pair essentially becomes less "related" or dependent on one another as a pattern in dissolutions. Dyadic partners who are closely connected suffer more trauma and loss upon uncoupling than do people who are not closely connected [284]. In addition to this global approach there are some more specific models of the dissolution process. For example, Altman and Taylor [6] specify that the "depenetration process" is generally the reverse of the penetration process, with the participants gradually withdrawing the rewards that they learned to provide for one another and the relationship moving from much sharing of core items to sharing more superficial information.

Conflict in the core areas contributes to rapid depenetration. If a dyadic pair has a conflict over a core topic such as sex, it reverberates throughout the rest of their system and, if left unmanaged, will undermine the rest of the relationship. Pineo found that during the course of a typical twenty-year marriage, there is a general drop in marital satisfaction, a loss of intimacy, increased loneliness, less reciprocal settlement of conflicts, and a decline in certain forms of interactions such as sex. According to Pineo, the "maximum fit" between two individuals is just before the marriage. A subsequent regression then sets in, with the partners becoming less "fit" to each other over time. In his research, the process of reduction in marital satisfaction was slow, with intimacy gradually being lost. All of these theorists set forth the same basic notion—that relationships fade out in ways similar to their development, except in reverse.

Duck [136] sets forth some general phases of relationship dissolution designed to track the overall events. The stages he lists in dissolution are:

Breakdown
Intrapsychic Phase
Dyadic Phase
Social Phase
Grave Dressing Phase

During the breakdown stage the person becomes dissatisfied with the relationship. Then in the intrapsychic phase there is a focus on the other's behavior, an internal evaluation of the other's strengths and weaknesses, and identification of some of the negative aspects of being in the relationship. In addition, the person has to face the issue of whether to "express or repress" dissatisfaction with the relationship. One also assesses the costs of withdrawal from the relationship [136]. One study by Baxter and Wilmot [28] on "secret tests" shows that people do engage in intrapsychic "tests" of the other person—and make judgments of them based on the test. In a dissolution movement, for example, you might think to yourself, "If he goes out once more with his friends instead of me, it is all over." If you don't tell him of this condition, then you are still in the intrapsychic phase—all the work is done internally without his awareness.

In the dyadic phase you shift from a focus on the partner to a focus on the relationship. You confront the partner with your dissatisfactions, express your discomfort, and deal with the partner's reactions to your viewpoints. The basic outcome after negotiations with the partner is a decision either to dissolve or to repair the relationship [136].

In a relationship where the two people do not reach some accommodation, they move to the next phase—the social phase. In this phase, one negotiates the postdissolution state of the relationship ("Will we be friends or enemies?"), initiates gossip with one's networks to justify one's decisions, and places blame on the other for the relational demise. If there is no intervention by others—family members, counselors, or the like—then the relationship is dissolved and the final phase, grave dressing, is reached. In this final phase, energy is spent "getting over" the relationship and dissolution. One looks back and tries to make sense of the relationship (e.g., "It worked well until he became so obsessed with his job"). One then distributes publicly one's version of the break-up story, telling others why one's actions were reasonable and his or hers weren't. The accounts given after a dissolution may be different than those advanced while one was going through the process [136]. The following is one person's account, compiled at the grave dressing stage of her terminated love relationship:

Why did Vic and Joan fail? They came from very different backgrounds, but that didn't matter, because Joan was in love. It also didn't matter that

Vic wasn't ready to settle down, or that he was a Greek Orthodox and Joan was a Lutheran, or that Joan felt like she could disclose to Vic topics of great depth, but Vic held a lot within himself, or that Vic gave Joan warmth, closeness, touching, the pleasure of satisfying him, a challenge of such a demanding person, and that she gave him only sex and a person to share supper at Perkins with, or that Joan and Vic decided to keep in touch over the summer and then Joan would send postcards and presents from Disneyland, letters from Phoenix, and birthday cards from Missoula, but yet Vic sent nothing, or that Joan finally got up enough nerve to call him after she hadn't seen or heard from him in almost a year, and then he was so very sweet and sounded so concerned about her, and he acted like no termination had ever taken place. . . .

—(CITED BY PERMISSION WITH ANONYMITY)

The advantages of Duck's phases of dissolution are that they call attention to the broader aspects, show us the shifts from intrapsychic to relational level efforts, focus on the attributions people give for breakups, and emphasize the role of the social network in dissolutions. It lacks a focus on the earlier stages of the relationship leading to the dissolution and suffers from a rather mechanistic view that disengagers are "goal-directed, rational, or strategic" [26].

One final description of the dissolution process comes from Knapp [260]. He is more descriptive of communication events and provides a somewhat different focus on the "coming apart" of a relationship. Combined with the steps of initiation, the entire sequence for "coming together" and "coming apart" would be like this:

1. Initiating.
2. Experimenting.
3. Intensifying.
4. Integrating.
5. Bonding.
6. Differentiating.
7. Stagnating.
8. Avoiding.
9. Terminating.

Differentiating is the process of beginning the uncoupling, just as integrating was the process of coming together. Former joint endeavors take on an "I do this" rather than "we do this" connotation. The possessions of each take on a more individualized cast: It is "her" house and "his" camping equipment. The participants work to get more space from each other and establish separate identities. Especially when the bonding stage was rushed, the couple needs to differentiate from each other in order to feel a sense of individual identity. Differentiating, of course, does not necessarily lead to the termination of the relationship—it can perform the function of establishing more separate identities that the individuals then fuse back together again.

During *circumscription* the communication becomes constricted—it decreases in amount and is restricted to certain topics. The communication tends to focus on more public and superficial topics with less breadth and depth [260]. If one of the partners ventures into a topic the other will close it off by saying something like, "Don't talk about that," or, "It's not worth discussing."

As the pair moves through circumscribing, the next stage is *stagnation*, where the relationship is "put on hold" and discussion of the relationship becomes taboo. Married couples in the stagnation phase feel that they know exactly what the other will say, so there is no sense discussing important topics. Of course, with little effort going into the relationship, it does tend to wither away slowly. A generation pair of parents and teenage children, as well as any other dyadic pair, can manifest stagnation by low levels of communicative exchange. The participants will often sit in the presence of the other for long periods of time and have nothing to say. This is painfully evidenced by the boredom and silence at some family holiday dinners.

In the *avoiding* stage the participants go out of their way to not be together. They spend energy actively making sure that they will not have to interact with the other person. Most often, the two try to avoid one another physically. I once observed a married couple sitting in a restaurant for fifty minutes. The man never once made eye contact with the woman or answered her questions. Finally, when he returned from the restroom she moved to the chair next to his to capture his attention. He just raised his newspaper between the two of them and kept reading.

During the *terminating* stage, one or more of the participants makes it abundantly clear that the relationship is over. This can occur, of course, in short-term relationships or in long-term commitments of many years. The participants signal the termination of open access and usually indicate what they want the future of the relationship to be. The typical lover lament, "She doesn't ever want to see me anymore," reflects a common termination condition.

Termination Tactics
The discussion of the phases of dissolution has been fairly general to this point, since the focus has been on the stages dyadic pairs experience in coming together and coming apart. The specific communication events in dissolution warrant closer examination. The speed with which people dissolve relationships, the specific communicative tactics they use, and the oscillation present in most terminations will be discussed. Following these three sections, the different experiences of the "leaver" and the "left" will be explained, the values of dissolving

Some relationships terminate by slowly "passing away," with the distance
between partners gradually increasing until the relationship cannot endure.

a relationship will be weighed, and the consequences on dyadic networks will be sketched.

Dissolution Speed.   Some dyads move slowly toward termination,
some rapidly. Murray Davis [116] calls them "passing away" and "sudden death." In passing away, the intimacy declines by almost imper-
ceptible degrees until the relationship can no longer endure. This is
typically brought about by the intrusion of a new intimate, by the
physical separation of the two, or by the aging of the participants over
time. We have already dealt with the question of the effects of a third
party, but it is equally true that the separation of two close friends or
romantic partners wreaks havoc on their relationship. One of the most
common experiences of modern life is moving and leaving friends
behind, then having to establish new friendships. The previous relationship slowly passes away, as if it were eroded by time. Those people
who endure the long separations brought on by military assignments
or jobs overseas experience tremendous change and readjustment
when the missing one returns home once again. Some relationships
endure the separations well—in fact, the two people can often thrive
on the separation. Sometimes this happens when a relationship is in
the building stages and the two people become so aware of the pain of
missing the other that they engage in extraordinary effort to fan the
flames. Or they may simply be used to it after many years. Two long-

distance lovers talked to each other three times a day and spent over $250 a month on phone calls. If the persons are not able to garner the resources to overcome the spatial separation by phone calls, letters, or other forms of frequent contact, they slowly drift apart. Some of the more recent literature on the relationships that fathers have with their children from previous marriages demonstrates that the most important variable in maintaining a close relationship over the months of separation is the father's income. (In years to come, if more fathers gain custody of their children, the same will apply to mothers.) If the parent can afford to make frequent calls and go for visits, the relationship with the children will endure. If the parent stops having contact with the children, the relationship is likely to fade away [525].

Separation is often consciously used by a person in order to let the relationship die slowly. The surest death to romantic or other intimate relationships is to let the energy ooze out of them; they do not have a life of their own independent of the two people. Letting a relationship die by increasing distance takes many forms. A college student, for instance, will increase the psychological distance between herself and another person simply by making herself unavailable. The typical maneuver is to let the roommate answer the phone and "tell him that I am not here." Similarly, people will change the routes they take to their classes or work in order not to encounter the other—knowing that the lack of contact lets the relationship die. People may just let the life slowly fade out of long-term relationships, often without being aware of the choices they are making—but the effects are the same. In the first stanza of the song "Isn't It Enough?," a young man is becoming aware of the slow passing of his marriage.

Isn't It Enough?

> Monday night and you're out somewhere dancing
> And I'm waiting here for you at home.
> You said you'd be at your office working
> But no one seems to answer when I phone.
> Working late is just your way to say we're on the skids, I know,
> I can see it in your eyes, I can feel it in your touch.
> And all I've ever wanted is to be your lovin' man,
> Is that too much,
> Or isn't it enough?*

In this case, the passing away is one-sided—one person vetoed the relationship. It has one element common to many one-sided dissolutions: one of the persons engages in relational sabotage. A person can let a relationship pass away by refusing to make choices that would arrest its decline. He or she may partially want the relationship to dis-

---

*©1977, Robert Geis.

solve and while protesting that the relationship is important, all effort is directed to producing its failure. The sabotage can also come from both people as they mutually work to let the relationship fade away.

Sudden death has the same effect as passing away, but the tactics are much more observable. In sudden death endings, the end is announced or made apparent with the swift stroke of death. While passing away is akin to starving, sudden death is similar to execution. Davis [116] maintains that sudden death is caused by (1) both people, (2) one person, or (3) neither person, with outside forces responsible. The most common form is when one person terminates the relationship and the other is not expecting it. Ted was a student who had an ongoing war with his roommate Marc for over a year. One day he came home to find that Marc had changed the lock on the door and moved all of Ted's belongings into the hall. People sometimes just disappear, without any warning or indication of their discomfort in the relationship. Similarly, a person may pass the word that "it is over" to their exintimate via a mutual friend. One man had his oldest daughter inform his spouse that he had left [525]. Or maybe the phone just won't ring anymore. The various tactics are as unique as the individual. One married man with two small children asked his wife if she would like to go to Hawaii. They busied themselves with the preparations and worked out all the details. Then, when sitting on the plane just before takeoff, the man turned to his wife, said, "Have a nice trip," and quickly disappeared. She returned from her traumatic vacation to a set of divorce papers and an empty house.

Why might a person engage in the "sudden death" tactic for dissolving a relationship? Two probable reasons are (1) some external event moves one to sudden action, and (2) it serves to balance out previous patterns in a relationship. Just as the elements of a conflict can stay underground until some "minor" event brings them to the surface, most relationships end with a triggering event [220]. Often the discovery of an extramarital relationship, a new job opportunity, a chance for a new career, or some other external event moves the people to action. It is precisely because the prospect of termination is so troubling to people that the tactics they use to end a relationship are often destructive and inhumane. How do you, after all, tell a person who still loves you that you want the relationship to end? Especially in relationships characterized by small amounts of metacommunication, the burden of talking about the ending is just too painful to bear. As a result, tactics are used that appear nonsensical to an outsider.

The second reason for quickly killing a relationship is a reaction to long-term patterns that the person feels he or she cannot alter. For instance, if a person feels less powerful than the partner, undergoes years of frustration, and feels that "talking about it" will only rob them of their personal power, a sudden death might be the chosen alternative. In more extreme forms, a person who has suffered abuse from another may find that the pattern of making up, abuse, making up, and abuse seems to occur regardless of what is done. Then, in an attempt to alter such patterns, one might make a final decision about the relationship, move to a new city and try to avoid all contact with the former partner. Sudden unexpected moves to dissolve a relationship can be seen as the ultimate power balancing act, with the one who feels less powerful finally bringing balance by one dramatic act [220]. Similarly, such overt, unexpected moves keep one from being vulnerable to the other's countermoves; if you intend to dissolve the relationship, you might not want the other to initiate the final actions [30].

Communicative Tactics.   One of the central factors influencing communicative tactics of dissolution is the fact that *it requires two persons to build a relationship but only one to destroy it.* As a result, the specific communication moves "strikes at the very nexus of cooperations that have been built up over the course of intimate relating . . ." [396]. Each participant can make choices to move the relationship toward dissolution, with or without the cooperation of the other person.

Baxter and Philpott [37] noted for us that the strategies used in termination show less variation than those used at the initiation stage of relationships. Such constriction of options is also present in the actual communicative choices of those moving toward dissolution. For example, friends in the process of dissolution most often do not self-disclose about the decline in the relationship. As Baxter [30] notes, their disengagements were nondirect. Disengagers seem to hint at a "desire to disengage by conversing only on superficial topics, hoping the other is socially perceptive" [30].

Overall, the tactics used by disengagers seem to reflect two basic dimensions: directness–indirectness and other–self orientation [34]. A direct tactic would be using open confrontation, telling the other directly that the relationship is in trouble or that you wish it to be over. Indirectness, as noted earlier, gives subtle clues about the deterioration of the relationship and any other type of withdrawal or avoidance. A self-oriented tactical move would be manipulating the other to accomplish the dissolution, whereas an other-oriented move would help the other by "letting him down gently."

Not only do the tactics you use affect how the termination is experienced, but the way you make sense of the failure of the relationship has an impact. Newman and Langer [354] surveyed divorced women and discovered that those who blamed their ex-spouse for the dissolution (he was selfish, lacked emotional maturity, had behavior problems, and others) adjusted less well to the divorce than those who made "interactive attributions." An "interactive attribution" would be attributing the cause for failure of the relationship to incompatibility, changing lifestyles, lack of cohesiveness or love, money problems, or lack of communication. A related finding by Wilmot, Carbaugh, and

Baxter [547] surveying long-distance romantic partners who broke up found a similar result. In this case, unilateral terminations yielded more dissolution pain than did mutual dissolutions. Clearly, how one goes about terminating a relationship affects the long-range outcome for both yourself and feelings about the prior relationship.

One final note about the communication behaviors during deescalation and dissolution. The "reversal hypothesis" holds that communication behavior during dissolution is the opposite of that during initiation and moves toward intimacy. Some recent research shows reversal occurring in some behaviors like self-disclosure, but not in those linked to one's knowing of the other [34, 32]. Put simply, if we know things about the other, they are often used in the dissolution process to harm the other.

Relational Oscillation.   It is easy to assume that the process of dissolution is straightforward and moves step by step without faltering toward a predetermined goal. For example, talking of "stages" or "tactics" can sometimes imply that disengaging is without attendant difficulties. But most of us know that the process is not linear and step by step. Rather, it more often reflects the dialectical tensions in relationships—as we try to get farther away from the other, we occasionally move closer. The relationship *oscillates* between closeness and distance, with the participants moving farther and farther away. The oscillation of the dyadic partners between closeness and apartness can sometimes cause distress for others involved in a dissolution. For example, if Phil has filed for divorce and has another romantic partner, she will probably be distressed if he engages in love making with his soon-to-be ex-wife. Yet such patterns of oscillation are very common. One young college male, in his words, "terminated seventeen times." After a few oscillations, the "on again off again arrangement is too painful to be sustained" [524]. Given all the oscillations, the repetitive moves toward distance have a cumulative effect, with the discord feeding back into the relationship. The partners move farther apart over time, until the relationship can be dissolved. The relationship tends to get into "autodisintegration," where the regressive spiral picks up speed until a dissolution is achieved.

The "lingering lover" syndrome, where the movement toward dissolution is less rational, straightforward, and sequential than many think it should be, occurs for many reasons. For one, the pain of dissolution does not hit many people ahead of time. But moving farther away makes them understand the positive features of the relationship, so they move closer. Upon moving closer together they are reminded of their dissatisfactions, and they move away again. A second reason for oscillation is that people often discover their goals after they act. One may move away from a friend, lover, or family member without consciously realizing it, then discover that one really does want to see the relationship end.

Oscillation is, in fact, the most common of termination trajectories. As Baxter says, "The most frequent dissolution trajectory was unilateral and indirect, requiring multiple 'passes' through the model, with no attempted repairs, and with an outcome of relationship termination . . ." [29]. Yet when asked what they regretted about their process of disengagement, the most frequently mentioned regret was the "overreliance" on indirectness [29].

The Leaver and the Left

When Betsy was in the first grade, her closest female friend turned to her one day and said, "I don't want to be your friend anymore—your overshoes squeak in the snow." Such explicit comment on the reason for the termination, while it occurs sometimes, is less common than the indirect approach. The research by Baxter demonstrated most relationships are dissolved by *unilateral indirect* moves. It is therefore a useful distinction to make between the *leaver* and the *left* in a relationship.

In the current college lingo, the one who is left has been "dumped." Most people, at some time in their history of intimate relationships, have been left by either a close friend or a romantic partner when they wanted the relationship to continue. Just as people fall in love at different rates, they also fall out of love at different rates. But whether you are the "leaver" or the "left," the emotional impact of terminating an important relationship is strong. The person who initiates the separation typically feels guilty and even anguishes over the damage done to the other. The one who is left usually feels traumatically rejected, misused, and aggrieved [525]. But *both* the leaver and left typically suffer, though when you have just been left it is hard to imagine that the other is also hurting emotionally. Even when the leaver has some other intimate to turn to, this third person cannot shield the leaver against the disruptions in family relations and sadness over loss of the relationship. The leaver has one big advantage, however, in having more time to work through the hurt of separating, whereas the bomb often just drops on the one who is left.

In nonintimate relationships, the process of leaving is not judged as harshly as in marital relationships. Whereas the lover "walks out," the business executive or college professor "moves on" when he or she dissolves relationships with associates. Often the one who leaves a work association for a better job is treated with warmth and kindness. The replacement of someone for nonintimate functions is seen as easier than for intimate functions, and therefore dissolution is not typically seen as negative. Also, outsiders often see good reasons for leaving. Young people who leave home are often seen as "needing to be on their own," and their taking leave of parents is considered natural. The heaviest moral judgments are typically saved by onlookers for the leaver of a committed romantic relationship.

The distinction between the leaver and left is a bit too simplistic for a complete view of the process, however. For instance, even though a husband's actions may precipitate the break in the relationship, in 70 percent of the cases the wife actually files for divorce [287]. One counselor maintains that in most of the cases she has handled, the man "sets up" the woman to be the leaver, at least technically. He then can claim that the divorce was her idea.

The leaver and left distinction may give the impression that the one who is left is more attached than the one who leaves. However, many an anguished romantic partner has terminated a relationship because the other does not love them as much as they love the other. Similarly, some people see the end coming and rush to be the first one to "call it quits" so they can tell themselves and others that the "breakup was my idea." Hill, Rubin, and Peplau [214] found that most people claimed the breakup was their own idea. I call this tactic the *First Strike Capability*, similar to nuclear attack. When you see the enemy building up missiles and poised to strike, you destroy them first. Many a person has said, "Just when I was thinking about cooling it with him, he breaks off the entire relationship. I just wanted to tone it down a bit, not destroy the whole thing."

Hill, Rubin, and Peplau [214] also found that college students structure their breakups around the times when external events can help them dissolve a relationship. Assuming that prior to a breakup one of the persons is less involved than the other, their patterns for timing the breakups differ. There is a strong tendency for the less-involved person to initiate breakups near the end or the beginning of school or during the intervening summer months. In contrast, if the more-involved partner is the one who initiates the breakup, it usually occurs during the school year, October to March. Of course, the summer months are when the students are more likely to be separated by natural forces—jobs and returning home to different areas. The less-involved person more often uses these natural breaks as a device to allow the termination to occur. And, of course, the ever-present summer romance gets in the way of the original dyad. For the more-involved partner, the intervening summer months often intensify the feelings for the other, whereas the less-involved person finds the feelings waning [214].

Hill, Rubin, and Peplau [214] also found that there are two sides to every breakup; each person sees the process differently. Typically, the two people have different interpretations for the breakup and even recall different events [525]. Not surprisingly, men and women differ in their orientations toward breaking up. College women tended to be more aware of problem areas in the relationship—they were more attuned relationally than were men. Women tend to fall in love more slowly than men and to fall out of love more quickly. This makes for different experiences during a dissolution.

Termination of an important relationship brings emotional trauma. The process *is* difficult, and during the process of termination a person often does many strange things. Not only are there "lingering lovers," but the entire process of decay is usually stormier than the process of building the relationship. And the misperceptions that each had before becoming committed to each other swing back in the other direction. The person often spends an inordinate amount of time saying, "I can't believe I stayed with her for so long. She is a true loser." The misperception continues, but this time differences between the two are accentuated.

Each person pays her or his own "disruption dues." The uncouplng process can be intense and calm, crazy and rational, all within a span of a few minutes. Lying occurs between people who had been each other's best confidant, objects are raided from houses and apartments, locks are changed, valuables are hidden with friends and in safety deposit boxes. Romantic relationships extract the largest disruption dues because of the intense emotions involved. The more exclusive the relationship, the more likely that the disruption will cause trauma for one or both partners. Disengagement from a relationship that one has invested in heavily is painful.

The emotional impacts from dissolving intimate relationships should not be treated lightly. One's definition of self usually comes into question, there are periods of guilt and remorse, and then there is the long, hard road to re-creating one's life. One must adjust to all sorts of unexpected happenings. One divorced woman, for example, received an average of fifty Christmas cards each year from the friends she and her husband had over the years. The first Christmas after her divorce, she got one card. Wallace suffered a chain reaction in his family from his divorce. His sister, to whom he had been close all his growing years, essentially "wrote him off" after he got his divorce, thus adding to the pain of redefinition. Two years later their relationship was still stalled and unsatisfying for both of them. The identity that one builds up with another person as a dyadic unit gets shattered. The dissolution of any important relationship is "like traveling to a foreign country. Few of us are eager for the journey; few can afford the fare; and few know how to cope enroute or what to expect when we arrive" [128].

There is one overrriding reason for so much discord and misunderstanding between the leaver and the left. The leaver, as we noted, often gives subtle hints about the desire to disengage. For example, such remarks as, "I'm really wanting some time for myself," "I need to study in an unbroken way this quarter," or, "I'm really tired of socializing" might be simple statements, or they might be disguised attempts to distance the other. When the leaver uses indirectness, the left does not get the hint. If you talk to the leaver, he or she says, "I don't know why it took so long for it to sink in—it was right there for all to see." Yet when you talk to the left, he or she says something similar to what Mike, who was left after thirteen years of marriage, said: "I knew she wasn't very happy, but I didn't know she was *that* unhappy. She was pretty cold for the last two years, but I didn't see it as threatening our family life."

The leaver and left have such different experiences because *they use unmatched relational frames* for interpreting the communication events. The leaver will think, "I'm going to get out of this, so how can I drop a clue? Well, I'll just make myself less available until he gets the point." Meanwhile, the left interprets the distancing and unavailability of the other as, "My partner just needs some space for awhile; we'll get close again after finals week is over." Of course, one *can* only need space and all attempts to move slightly farther away do not signify an impending termination (which, of course, makes predicting even more difficult). But when the moves do hint at termination, the other misinterprets the moves. That is why at the end of a dissolution process, one person says, "I just can't see how he didn't know it was coming," and the other says, "I had no idea this was going to happen, but she had decided two months earlier."

Once one person in a dyad starts to believe the relationship is "dead" or "fated for destruction," it often is. When the relational interpretative frame becomes negative, one of the persons sees everything in negative terms, and communication events just reinforce the negative perception of the relationship. People act on their expectations whether they express them to the other person or not, and their beliefs about the relationship become a self-fulfilling prophecy, with demise just around the corner.

Sometimes, the "left" will fight back and struggle against the impending dissolution. One man, whose spouse left him in Seattle and moved to Missoula, rented billboard space on the major thoroughfare in town. The large billboard said:

Unfortunately, since I did not know them, I can't tell you if they got back together.

Values of Termination

If dissolution of an important relationship is difficult for people, why do they engage in termination? Obviously, there must be something in it for people to engage in a painful process—some goal that counterbalances the difficulties.

A relationship can stabilize or dissolve for hundreds of reasons. Basically, however, the decision to dissolve a relationship is the flip side of the decision to continue. People may stay in a relationship that is unsatisfying because of lingering attachment to the other, feelings of obligation to the spouse or children, not wanting to hurt oneself or the other, fear of the unknown, the difficulties of constructing a single lifestyle, financial uncertainties, or the willingness to be faithful to one's wedding vows [525]. A person evaluates the attractions of the current relationship, the barriers to dissolution, and alternative attractions available [287]. If one decides to not terminate an important relationship and to become more committed to it, one can stabilize it by (1) increasing the attractiveness of the relationship, (2) decreasing the attractiveness of alternative relationships, or (3) increasing the barriers against a breakup [286]. When family and friends make it clear that they will no longer consider you worthy of family love and support if you divorce, they are trying to increase the costs of termination so you will not divorce. On the other hand, when your close friend says you can have "anyone you want" as a romantic partner, he or she is trying to assure you that alternative relationships are attractive and accessible to you. One's "comparison level" for available alternative relationship has a marked impact on the willingness to terminate an ongoing relationship. If, as is the case with a large number of people, you are involved in an outside relationship, it affects your level of comparison. You literally can compare the rewards of the two (or more) relationships to see which is more fulfilling. Similarly, a popular person can linger longer over falling in love because of the available alternatives. In an ongoing relationship, if a person's outcomes fall below a critical point of comparison, he or she terminates it [227]. People terminate their relationships when the rewards are no longer sufficient to offset the costs.

A precise estimation of the rewards and costs of termination is difficult for most people. One man terminated a marriage and was surprised when his ex-wife moved 1200 miles away with his two children. He had anticipated having an ongoing daily relationship with the children. Another man who terminated his marriage found himself unable to deal effectively with his guilt. As a result, at the last minute he gave his wife the house, bought her a new car, and voluntarily agreed to give her 75 percent of his take-home pay each month. Now, two years later, he cannot afford to travel to visit his children more than once a year. Many ex-spouses, whether male or female, experience economic distress—the cost of maintaining two households is greater than maintaining one. Many a father has been strapped by heavy financial loss and obligation and many a mother has been left without viable economic means. It is more common than not that after a period of time the man (or woman) stops paying child support and maintenance. Such turns of events are difficult to anticipate when trying to weigh the advantages and disadvantages of termination.

The rewards of dissolving a relationship are as varied as the reasons for staying in a relationship. Many people who terminate a relationship feel a positive emotional impact from "becoming free again." Some, in fact, report an almost "immediate emotional uplift" [290]. Especially when one has been in a frustrating, debilitating relationship and has put a lot of effort into making it work, the decision to terminate can ease a heavy burden. In addition, a termination of a relationship allows for a new relationship—one can "start over." Often one finds someone else who "fits" better—who shares more of the same values, responds more fully to one as a person, and generally provides more rewards. The new intimate often provides the functions the previous one did not. If the first partner did not openly share feelings, the second probably does. Similarly, the new intimate may become proficient in carpentry, cooking ability, avant-garde attitudes, or whatever skills the first partner lacked.

Termination also directly affects one's self-concept. In many destructive relationships it can be a choice between "saving the relationship" and "saving yourself." In such cases, the choice for termination can allow one to grow and change in ways that would not be possible with a continuing commitment to the first person. In a new relationship, new parts of the self can become activated. Following a divorce from an unsatisfying marriage, many people find themselves more open, caring, and expressive than they thought possible. Carl, a man of forty-seven, was unable to touch people physically or express openly any concern for them. Three years after his divorce, he has become a gregarious, physically affectionate, expressive person. One's "personality" can change as a result of a dissolution.

Another positive feature of some dissolutions is the effect dissolution has on your other relationships. Not only might you have a more successful replacement relationship and have an increase in self-esteem, but other relationships can be enhanced by the dissolution. Two friends who stop seeing one another because one of them has fallen in love may find it easier to spend time together when the lover has left. Similarly, many a parent has discovered that after the trauma of a divorce, relationships with the children improve. Removal of someone from the family system can open new possibilities.

Just as staying in a relationship is not a guarantee of happiness, neither does dissolving a relationship always lead to positive outcomes. Dissolution, being part of the dialectic of relationships, brings both pain and release and is rarely only noxious *or* ecstatic. But terminations happen because one of the partners expects some positive value from it. The experience may be different for the "leaver" and the "left," but in most terminations some positive result ensues.

RELATIONAL REDEFINITION

Termination Myths

Throughout this chapter the words *termination* and *dissolution* have been used to characterize the process of the weakening of the dyadic bonds between a formerly close dyadic pair. Just as saying a dyad "decays" implies that the dissolution is necessarily negative, to talk of termination and dissolution implies that the relationship between two people stops.

The everyday language that people use to describe the deterioration of a relationship gives the impression that after termination a relationship comes to an abrupt halt. Rejected lovers speak of "being dumped last Friday," and the person who "called it off" may well say something like, "I told her that our relationship was over." The participants attribute the drastic alterations of their relationship to a "termination." Actually, when a relationship is "terminated" it is usually *redefined.* The uncoupling process will drastically alter the patterns of interaction and put the dyadic participants at different places geographically, but in a very real sense, the old relationship cannot be stopped dead in its tracks. The influence of the other lives on, even in minute amounts, throughout the person's lifetime.

Divorce, or any other dissolution, "does not break clean." There is always a residue to be dealt with [65]. Our past relationships haunt us; the ghost of the other hovers about, ready to pop up at inappropriate times. The active, ongoing transactions with the other may come to an abrupt end, yet the dyadic influences may linger for years. And the longer and more important the previous relationship, the stronger the residual influences. More than one person has rushed into a second or third marriage on the "rebound," in an attempt to erase the influence of the other. However, just like an eighteen-year-old who does exactly the opposite of what his or her parents want, if the previous partner is your frame of reference the relationship still has influence. In a very real sense, then, any important relationship is never just "ended." It is dramatically transformed; but the influences linger on. Many people can describe quite graphically the loved one who left them, and they never quite get over it. For some, the friend who suddenly terminates a relationship remains a source of confusion for years. If the participant says, "Well, the relationship just ended on that Friday night—Bam!!

it was over," the odds are that the relationship has more influence on the person's feelings and current choices than we would ever guess.

Further evidence of the lingering effects of a past relationship commonly is found. For example, Julie had broken up with Stan and was involved with Kirk for over five months. One day she was hiking with Kirk in Montana's Bob Marshall Wilderness Area and she turned to him and said, "Stan, I. . . ." Many a person has reacted to some stimulus and used the name of a former loved one for their current partner. Julie used to hike with Stan, and being back in that situation triggered her use of his name for Kirk. As Dean Pioli, a former student of mine, once said, "Termination is often more of a *transitional* than a terminal phase." The influence remains, either apparent to all or just under the surface.

The person who was left often harbors resentment about the relationship for a long period of time. The scorned lover, for instance, may react to the "end" of the love affair by moving to Alaska to be a smoke jumper, quitting a job, or drastically changing a lifestyle—all attempts to get away from the former relationship. The person makes many decisions in such a way to state loudly and clearly to the world that he or she is not being influenced by the relationship. People move away to show they are *not* tied in with the former partner. But the forces of the relationship linger still. Many a man or woman has been dragged into court by an ex-spouse who continues to exercise influence, albeit in negative ways. One's wife or husband becomes an ex-wife or ex-husband, but never a nonwife or nonhusband. Only those we have not been in a relationship with can be nonintimates; others are ex-lovers, ex-friends, or ex-spouses.

Instead of just wanting a former intimate to no longer be important, one can actively work to redefine the relationship. Just as two participants worked to define their original relationship, they can cooperate to redefine the waning relationship. In one class of forty students studying the process of development and dissolution, I asked how many had been successful in redefining a former love relationship into a friend relationship. Five people were able to give accounts of a successful transformation of the basis of the relationship from romance to friendship. Jim told us that the woman in each of his four previous romantic relationships still considered him a friend.

Relationships *can* change their bases if the participants are willing to continue to invest time and energy in assisting one another work through the processes of change. Of course, this demands a lot from the participants. It is difficult to be both a prosecutor of relational change and a counselor to the other at the same time. But the rewards that people reap from redefining their relationships remove many of the traumatic effects of the terminations. I know three divorced couples in which the ex-spouses still consider themselves friends. They actively assist each other, give a few limited favors to each other, and generally act as valued friends, although they are not as close as when they were romantic partners. In fact, many people who have success-fully redefined a romantic relationship report it *more* satisfying to be the person's friend than it ever was to be their romantic partner. Whole areas of personality do not have to be worked out, synchro-nized, and negotiated. The relationship may take on the character of a brother–sister relationship. And once the partners are far enough away from their own dissolved romantic relationship, they can offer words of encouragement and advice to each other, even for how the other can be more effective in his or her current romantic relation-ships. Obviously, if the romantic couple are parents of children, such a friendly relationship can work to the advantage of all concerned. Don and Lisa had three children before they divorced. Within two years, each had remarried. Now, four years later, Don and his wife live four blocks from Lisa and her husband, and the children have two homes where they are loved and welcomed. The two couples even belong to the same church and are supported by a network of friends. Don and Lisa are an exemplary case of two former romantic partners who have productively redefined their relationship.

Relationships other than romantic ones can also be redefined. For-mer friends can spend less time together and return to an early stage of being friendly but not integrated as friends. Counselor and client can alter their aider–aided dyad to allow themselves to be peers. Roommates can move to being casual acquaintances, and a parent–child relationship can change into an essentially peer relationship—two adults meeting and sharing. Former teachers can be redefined as friends or as strangers, depending on your preferences. Any relation-ship can be redefined to a lesser or greater level of intimacy, and if you were once very close to someone, you have the option of having a changed relationship in the future.

The dissolution of a dyadic relationship, therefore, is not quite as simple as it sounds at first glance. In most cases the effects of the rela-tionship continue to arise occasionally, and in some cases the partners are able to negotiate a new relationship. Of course, whether we are speaking of a romantic pair or a friendship pair, the continuing rela-tionship can be redefined.

Network Realignment

A relational dissolution does not occur in a vacuum. Our networks of relationships both affect the dissolution and are affected by it. Parks and Adelman, for example, found that, "Individuals who received more support for their romantic relationship from family and friends . . . were less likely to terminate their romantic relationship" [379]. And, of course, when a dissolution occurs, it affects those close to the two people involved. Every divorcee experiences the "community divorce," with the alterations in family members, friends, and others in the wider community as a result of the dissolved relationship [65]. And, of course, a married couple with children have an "irreversible, indissoluble relationship with each other" [324] through their connections with the children.

A divorce has the most profound impact on the couple, followed closely by the impact on the children. At the present time, more than 60 percent of divorcing couples have children at home, and the impact of a divorce on children cannot be ignored. The effects on children are, of course, as varied as those on the primary dyadic partners. Bob illustrates one viewpoint. He says, "If I ever see my father again, I'll kill him. He ran out on us when we needed him and my mother had to scrape for years just to put food on the table." Yet Becky says, "My father left my mother when I was a teenager. It was the best thing that ever happened in our family. I love both my mother and father now and I didn't before." Children are profoundly affected, and some recent studies suggest that after a year most of the children "return to normal developmental progress" even if they have been negatively affected [525]. There is much research currently being conducted to assess the impact that divorce has on children of all ages, but one of the common themes is that the child will often blame himself or herself for the parents' relational termination. Lamar, a seven-year-old, says that there are two kids in his class with the same "problem": each has a father and a stepmother and a mother and a stepfather.

At the current time, some 17 percent of all children—one in six— are living in families headed by a single parent, with an increasing number of those single parents being fathers. There are cases of single women bearing children with the intention of raising them themselves, homosexual couples raising children together, and single men and women adopting children—which was unheard of a few years ago. The notion that the ideal family consists of a mother, father, and children living as an intact unit, with the father working and the mother at home, is rapidly fading [285]. For instance, in 46 percent of the families with children under eighteen, both parents work. And future trends are even more shattering to the traditional American ideal of the family unit. It is projected that 45 percent of those children born in 1977 will live in a single-parent home sometime before they are eighteen [285].

The family is not dying, but it is being rapidly transformed and altered. Children are being raised in configurations of relationships thought impossible just a few years ago. Our language hasn't even kept pace with the changing reality for a significant number of children. When the parents remarry, for instance, and the children are living with the mother, they have a mother and a stepfather. Yet the natural father, who is also remarried and maintains close contact, still exists— so the stepfather really does not meet the classic definition. Then, what of the father's wife? If she and the father do not have custody, then is she to be considered a "stepmother" who has replaced the mother? Margaret Mead makes the point that when the parents remarry we need terms for "father's wife" and "mother's husband" to be used openly and freely by the children [324]. It is very confusing for all concerned.

We need to remain open about the possibilities for definition of families. It might be more constructive to work out other options creatively. For instance, some family-therapy specialists are calling for "retribalization," the bringing in of significant others from the extended family to help a person in a time of crisis [470]. A similar concept could be invoked to discuss the raising of children when the natural parents are no longer around. The central issue is whether children will have loving and nurturing adults in their world who will care for them—not whether those adults are the natural parents. Often children get more love from concerned friends and extended family members such as cousins than from the nuclear family unit.

Not only does a relational dissolution cause difficulties for dependent children, but other people in the network of the relationship also have to undergo change. Parents of the dissolved couple must face a newly defined relationship and usually have to adjust to the presence of a new intimate of their son or daughter. One woman's parents were close to her former husband, and the symbol of closeness in the family was camping. After the divorce, the ex-husband continued to go camping with the parents every summer, although the daughter did not go along. The daughter, now remarried, has been successful at integrating her new husband into her family's inner circle. Each summer, she and her new husband also go camping with her parents.

The network effects of a divorce not only affect children, parents, and others of the immediate family, they also affect friends. Earlier the case was cited where the young woman didn't get the number of Christmas cards she expected. Friends, just like family members, have diverse reactions to a relational dissolution. Miller [331] suggests some of the ways that friends may react to a divorce. They also apply to anyone else in the divorcee's close network of relationships.

- anxiety
- shame
- inordinate preoccupation with the divorce
- desire for a sexual relationship with one of the divorcees
- pleasure about the divorcee's suffering
- feelings of superiority
- surprise and incredulity
- experience of emotional loss and grief

- conflict over allegiances
- disillusionment about friendship
- crisis about personal identity
- preoccupation and curiosity about the settlement

Most persons who divorce have someone in their network who responds in these ways. One jolting example of a reaction to relational change comes from Linda, Elaine's six-year-old niece. Linda had seen Elaine get married and subsequently divorced. Then, when Elaine got married a second time, Linda said, "Elaine, your weddings are so much fun I want to go to *all* of them!"

Some evidence exists that divorce is contagious, and once one person in a social group divorces, others follow suit. The friends or family members see the person go through the grief and pain of a divorce and then realize that the person lived through it. They then may decide to divorce also. More than one family with a large number of children has witnessed brothers and sisters getting divorces one after the other. When multiple divorces occur, the friends and acquaintances then regroup into new configurations. Bohannan [65] cites the example of a "divorce chain," which is becoming more and more common. A man A has been married three times and is currently living with his third wife. Here is the constellation of relationships that developed the few short years after his divorce from his first and second wives:

1. The first wife got remarried to man B. Over the time of some business trips and visits to B's and his ex-wife's house, A and B became business associates.
2. The second wife of A also remarried. She became friends with A's first wife.
3. The third wife of A was the first cousin of B, the man that A's first ex-wife married [65].

There is nothing that automatically precludes men who are married to sisters (and both divorced from the sisters) from remaining and becoming even closer friends. Similarly, Paul is a man in his early twenties whose former in-laws keep in touch with him and treat him with more affection than they do their own daughter. And former wives and husbands do actually join the same social circles in extended friendship networks. The possible combinations of family and friend networks are rich and varied. Some cases are so complex and fascinating that they are difficult for outsiders to believe. Former lovers, ex-spouses, and current friends can be intermingled in complex, supportive, and loving groups.

Relational turnover is part of our lives. With sensitivity and openness toward others, however, satisfying relationships can continue to be built. This chapter may have been troubling to you, for these are difficult issues that must be faced on an individual basis. One of my students, after an intensive reading of some of the literature cited here, said at a party, "Yeh, it is an interesting course. If you take it you may end up with a divorce." The intention is not to drive people to make the decision to dissolve their important relationships, but to help us all become sensitized to the realities around us. If you personally do not undergo a divorce, you will have a close friend who will suffer and agonize from the dissolution of an intimate relationship. It is hoped that you will be able to assist someone who is dissolving a significant relationship. Divorcees are not lepers, and neither are people who stay in long-term relationships and refuse to dissolve them. Each person makes his or her own decisions within the context of the primary dyadic unit. Understanding the processes of initiating, stabilizing, and dissolving relationships may help us to put them into better perspective. How you handle a dissolution of a relationship is no less important than how you initiate or maintain it.

SUMMARY

We all experience a high degree of relational turnover, the replacement of acquaintances, friends, romantic partners, and others. The processes of initiation, stabilization, and dissolution of relationships have some common elements that apply to all forms of dyadic relationships. Most relationships are initiated in an incremental way, become stabilized at some agreed-upon definition, and dissolve. The process of dissolution is clouded in hurt and mystery, but, just like the initiation stages, it can be described as following a systematic course. Most terminated relationships involve some redefinition, with the former friends becoming acquaintances or the former romantic partners becoming friends or enemies. Whenever an important relationship dissolves, there are effects on an entire network of people, including the family and others. Understanding the processes of initiation, stabilization, and dissolution can assist us to cope with the turnover we experience in our own relationships.

Chapter 7

Relational Competence and Enhancement

Conversational Management

Communication Apprehension
Conversational Skills

Relationship Enhancement

Communication Skills Training
Confirmation of the Other
Closedness–Openness

Relational Visions

Summary

All dyadic relationships, regardless of their type, are built, modified, and redefined through individual communication episodes. For instance, if you think about your relationship with your father or mother, you can characterize some of its features. This definition is created by the thousands of transactions that you have experienced together. Although some of our dyadic relationships are composed of such large numbers of transactions, others are built with fewer than 100 episodes (like your relationship with a professor during a school term), yet most of our relationships consist of only a small number of encounters. Whether you are in a life-long or a fleeting relationship, the quality of the communication will determine the nature of each relationship. As Spitzberg and Cupach note, our *relational competence* is a function of the appropriateness and effectiveness of our communication behaviors [473]. And although the demands of each relationship are diverse, there are some common denominators necessary for effective functioning in any relationship. This chapter will examine the communication skills necessary for (1) conversational management, (2) relationship enhancement, and (3) relationships across the life span. The final section will highlight different "visions" or views of communication and relationships.

CONVERSATIONAL MANAGEMENT

Managing the flow of communication in conversations is not simply a "frill" that has no consequences. We construct our relationships— those with friends and romantic partners, those in the family and on the job—with our communication skills. The lack of communication skills has a profound impact on the types of relationship experiences we have. Therefore, such skills are a crucial step in connecting with others.

Communication Apprehension

Someone who has difficulty communicating with others is variously seen as shy, reticent, or afflicted with communication apprehension [253]. McCroskey calls such communication apprehension a "fear or anxiety associated with either real or anticipated communication with another person or persons . . . " [319]. Whether one's apprehension is general across all situations or limited to a specific type of communication event [377], when one faces a situation that provokes anxiety or possible poor performance, it can be quite devastating. People with communication apprehension are perceived as likely to

- Be less socially attractive.
- Be less competent.

- Be less sexually attractive.
- Be less attractive as a communication partner.
- Be less sociable.
- Be less composed.
- Be less extroverted, but of higher character.
- Drop classes more.
- Talk less in small groups.
- Avoid communication that is threatening to them (e.g., giving a speech).
- Prefer large classes.
- Choose classroom seats at the periphery.
- Prefer occupations that require less communication.
- Have lower overall college gradepoint averages.
- Have lower scores on standardized tests given upon high school graduation.
- Develop negative attitudes toward school in both junior high school and college [319].

Communication apprehension has an indirect effect on the lives of a wide range of people. Because those with high apprehension avoid or withdraw from communication, they are perceived less positively than others, and the withdrawal plus the negative perceptions of others leads to negative impacts on their "economic, academic, political, and social lives" [319]. For example, people who have high apprehension are more likely to be lonely than others [559, 558, 44] and to feel alienated from others [376]. Although people with low apprehension may sometimes find themselves in difficulty too, it is clear that high apprehension has demonstrably negative results. There are some training programs for apprehensive individuals to help them with fear and anxiety, but not nearly enough services are available to affect a large number of people who have difficulty communicating.

Quite clearly, communication competence in individual episodes is important to our lives. Moreover, Zimbardo has stated that fully 40 percent of his respondents considered themselves shy and had difficulties in communication situations. Phillips [390] conducted a detailed analysis of the fears and difficulties college students face. The following items consistently emerged from the students' reports:

1. Inability to open conversation with strangers or to make small talk.
2. Inability to extend conversations or to initiate friendships.
3. Inability to follow the thread of discussion or to make pertinent remarks in discussions.
4. Inability to answer questions asked in a normal classroom or job situation.

5. Incompetence at answering questions that arise on the job or in the classroom, not through lack of knowledge but through an inability to phrase or time answers.
6. Inability to deliver a complete message even though it is planned and organized.
7. General ineptitude in communication situations characterized by avoidance of participants [390].

Finally, Wiemann, who studied the perceptions that members of a sorority had of the other women in the house, discovered that the moment-to-moment conversational behaviors of each woman distinguished whether she was judged as a competent or incompetent communicator by the others [536, 537, 538].

The good news is that, "Even relatively small changes in conversational management result in large variations in how others see our competence" [536]. Why is this ability to manage transactions successfully so central to how we are seen in terms of our social competence? Rushing says it best:

> Ordinary, basically honest people give much thought to, and develop a considerable degree of skill in presenting themselves in front of other people. The self is everyone's most valuable possession; one does not present it to the world without protection [426].

In the course of our transactions with others, we confirm both our own and others' selfhood. Goffman states that competence at managing transactions is inextricably linked to the ability to "maintain face" [178]. The need to be a competent transactor is so pervasive that when someone is a "faulty interactant" (to use Goffman's term), that person is called a "cold fish," a "wet blanket," a "weirdo," or some other negative term. To make a transaction flow smoothly, one has to work to accept the other's moves and to structure responses that build on what has come before.

Effective transaction management involves being able to (1) initiate a conversation, (2) maintain that conversation, and (3) bring it to a smooth close. Whether your dyadic partner is your business associate, teacher, friend, lover, relative, or acquaintance, *the management of the separate transactions is the single most important determiner of the quality of the relationship.*

Conversational Skills

The first important skill in transaction management is the ability to initiate a conversation with another. In every episode there is an "initiation imperative," the force demanding that the participants acknowledge one another [158]. As Frentz and Farrell [158] note, the

copresence of the two participants puts pressure on them to acknowledge one another and manifest a willingness to enact an episode. For
instance, when you sit in a room with someone else, unless you both
busy yourselves with some external object such as a magazine, you can
almost feel the pressure to make contact. Nofsinger [357] notes that
people learn to develop a "demand ticket"—they make statements in
order to take the floor and entice the other into the conversation. One
example that he lists is:

A: "You know something?"
B: "What?"
C: "It's time for lunch" [357].

Person A has successfully gotten the attention of person B by making
a demand for it. Children soon learn that if they are to get the attention
of adults, they sometimes need to demand it. When a child says, "Hey,
Mom," he is giving a demand ticket. The statement obliges the other
to respond and be available—or else make an open refusal to do so.

Our greetings to others serve some important functions. Krivonos
and Knapp [265] note that greetings or initiations (1) mark the transition between a period of absence and greater access, (2) reveal information about the state of the relationship, and (3) serve to signal your
accessibility for further talk. The specific cues used to greet others
have also been isolated. One can use these verbal avenues: *verbal
salutes* ("Hi, John, you character you!"); *references to the other* ("Nice
coat you have."); *personal inquiry* ("How's it going?"); and *external
reference* ("Nice day for 40 below, isn't it?"). Nonverbally we open up
for conversation by mutual glances, making head gestures and smiling.
Taken collectively, these verbal and nonverbal cues signal to the other
that we wish to initiate a conversation.

Once the other is engaged in the conversation, the transaction must
be continually moved forward. Each participant employs techniques
for continuing the transaction. After making contact one must be able
to "share speaking turns, and have the interaction flow smoothly"
[208]. And one needs to maintain topic flow while contributing to a
relaxed atmosphere [73]. Wiemann labels the skills as supportiveness,
social relaxation, empathy, behavioral flexibility, and interaction management [536]. If you can "take and make" conversational turns for
you and the other, you will be judged as communicatively competent
and will contribute to a good experience for both you and the other
[323]. You need to signal verbally and nonverbally, "OK, I'm finished
now and it is your turn to talk," not switch topics too frequently, and
help provide for reciprocity for both of you. If you take more than
your share of the "talk time," you can be assured that others will feel
negatively about it, and if you don't contribute, they will see you as
less competent. Talk time needs to be balanced between self and
other.

Showing involvement is an important conversation skill.

One of the most essential skills for maintaining conversations is the art of asking questions. Stech's research showed that closed questions (e.g., "Did you sleep well last night?") elicit simple statements of fact, such as "Yes." On the other hand, open-ended questions (e.g., "How was your night?") are more likely to get extended answers from the other. The art of asking questions and the impact it has on conversations and others' views of us are not fully explored. It is reasonable, however, to assume that good question askers are sought out by others and seen in a positive light.

We must also indicate our *involvement* in the conversation. Those who are involved have a better sense of their own and others' behavior [96], and meet the "involvement obligations" that are present in all interactions [159]. Lack of involvement is manifested in numerous ways. If you are externally preoccupied (watching the skydivers on the horizon while the other is talking) or are too self-conscious (focusing attention on yourself rather than on the other), you are showing alienation from the transaction. Similarly, if you are too conscious of the ongoing transaction (by calling attention to what you are doing in the process of doing it) or if you are too conscious of the other (and show that you are really trying too hard to make an impression), the quality of the transaction suffers.

Once someone produces a sequence of inappropriate behaviors, the uneasiness that occurs is usually contagious—both participants are affected. Goffman [181] says that we all cooperate in supporting the face of the other during the transaction by engaging in a single focus, correctly adhering to rules for switching, changing turns, and making sure that others do not interrupt us. Whenever a person offers a statement, he or she is offering himself or herself for involvement in helping facilitate the exchange.

Seen in the context of protection of the "face" of self and other, the dramatic effects of disconfirming messages seem reasonable. When people give tangential responses, they are making it clear to you that they are not interested in your welfare or your participation in the episode. Similarly, when people give incongruent responses, they are putting an extra obligation on you to work out the inconsistency so that the transaction can continue. And, as Goffman specified, using one-up responses in a conversation is an attempt to make a favorable image of the self at the expense of the other. Clear, congruent, confirming communication best facilitates the participation of each person in the transaction.

The process of terminating an episode is no less important than the processes of initiating and maintaining a conversation. Knapp and his associates [262] have identified the three functions that are performed when ending a transaction. A participant (1) signals inaccessibility for continuing the episode, (2) signals supportiveness of the other participant, and (3) summarizes the essence of the transaction to put it into perspective. These three functions are signaled by both subtle and direct behaviors, including breaking eye contact, showing appreciation for the other ("I really want to thank you"), using an external reason for easing out ("I can see that you are busy"), expressing concern for the other ("Take it easy") or simply referring to the self by legitimizing the parting ("I guess I'm finished"). The study demonstrated that both verbal and nonverbal behaviors provide cues to the impending termination of the conversation. In our everyday transactions, these functions can easily be isolated. For instance, on leaving someone with whom you have had a conversation, typical comments would be: "It's been nice talking to you" (summarizing and supporting); "Well, I have an appointment in ten minutes" (signaling future inaccessibility); and "Thanks for your time" (signaling supportiveness).

There are numerous cases where the ritual of leave-taking is violated, much to the consternation of the participants. I once had a colleague who would stand in the doorway of my office and engage me in very productive, lengthy chats. Then all of a sudden he would disappear without warning. I was always puzzled by my colleague's behavior because there was no termination behavior—no comments, no signaling of supportiveness, just the disappearing act. Similarly, many participants often do not pick up on cues used to signal impending inaccessibility. Tom has become a legend among my co-workers because of his inability to (or desire not to) attend to impending terminations of transactions. Even when someone would say, "Well, I have to go now," Tom would counter with, "Where are you going? I could walk with you." One of Tom's instructors was forced to use extraordinary measures to terminate their conversations. One day, after many feeble attempts to terminate a conversation, the instructor introduced Tom to another instructor by saying, "Tom, this is my colleague Jean. She is really interested in the topic we have been discussing." Then the beleaguered instructor walked away, leaving Jean to deal with Tom's unwillingness to process leave-taking cues.

Albert and Kessler [2] have summarized the reasons people give for ending social encounters. First, they note that there is a socially learned predisposition to provide an external justification for the termination. For instance, an external justification would be, "I have an appointment now," implying that the force of the appointment compels the person to leave. External justifiers can be the physical environment ("Let me walk you to your elevator"), the social environment ("There is Charles, he has been looking for me"; "I have to meet my girlfriend"), or the temporal environment, referring to the external dimension of time as a motivating force ("We have been at this a long time"). Whenever convenient, the person who wants to terminate the conversation will give external reasons for leaving in order to save the face of the other.

If a person uses an internal justification to end a social encounter, he or she normally attempts to present it positively. The use of the summary, pointed out by Knapp et al. [262] does this job well. When someone says, "It was certainly nice seeing you again," he both summarizes the transaction and provides a force for ending the transaction. Often if the summary is inaccurate or unsatisfactory to the other party, the two participants continue the episode in an attempt to find a mutually satisfying conclusion. And often, each person will have a dual summary—one that is expressed publicly and one that is thought privately [2]. The publicly expressed summary will serve the function of stopping the exchange, and the private one will allow the participant to capture the essence of the transaction for her own memory. In the following example, man *A* and woman *B* are saying goodnight after being out on the town together. The public summary is listed first; the words in parentheses are the private summary.

A: "Sue, I sure did enjoy the evening." (Whew—she almost drove me bananas with all her talking during the movie.)
B: "Bob, it was nice. I liked the movie." (What a dull evening it has been. He didn't talk to me even when I tried all evening to engage him.)
A: "Goodnight—see you around campus." (Not if I can help it.)
B: "Goodnight—yes, see you around." (Like in the next century.)

The process of ending an episode is so potentially stress-producing for people that all kinds of pledges and oaths are made about the future of the relationship that may or may not be realistic. Persons will routinely pledge continuity ("See you later"), express good wishes ("Take care"), and generally deny that the termination of the episode means that there will be no further meetings [2]. We are all so used to these norms that many people are offended when someone does not pledge continuity even though both parties know that they will work hard to avoid one another. Frentz and Farrell [158] note that participants effectively end conversations by (1) expressing a mutual desire to conclude the episode, (2) expressing satisfaction with the accomplishment of goals, and (3) proposing the enactment of future episodes.

The effective management of dyadic transactions is at the heart of competent communication. It entails the skills of initiating, maintaining, and terminating individual transactions—whatever the type of dyadic relationship. Hecht's work demonstrates that the effective management of transactions is the key to feeling satisfied with an encounter with someone [206, 207]. His respondents reported that if they felt that a conversation flowed smoothly and that something was accomplished, then they were satisfied with the conversation and wanted to have another conversation with the same person. This applied to transactions with strangers, acquaintances, and friends. While satisfaction with a communicative transaction is dependent on the context [206, 207], the smoothness of the transaction will probably be a factor in most cases. One's transactional management is the best indicator of competence and is related to satisfaction with encounters.

RELATIONSHIP ENHANCEMENT

Maintaining a long-term quality relationship is one of the prime difficulties for people in our age. The "relational turnover" mentioned in Chapter 5 is a reality; people move in and out of our lives. Yet we often want to sustain a satisfying relationship. Members of our family, best friends, and romantic partners all are central to our sense of well-being, and we often want relationships with them to have staying power.

Relationships fail mostly through neglect, and sometimes because of a "bad match." Many people who have witnessed the high divorce rate are pessimistic about relationships and say, "They will all fail," or, "It was meant to happen sooner or later." People spend energy at fixing up a car that is faltering, but often sit idly by and watch a previously good relationship deteriorate into dissolution. Often they take no action until the relationship is beyond repair.

Relationships can be enhanced and improved. Unfortunately, many people do not spend time and energy to improve their relationships. This is not surprising in a culture where, "We wait until families are in serious trouble before we offer any intervention" [268]. It is shocking to realize that in the budget of the National Institute for Mental Health, *less than 2 percent* is allocated for the prevention of mental illness. "Relational illness" is also usually dealt with when it has become severe. We need an ethic of "relational wellness"—putting effort into relationship improvement.

Not all dyadic relationships have received the same amount of research effort as marriages, but we do know the characteristics of satisfying marriages. For example, Lewis and Spanier reviewed over 200 studies and found that satisfied couples experienced positive regard, emotional gratification, effective communication, and considerable interaction with one another [297]. Similarly, it has been found that satisfied couples, compared with dissatisfied couples,

- Reward each other at equal rates.
- Blame and threaten less.
- Emphasize the importance of the relationship when they disagree.
- Resolve conflict more effectively.
- Confirm each other.
- Use more positive statements in response to the other.
- Reciprocate pleasing behaviors.
- Perceive their partners more accurately.
- Agree more on the status of their relationship.
- Disclose more to one another [266, 237].

The communication differences between satisfying and unsatisfying marriages are clear. Similar findings are true for entire families. As a result, one approach for enhancing a relationship is to improve the quality of communication between the partners.

Communication Skills Training

There are some programs for relationship enrichment that offer help for some relationships. Keeping in mind that friendships, work relationships, gay and lesbian relationships, and many nonmarried romantic relationships are not accorded the same attention as marriages, the marital improvement programs are worthy of note. Enhancement or enrichment promotes relational growth by "encouraging the couple to discover and claim their unappropriated relationship potential" [307]. Most skill development programs emphasize systematic training, taking small steps at a time, focusing on process rather than content, and having the skills reinforced by the spouse [237]. The programs also center on a systems perspective (seeing difficulties within the context of a particular relationship), use learning theory principles, and span a short time such as a few weeks [366].

One representative program uses "listening, measured self-expression, selective request-making, provision of positive and corrective feedback, and clarification of intended meanings" as its central focus [480]. Olson [368] sets forth a clear description of a program designed for couples both before and after marriage. Its components are:

Premarital Inventory

- Increase a couple's awareness of relationship strengths and potential problem areas.
- Facilitate a couple's discussion about their relationship.
- Establish relationship with clergy, counselor, or married couple.
- Prime for postwedding enrichment or counseling.
- Refer for intensive counseling if serious problems arise.

Couple's Discussion in Small Groups

- Increase couple's ability and willingness to share with other couples.
- Develop other couples as friends.
- Learn how other couples relate and deal with issues.

Communication Skill Training in Couple's Groups

- Build communication skills like sympathy, empathy, and self-disclosure.
- Build skills for resolving conflict and problem solving [346].

At this point, programs under the guidance of a trainer seem best. But research by Hocker [217] suggests that couples can "make some gains" using self-help materials without much trainer contact [217]. Like any program, marital or relational enrichment is not a cure-all [469, 162]. For example, marital enrichment programs focusing on communication are not much help for distressed couples [66]. Their relationships have already deteriorated so much that they cannot "put into practice the communication skills that would help them lessen their distress" [217]. Nevertheless, if you are interested in marital improvement programs, a good starting point is the review by Galvin and Brommel [162].

One of the key skills that appears in almost all lists for relational enhancement is conflict management. A conflict is an "expressed struggle between at least two interdependent parties who perceive incompatible goals, scarce rewards, and interference from the other party in achieving their goals" [220]. A conflict is set into motion when we see someone as "blocking" us from getting what we want, whether that be money, attention, intimacy, or other objects. The study of conflict is complex and fascinating. For example, the styles that people use, the way power is exercised in personal relations, and the way people fight over content when the distress is really on the relational level are all important topics. For the present, however, suffice it to say that conflict choices have dramatic effects on our personal relationships. For example, Sillars has demonstrated that choosing an integrative strategy (such as problem solving with the other instead of blaming or threatening) is related to greater satisfaction in the relationship [457].

Some central conflict management skills one can use to enrich rather than impoverish their relationship are (1) self-regulation and self-expression, (2) negotiation, and (3) reaffirmation of the relationship. Self-regulation is learning to monitor oneself, not to say all the hurtful things that you might be tempted to blurt out. It is far better to "edit" than to say later, "I wish I hadn't said that." Self-expression is learning to "level"—to tell the other what you are thinking and how you are reacting to them and the relationship. Negotiation is the skill of working with the other so that you will both get some of what you want. Often two people get locked in a struggle and the struggle becomes more important than the relationship. They want to "win" no matter what the outcome. With negotiation, one can learn to reach agreements irrespective of initial bad feelings. Finally, since most of us do not like to have others "come at us," when we engage in conflict with someone who is important to us, we should let them know we value the relationship. Saying, "I really like what we have had and want to get back to that point, but I need to work this out so we can" has a much more productive impact than saying, "Let me tell you what is wrong with you." Metacommunication (talking about the relationship) can give us a buffer for working through difficult spots that arise between us and the other. Two other skills are worthy of more detailed attention—confirmation and sharing information with the other. With this repertoire of skills, one can make strides in improving relationships [220]. (For a more complete treatment of conflict, consult Hocker and Wilmot.)

Confirmation of the Other

It was noted that reciprocity, positive affect, and empathy are all central contributors to a relationship that is being improved. Confirmation involves more than just noticing the other; it entails responsiveness, "tuning in" to them, and enacting appropriate conversational and relational skills. As such, confirmation is one of the most effective ways to receive positive responses from another person, whether it is your boss, subordinate, counselee, or intimate. For instance, if someone comes to you with a personal problem and lets you know his life is a shambles, your attentive listening and responding to him will often be of considerable help. It is amazing how curative it is for people just to have a receptive listener—one who does not castigate them but rather, participates with them in working through the problem. Watzlawick, Beavin, and Jackson [519] have demonstrated that you can respond to another by accepting, rejecting, or denying them. Whether you accept others' ideas or openly disagree with them, you are still confirming their existence, which is an appropriate response. Denial of the other person's existence, however, is a disconfirming response. If the other says, "I have been really feeling bad about us," and you turn and walk away, you disconfirm the other.

The most effective responses are those that acknowledge the other, clarify what he or she said, give a supportive response, agree about content, or express positive feelings [456]. Confirmation is present in all these acts. Conversely, a disconfirming response is one that is irrelevant, tangential, impersonal, incoherent, incongruent, or impervious. Confirmation, therefore, involves showing that you believe that the other is worthy of notice. A message sent to another, whether it agrees with the content the other expresses or not, is perceived as confirming to the extent that it:

1. Expresses recognition of the other's existence as an acting agent.
2. Acknowledges the other's communication by responding to it relevantly.
3. Is congruent with and accepting of the other's self-experience.
4. Suggests a willingness on the part of the speaker to become involved with the other person [455].

Watzlawick, Beavin, and Jackson [519] speculated that agreement with the content was not a necessary part of confirmation. Subsequently, however, a number of researchers have found that agreement with the content of the other's message seems to be important to the perception of being confirmed. Young children, for instance, use content disagreement to disconfirm the other. When the older brother says, "Carina, you are wrong. That is not how you spell it," he is not only disagreeing on the content level, but also sending a barbed relational message. Carina, in retaliation, will assert her right to know how to "do it herself" in an attempt to regain her feeling as a person who has some influence. Certainly agreement with the other can aid her in feeling confirmed, but whether or not it is a prerequisite is unclear [100]. One thing remains apparent: Confirmation is basic to all social contexts and is a communication factor that has consistently appeared in numerous studies as being important [100].

One of the best ways of understanding confirmation is to see examples of disconfirming messages. Virginia Satir says that all our messages can be characterized as "validate me" messages, and when the other person pretends that we do not exist, or disconfirms us by transacting in a bizarre way, it undermines our confidence [432]. When someone sends a message to another, it has the following four parts:

1. I (the sender)
2. am saying something (message)
3. to you (the receiver)
4. in this situation (context) [432].

When someone sends a disconfirming message, it places an extra burden on the receiver. Someone who tells you to "come closer, darling" but stiffens when you approach is sending a message that is incongruent and unclear [432]. You the receiver cannot easily decode the relational message.

A disconfirming message is usually unclear about who the sender is, what is said, whether it applies to you as a receiver, or whether it is apropos to the context [191]. An example of denying who the sender is occurred between Linda and her mother. Linda, a woman of twenty-eight, was living at home while her husband was stationed overseas. Her mother told her, "Linda, the neighbors think that you should not stay out late partying." When Linda said, "Mom, are *you* the one who thinks that I shouldn't stay out late?" she replied, "No, I personally don't have an opinion. But the neighbors are concerned about you." The mother denied that she was the one sending the message. Other forms of this communicative denial are to claim that one is in a trance or that one is possessed by a spiritual force beyond one's control. In addition, people may try to absolve themselves of responsibility by claiming that nothing was intended. One time a relative of mine, rather miffed over some personal decisions of others in the family, slammed the mail down on the dining room table and stomped out of the room. If confronted, she would have said, "I didn't mean anything. I just gave you the mail." Denying one's nonverbal messages is a form of denying message responsibility and places an extra burden on the receiver.

Talking in overly general terms is a common way to deny that a message is aimed toward a given person. If you are at a family gathering and someone says, "College students sure are an irresponsible lot these days," you can rightly feel a bit thrown off balance. It is unclear if the message is meant for you. The parent who shouts, "People in this house sure are messy," may or may not be sending the message to you. Finally, a person can deny that the message was meant for the particular situation by claiming that what was said was meant for a future time, not for the present. Whenever someone denies sending a message yet is still sending it, he or she is placing extra responsibility on the receiver, an action that is potentially disconfirming. We all err in being unclear, unsupportive of others, and disconfirming at times. But the first step in constructing confirming messages is to take responsibility for the messages and be clear about who they are addressed to and what they are intended for. Confirmation is undermined by lack of clarity.

In addition to the four basic forms of denial, people have an unlimited array of techniques for disconfirming others. Some of these techniques will be reviewed so you can recognize and respond appropriately to them.

Disconfirming responses usually make the recipient feel confused, unworthy, manipulated, or just plain devalued. It helps to be able to identify these responses. Several writers have isolated various types.

One of the earliest persons to study disconfirming responses was Piaget [393]. He noted that children often engage in parallel play; they are in close physical proximity yet play independently of each other. Each one carries on his or her own conversation irrespective of what the other says. Adults, too, engage in "collective monologues," with each person continuing a conversation independently of the other's responses. There are two conversations occurring under the guise of one; therefore each person is disconfirming the other.

Ruesch [423] identified a type of disconfirmation that he labeled the "tangential response." A tangential response is one where the reply (1) inadequately fits the initial statement, (2) has a frustrating effect, (3) is not geared to the intention behind the original statement, or (4) emphasizes an aspect of the original statement that is incidental. The most common form of tangential response is when someone continually switches the topic. Here is an example:

HE: Sally, would you like to go to the park this Sunday?
SHE: You mean Playfair Park? Why that park is really overrun with people during the weekend. I much prefer larger parks with fewer people. In fact, did I ever tell you about my trip to the backcountry of Yellowstone? It was 1972, and we had just decided that the city was unbearable. Then we . . .

She fails to confirm his communication attempt by switching topics. Tangential responses occur for many reasons. Sometimes people just want to talk about their own ideas, sometimes they are consciously giving a one-up response, and at other times they are simply unable to keep up with the flow of the other's conversation and, as a result, switch topics. A tangential response is disconfirming because it undermines the other's attempt to get recognition and confirmation for his or her own topic. The example of a tangential response between a mother and child that Ruesch provides is a classic:

BOY: Look, Mom I found a snail.
MOM: Go wash your hands.

Ruesch refers to the tangential response (and others) as being "disturbed messages" and provides an interesting poem that captures the essence of all forms of disconfirmation.

Too much,
Too little,
Too early,
Too late,
At the wrong place,
Is the disturbed message's fate [421].

Searles [445] has provided an interesting list of messages that can literally "drive the other person crazy." First, one fosters emotional conflict in the other by questioning the other's adjustment. When Jim
says, "Anthony, you really have a severe problem there. It seems to
me that you are in need of some intensive help," Jim is questioning
Anthony's adjustment. Second, one can deal on two levels of relatedness simultaneously. Satir [432] calls this the incongruent response, in
which the verbal and nonverbal messages do not correspond. Searles
provides an example of a woman patient of his who engaged him in a
very high-level philosophical discussion and at the same time sent very
obvious nonverbal sexual signals. The two levels do not fit together,
and responding to either level left the other message unanswered.

The third way to drive the other person crazy is by the sudden
switching of emotional wavelengths. For instance, in the middle of a
very rational discussion with you about career choices, the other person may suddenly begin screaming at you. Then, just as unexpectedly,
he or she returns to the calm, rational tone. This emotional switching
is difficult to follow. Finally, the continual, unexpected switching from
one topic to another (the tangential response) is an effective way to
challenge the other person's view of a sane and orderly world. Each of
the four ways to drive the other person crazy undermines the other's
confidence in the reliability of his or her own emotional response.

Research on disconfirmation demonstrates that inconsistent or disconfirming messages do have a disruptive effect on the listener and
produce some anomalous behaviors in the receivers as well [281]. People who receive such messages first try to determine the literal meaning, then try harder to figure it out, and finally withdraw from the
interaction. Of course, the one who produces the disconfirming messages does so for reasons. Janet Beavin-Bavelas and her colleagues
have investigated why someone might produce such disturbing messages. They found that disqualifying messages are a "reasonable
response to an impossible situation" [28]. Further, they argue that dis-
qualifications appear in normal conversations when one wants to avoid
a more direct message. The direct message is seen as having negative
consequences, so the disqualified message is a "good solution to a difficult problem" [28]. Regardless of *why* the message is produced, the
receiver must deal with the messages.

One can deal with disconfirming messages [465] in a variety of
ways. Sluzki and his colleagues have described four possible responses

to disconfirming messages.* Some options for responding to disconfirming messages are as follows.

1. *Explicit comment.* You can comment on what the person is doing. For
   instance, when the other gives you a tangential response you can say,
   "I am frustrated by talking to you because you seem to switch the
   topic on me almost every time I bring up something that is
   important." Or if someone suddenly switches emotional wavelengths,
   you can immediately tell her what she has done. The basic notion
   behind explicit comment is to isolate accurately what the other is
   doing and then point it out to him or her. Often people get used to
   communicating in disconfirming ways without becoming aware of it.
   When I was in my first year of college teaching, a student
   approached me and pointed out some disadvantages of my style of
   communicating. (I was like a machine gun rattling off studies.) To this
   day, his explicit comment has helped to clarify and improve my
   communicative style.

2. *Withdrawal.* This is a common strategy for dealing with
   disconfirmation. When you can't reform the other, just leave. Often,
   however, if you are in continual contact with the person (for
   instance, a work associate), withdrawal continues to build tensions.
   You can withdraw by refusing to transact further or by physically
   withdrawing from the person's presence. Withdrawal works best
   when the reason for the action is given, for example, by saying, "I
   don't feel we're getting anywhere in this counseling session. You are
   changing the subject while saying you want my help. Since I can't
   help you under these circumstances, I suggest we call off our sessions
   for the present."

3. *Acceptance of only one level of the message.* When faced with
   messages that are incongruent or contradictory, just pick the one
   level that you choose to respond to. For instance, someone may be
   putting the "martyr" routine on you, saying with a downcast face and
   stooped, heavily laden shoulders, "It is okay with me if you go and
   have a good time, I'll just stay home and do the cleaning." A possible
   way to respond is by ignoring all the nonverbal cues and saying,
   "Well, since you say you want me to have a good time, I sure will.
   Thanks a lot. See you later." This is called "fogging" in assertiveness
   literature. Of course, you could choose to respond to the other level
   of the message by saying, "The way you are looking tells me that you
   want me to stay."

4. *Counterdisqualification.* Sometimes it is effective to respond to the
   person by counterdisqualifying her or him. If you are placed in a
   position where no correct response is possible, it can be a great
   tension reliever to give equally disruptive responses. Often it will
   shock and upset the other to the point where the issues between you

---

*Sluzki et al. [456] also present additional forms of disqualification which overlap somewhat
with those mentioned earlier, but with a slightly different focus.

will have to be dealt with openly. This is not, however, a blanket license to engage in put-down contests.

The key to confirmation of the other is to communicate as clearly and congruently as possible. By taking responsibility for your messages, by specifying to whom they are sent, and by not engaging in the forms of disconfirmation mentioned earlier, the communicative transactions between two parties can be more effective and fulfilling. Of course, all of us engage in some of these patterns once in a while. But when someone continually disconfirms others, the smooth flow of communication between the participants is disrupted. If both participants have an implicit rule that when they kid around their crazy messages aren't to be taken seriously, then very bizarre patterns can be functional for them. But if one of the participants is confused, is angry, or feels guilty about the transaction, then some disconfirmation has occurred. It has been fairly well documented that disconfirming responses occur with considerable frequency in transactions between disturbed individuals [276, 419, 420, 421, 422, 423, 432, 464, 519, 527, 541]. Conversely, confirmation is "probably the greatest single factor ensuring mental development and stability . . . ." [519].

Closedness–Openness

All dyadic participants decide how much information to share with their partner. In all our dyadic relationships—whether with our romantic partner, friend, family members, work colleagues, or others—we decide, in some cases, to express ourselves and at other times to withhold information. Many parents, for example, are often shocked when they discover some of the events their nineteen-year-old children have participated in; upon discovery say, "Why didn't you tell me?" As noted in Chapter 5, there are dialectical tensions between expressiveness and protectiveness, choices we make about how open or closed we are with others.

No other communication behavior is so closely linked to close relationships as being open—engaging in self-disclosure. As relationships increase in intimacy or closeness, there is an increase in the depth and breadth of information, more exchanging of personal disclosures, expressiveness, "candid self-disclosure," and mutuality of disclosures [531, 170, 55, 6, 341, 284, 288, 450, 155, 413]. As a relationship develops over time, it is characterized by more and more self-disclosure to the point of maximum closeness. In the early stages of interaction people exchange information of a surface level; more delicate information does not occur in conversations until a close relationship has been constructed by both people [46].

Self-disclosure is also incremental; it slowly increases over time in a relationship until it reaches a maximum level. We literally "try out" others by revealing some information and seeing how they respond. If all goes well and they still accept us, we slowly open up more and more over time. Similarly, the other person is incrementally disclosing to us. This "dyadic effect" [242] comes from disclosure prompting disclosure—we disclose to those who disclose to us. As the relationship becomes closer, both people will likely disclose more about themselves. Highly negative disclosures ("I burned down my neighbor's garage when I was seven") are reserved for the most intimate relationships, and women usually disclose more than do men [170, 155].

Just what is self-disclosure? Self-disclosure occurs when you let someone know about you. It occurs "when one person voluntarily tells another person things about himself which the other is unlikely to know or discover from other sources" [386]. Whenever you share personal information with another, you are disclosing yourself to him or her. There are many types of self-disclosure, depending on the type of relationship. For example, the norms for effective self-disclosure are different when you are in therapy or counseling than when you are at work or in your family. What is appropriate disclosure for one context usually is not for the next. Just imagine for a moment all the things your best friend knows about you that others (your supervisor, for example) do not. Usually it is quite a long list.

It is easy to confuse disclosure with evaluation. Some people say, "I want to be open and honest with you—I need to tell you that I think you are a dirty, rotten bum!" Such "openness" is not disclosure; it is evaluation of another in the guise of openness. True disclosure implies risk. You share information with another about yourself that could be damaging to the relationship. You place yourself in a vulnerable position with the other, which indicates trust, and builds the foundation for closeness. We disclose to those we trust and we trust those to whom we successfully disclose.

Disclosure is such an important communication skill useful for relationship enhancement that it is easy to overstate the case for it. Although it is true that all close relationships are characterized by high levels of disclosure, it is equally true that most of our productive and healthful relationships with others are neither intimate nor close. To assume that all our relationships have to be close and personal is to fall for the trap of "ideology of intimacy"—only valuing those relationships that are the most intense [379, 63].

Second, there are limits to the relationship between disclosure and psychological adjustment. In Jourard's early work, he noted that people are attracted to high disclosers and that mentally unhealthy persons are characterized by low rates of disclosure [242]. However, later work by Gilbert [168] showed that highly disclosive behavior in a short-term relationship is seen as inappropriate. Similarly, it has been found that use of intimate disclosure of negative items reduces others' early positive impressions of you. Finally, it has been demonstrated

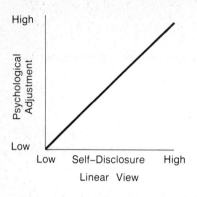

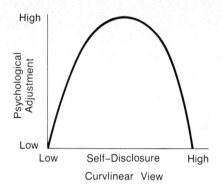

Figure 7-1.   Two views of self-disclosure.

that people who are extreme low or high disclosers are seen by others as psychologically maladjusted. The two views of the relationship between disclosure and adjustment are shown in Figure 7.1. The "linear view" of early formulations implies that the more disclosure the better. But as we all know, randomly walking about and disclosing to everyone you meet is not a sign of good adjustment, nor is "totally opening up" upon first conversing with someone. Rather, the "curvilinear" view is more accurate; both the lack of disclosure and excessive disclosure indicate some form of maladjustment.

Because our focus is on relationships rather than individual psychology, one more limitation to "endless disclosure" needs to be given. In most long-term relationships, once the social penetration process has moved into considerable breadth and depth, it does not continue unabated throughout the life of the relationship. Put another way, we maximally disclose in our closest relationships during the process of building to the level of intimacy we desire. Then there is usually a leveling of amounts and types of disclosure, with occasional dramatic increases in disclosure during times of conflict or of relationship enhancement. The role of disclosure in ongoing, intimate, and successful relationships over time has yet to be adequately researched. Most research has not focused on changes in self-disclosure over long periods of time in a relationship.

All these cautions about disclosure really boil down to one point. Self-disclosure has to be geared to the type of relationship the participants are developing. Self-disclosure is appropriate and effective when it

1. Is a function of the ongoing relationship.
2. Occurs reciprocally.
3. Is timed to fit what is happening.
4. Concerns what is going on within and between persons in the present.

5. Moves by relatively small increments.
6. Is confirmable by the other person.
7. Takes into account the effect disclosure has on the other person(s).
8. Creates a reasonable risk.
9. Is speeded up in a crisis.
10. Shares the context mutually [303].

If your goal is to build a close personal relationship with someone, self-disclosure can be used both to construct and to enhance the closeness. Although it is not "foolproof," self-disclosure can bring people closer together over time.

Openness or expressiveness is represented by disclosure. The other end of the dialectic spectrum, closedness, restricts information flow to the other. Just as people open up information to accomplish goals (to be closer), they also restrict or alter information to accomplish goals (such as protecting themselves). At the least, most of us do not disclose everything; we hold something back [216]. Rosenfeld, for example, found that when men don't self-disclose it is because of a fear of losing control, and women choose not to self-disclose in order not to be vulnerable [412]. As Rawlins puts it, "It is imprudent to make ourselves or our friends excessively vulnerable through conversation" [398]. There are just as many reasons for us to constrict the information flow about ourselves as there are to open the flow.

People withhold information not only about themselves, but about other important topics as well. In close relationships, for example, Baxter and Wilmot found that certain topics are off limits. When asked what topics were taboo their sample of ninety students listed the following: (1) current state of the relationship, (2) extra-relationship activity, (3) relationship norms, (4) prior relationships, (5) conflict-inducing topics, (6) negative self-disclosures, and a few others. Although each topic was taboo for slightly different reasons, some patterns were evident. When asked why a topic was taboo, some of the responses were (1) "Talking about the relationship destroys it"; (2) "If you talk to another, you are vulnerable"; (3) "It is more effective to do things tacitly and implicity"; (4) Talk is futile"; and (5) "Talking about a relationship signals the other that you want to be close, and you might not want to reveal that." Other reasons for not talking about selected items had to do with rights to privacy, fear of negative effects on the relationship, avoidance of embarrassment, and so on [38]. Clearly, people do restrict information in a relationship, and for some good reasons.

Not only do dyadic partners close off information, they also deceive and tell untruths. Some of the forms of misinformation are "make-believe, exaggerations, tall tales, lies, evasion, and misleading" [225]. People justify their lies as a way to cope with external demands [89]. Turner's study [507] found that people lie in order to save face, guide social interaction, avoid tension or conflict, and achieve interpersonal power.

Dyadic partners are also closed in yet another sense. They sometimes will work to not make things clear, a process Laing [273] calls "mystification." Here someone confuses a partner, friend, lover, family member, or other as a way to "maintain the status quo." The forms of disconfirmation mentioned earlier serve to keep the other off balance and "out of the know." If you have a strong desire to be forthright about what is happening in a relationship (you prefer openness), such mystifications and disconfirmations will be very frustrating to you. One way that some people keep others from knowing what is occurring, is to perform "secret tests" on the other [39]. In carrying out a "secret test," one essentially puts forth a test for the other person without telling that person that he or she is being tested. For example, in a budding romantic relationship, one young woman reported this test: "I would intentionally leave him alone in the room with my roommate and then ask him when I returned 'What have the two of you been up to?' If he acted uncomfortable, I'd know that he wasn't faithful (or at least that he was thinking of being unfaithful to me!)." A young man reported his romantic partner putting him to the test in the following way: "During the break, she wrote to me to see if she could come and visit me for a few days. The thing was that I would have to drive 500 miles to pick her up. It was a test to see how much inconvenience I would stand in the relationship." Such tests come in a variety of shapes and forms [39], but the essential point is this: Even in close relationships people see reasons for restricting information from the other and not being totally open.

RELATIONAL VISIONS

We all have visions of relationships, including the presumptions we make about them, what we feel constitutes a good relationship for us, and the way we think relationships ought to be. Many of these views are reflected in popular magazines. A study by Virginia Kidd [256] isolated the predominant visions presented by popular magazines over the past twenty years. Vision I sees relationships within the context of a world that is unchanging, where behavior is seen as right or wrong, and where males and females are supposed to behave according to traditional sex roles. Typically, women are presented as passive homemakers and men as aggressive breadwinners, and if they deviate from the norms, dire consequences follow. You should, according to vision I, put the other first and avoid causing conflict or disagreement with another. As a result, "Vision I offered little outlet for creativity in communication, for formulating new ways of expressing relationship mes-

As a relationship becomes more intimate, the participants engage in more self-disclosure.

sages, or for forming new ways of relating which were not prescribed by the vision" [256].

Vision II, which began emerging in the early 1960s, challenges the idea of permanence. It sees life as changing, and consequently, relationships are also seen as being in flux. The theme that individuals could "talk it out" and that unexpressed conflict would not go away but would continue to affect the relationship led vision II advocates to prize the expression of feelings. In vision II, community and social norms are no longer seen as the final arbiters of relationships. The individuals in the relationship are seen as the best judges of the value of the relationship.

The fact that an enormous number of articles and books deal with the theme of human relationships indicates the importance of the issues. This book also has presented a vision of relationships that by now should be fairly obvious. It reflects a philosophy similar to vision II: that (1) relationships do change, (2) relationships require attention, (3) good relationships are those that meet the expectations of the participants, and (4) relationships can be improved by dealing directly with relational issues.

First, all relationships undergo change. Try as we might, it is impossible to "freeze" a relationship at a given stage. For instance, the excitement that comes with first meeting and getting to know a romantic partner cannot continue to exist to the same degree. As you come to know each other, you respond differently to the relationship, thus effecting change. If you try to preserve the initial excitement by "putting the relationship on the shelf" for a while, you will be disappointed. Change in participants and in relationships is inevitable. "The relationship must undergo metamorphosis at each major turning point in the personal career of each participant" [316]. If the participants are not willing to accept the inevitability of change, difficulties arise. In marital dyads, for instance, many spouses interpret change in the other partner (and therefore change in the relationship) as a betrayal of trust [283]. If the participants change but are unwilling to accept change in their relationship, the relationship will "fade away or be destroyed" [316]. The first step, therefore, in analyzing any relationship is to realize that relationship change is inevitable.

Not only do relationships change, in their formative stages the changes are sequential. Chapter 6 traced the development of interpersonal relationships. Put succinctly, social transactions proceed "gradually and systematically from superficial to intimate topics." As a result, incorrect timing of behaviors, such as revealing very personal information on a first meeting, disrupts the pattern of slow increments and puts strain on the relationship. One's behaviors have to be attuned to the other's expectations. Especially in the case of self-disclosure, when one person honestly shares personal information with another, the timing of the remarks is crucial. The self-disclosure occurs incrementally over time, and as one person increases his disclosure, so does the other person [386]. From the transactional perspective, each person's disclosing behavior is in part a function of the other's, and disclosure at too early a stage is inappropriate. It should be clearly recognized that all continuing dyadic relationships progress through stages [6]. Not only do we sequentially and selectively move toward commitment, but relationships also continue to change after commitment has been made. As we saw in Chapter 6, relationships are initiated, maintained, and terminated; they are continually redefined.

Second, relationships require attention. Because relationships undergo change, the participants need to give their attention to those changes. A romantic pair that marries and has children soon discovers that the old assumptions about the relationship need to be reexamined. Even if no dramatic change occurs in a relationship, attention is required for maintenance of a good relationship. In the case of any committed pair, participants have to *keep working on their relationship until the day they die* [244]. If we all worked on our relationships as much as we did our jobs, we would have a richer emotional life. To assume that your relationship will maintain itself is very naive; it requires time and work. If you pay no attention to your important dyadic relationships, they will fade away.

Third, a "good" relationship is one that meets the participants' expectations. Our dyadic relationships obviously serve different functions for us. We expect to achieve different goals in different dyads. Relationships with spouse, friend, and relative typically serve goals that, although they may overlap, are not the same. Furthermore, one marital dyad may not have the same function as another marital dyad. What is important is the function the dyadic relationship serves for the particular participants.

A good relationship is one that serves the functions for which it was formed [47]. If two people get married in order to increase their joint income and expect and receive little emotional satisfaction, the marriage is a "good" one. Although someone else may observe the marriage and conclude, "I don't see why they stay married. They seem to have little emotional commitment," this is applying one's own goals to their marriage. The two participants may be perfectly satisfied with the relationship.

Bennis et al. [47] have suggested a classification for the primary functions that relationships serve. Type A relationships are formed for emotional–expressive purposes. Emotional–expressive relationships are formed for the purpose of fulfilling emotional needs. Typical dyads in which these functions are prominent are romantic and friendship pairs. Type B relationships are confirmatory; they exist in order to establish reality. As a participant in this type of relationship, you receive (1) information about yourself from the reflected appraisals of others, and (2) information about the situation, your perceptions and definitions of the situation being validated by others. When confirmation is not forthcoming, there is a lack of consensus about reality. Confirmation is obviously crucial in all dyadic pairs, but especially so in the dyads typified by the more personable qualities of friendship, romantic, and generation pairs.

The primary function of type C relationships is change–influence. Some goal is desired, and change or progress toward that goal is the basis for evaluation of the dyad. Typically, the goal has to do with another person, as in an aider–aided dyad. The teacher, the psychiatrist, or the coach has the role of producing change in the other participant. As a result, attaining the goal is a sign of success. In instrumental relationships, type D, the goal is a task; the relationship is formed in order to produce or create. Joining together in a business relationship is one of the simplest examples of this type of relationship often found in superior–subordinate dyads.

The basis for a relationship can shift over time. A teacher–student dyad may begin as a change–influence or instrumental relationship and shift to an emotional–expressive one, the two ultimately getting married. In fact, if the participants want it to, the basis for a relationship may shift many times. As long as the relationship fulfills the functions the participants want, it is a good relationship. However, when a shift of functions occurs that one or both participants do not accept, necessary adjustments must be made. The classic case of a romantic relationship leading to marriage, then, being transformed over time into an instrumental relationship is a case in point. If one person still wants emotional–expressive functions and the other only wants task-oriented behaviors, adjustments are required in order to bring satisfaction to both participants.

Relationships become exceptional and extremely satisfying when they exceed the minimal expectations of the participants [47]. When the behaviors go above and beyond what the role requires, the relationship moves to a new elevated plane. As a teacher, I find that when a student and I become good friends, the relationship becomes something special to us both. The relationship may have begun as instrumental or change–influence based but then moves to a confirmatory or emotional–expressive relationship. In a word, it becomes more personal. When the romantic partner also becomes a friend, the student a colleague (or the professor a friend), and the employee a committed worker, minimal expectations are far surpassed. A good relationship is one that fulfills its functions; a bad one does not. And a superior one exceeds the minimal expectations set for it.

The fourth assumption underlying this work is that it is worthwhile to understand relationships and to deal directly with them *as relationships.* Understanding the relationship you are in, knowing what function you wish it to serve, and being aware that the rules for it are set forth by you and the other participant are the first steps toward improvement. Often, however, these steps come about only when the relationship has begun to deteriorate. When someone recognizes that the relationship is beginning to run out of control, corrective action is necessary. Relationships have synergy, almost a life of their own, and this momentum has to be pointed in constructive rather than destructive directions.

When conflicts arise, the relationship tends to build upon itself in the fashion of spirals discussed in Chapter 5. But a spiral can be changed by some techniques available to everyone. If an issue disagreement starts a relational disagreement (and it almost always does), then *metacommunicate.* Communicate about your communication. In this "stop the world, I want to get off" device, the participants probe for the relational perspectives and metaperspectives of their partners. Tom and Sam reached the point in a disagreement where Tom said, "Anybody who believes that is a fool," and Sam replied, "You think you're so smart that no one else can contribute anything." It makes no difference who alters the spiral, but one must want to metacommunicate in order to deal with the relational conflict. If in this case Tom were to reply, "What is it I do that gives you the impression that I don't want to listen to your ideas?" the way has been opened for Sam to begin sharing his relational perspectives. The key to altering relational spirals is to break out of the pattern of the "natural" response.

If both participants are able to return only hostility to hostility, then those interpersonal "reflexes" will push the relationship so far out of control that it cannot recover. The task is to influence regressive spirals and give them the opportunity to become progressive.

Metacommunication is only one of the possible ways to break the cycle of accusation, defense, and counteraccusation. Instead of seeking to place blame, a participant must accept the situation as given and merely ask himself, "What can I do about it?" [428]. Solutions are preferable to accusations. Participants can also stop the transaction and begin again after a "cooling-off period"—a Taft–Hartley injunction for dyadic relationship. And obviously, they can seek the help and counsel of a third party—friend, co-worker, or professional counselor. The participants, with or without professional help, can also analyze their views of conflicts, the style each person uses to express the conflict, and the structure of the conflict, thereby assessing their relative relational power [220].

Our dyadic relationships are the fundamental units of social exchange. They are both troubling and exciting, both frustrating and fulfilling. When you activate a transaction with another, the relationship is formed, even if briefly. And different relationships bring diverse demands with them.

Because our communication is relationally grounded, persons who are able to adapt to different relational situations are "rhetorically sensitive" and seen by others as competent communicators. The rhetorically sensitive person is able to accept role taking as a necessary part of life, avoid stylized behavior, undergo the strain of adaptation to others, and realize that the other person is a primary constraint on communicative choices [198]. Competent communicators can accomplish their goals in a variety of encounters, and that necessitates the ability to adapt to very diverse requirements. If one follows vision II, one will be interested in enhancing and improving one's dyadic relationships regardless of their level of closeness. All the relationships are important, and all are subject to improvement—and it's worth the effort.

SUMMARY

Relational competence and enhancement is a function of your skill in managing conversations and ability to deal with long-term relationships. People with communication apprehension have anxiety in one or more communication contexts; skill training can help overcome such difficulty. Furthermore, we can all profit from appropriate conversational skills—initiating, maintaining, and closing individual episodes with others. Relationships can be enhanced and improved with specific attention to communication skills, for it is through our communication that we construct our relationships. Of the many important skills, conflict management, confirmation of others, and self-disclosure are some key elements. All of us must deal with the dialectical forces of closedness and openness; as a result we both open up to others and restrict information flow to them. It is hoped that you will have a vision of your relationships that will lead you to enrich and improve your relationships at every stage of life. This book has stressed that (1) relationships change, (2) relationships require attention, (3) good relationships are those that meet the expectations of the participants, and (4) relationships can be improved by dealing directly with relational issues.

References

1. Ackerman, Nathan W. (ed.), *Family Therapy in Transition*. Boston: Little, Brown, 1970.

2. Albert, S., and S. Kessler, "Processes for Ending Social Encounters: The Conceptual Archeology of a Temporal Place." *Journal for the Theory of Social Behavior* **6**(1976):147–170.

3. Alexander, Bruce K., and Gary S. Dibb, "Interpersonal Perception in Addict Families." *Family Process* **16**, No. 1 (March 1977):17–28.

4. Allport, Gordon W., *Pattern and Growth in Personality*. New York: Holt, Rinehart and Winston, 1961.

5. Allport, Gordon W., "Is the Concept of Self Necessary?" in *The Self in Social Interaction, Vol. I: Classic and Contemporary Perspectives*, Chad Gordon and Kenneth J. Gergen (eds.). New York: Wiley, 1968, pp. 25–32.

6. Altman, Irwin, and Dalmas A. Taylor, *Social Penetration: The Development of Interpersonal Relationships*. New York: Holt, Rinehart and Winston, 1973.

7. Anspach, Donald F., "Kinship and Divorce." *Journal of Marriage and the Family* **38**, No. 2 (May 1976):323–330.

8. Apfelbaum, Erika, "On Conflicts and Bargaining," in *Advances in Experimental Social Psychology*, Vol. 7, Leonard Berkowitz (ed.). New York: Academic Press, 1974, pp. 103–156.

9. Argyle, Michael, *Social Interaction*. Chicago: Aldine-Atherton, 1969.

10. Argyle, Michael, and Marylin Williams, "Observer or Observed? A Reversible Perspective in Person Perception." *Sociometry* **32**, No. 4 (December 1969):396–412.

11. Asch, Solomon E., "Forming Impressions of Personality." *Journal of Abnormal and Social Psychology* **41** (1946):258–290.

12. Ayers, Joe, "Uncertainty and Social Penetration Theory Expectations about Relationship Communication: A Comparative Test." *Western Journal of Speech Communication* **43**, No. 3 (Summer 1979):192–200.

13. Ayers, Joe, "Relationship Stages and Sex as Factors in Topic Dwell Time." *Western Journal of Speech Communication* **44**, No. 3 (Summer 1980):253–260.

14. Ayers, Joe, "Perceived Use of Evaluative Statements in Developing, Stable, and Deteriorating Relationships with a Person of the Same or Opposite Sex." *Western Journal of Speech Communication* **46**, No. 1 (Winter 1982):20–31.

15. Ayers, Joe, "Strategies to Maintain Relationships: Their Identification and Perceived Usage." *Communication Quarterly* **31**, No. 1 (Winter 1983):62–66.

16. Ayers, Joe, "Four Approaches to Interpersonal Communication: Review, Observation, Prognosis." *Western Journal of Speech Communication* **48**, No. 4 (Fall 1984):408–440.

17. Bach, George R., and Peter Wyden, *The Intimate Enemy*. New York: Avon Books, 1968.

18. Bales, Robert F., and Edgar F. Borgatta, "Size of Group as a Factor in the Interaction Profile," in A. Paul Hare, ed., *Small Groups: Studies in*

Social Interaction, Edgar F. Borgatta and Robert F. Bales (eds.). New York: Alfred A. Knopf, 1965, pp. 495–512.

19. Bandler, Richard, and John Grinder, *The Structure of Magic*. Palo Alto, CA: Science and Behavior Books, 1975.

20. Bandler, Richard, and John Grinder, *The Structure of Magic*. Palo Alto, CA: Science and Behavior Books, 1975.

21. Banks, Stephen, Ron Sept, and Janet Fulk, "Metacommunication: Toward a Reformulation Through an Interpretation of Intersubjectivity." Paper presented at the International Communication Association Convention, San Francisco, CA, May 1984.

22. Barbatsis, Gretchen S., Martin R. Wong, and Gregory M. Herek, "A Struggle for Dominance: Relational Communication Patterns in Television Drama." *Communication Quarterly* 31, No. 2 (Spring 1983):148–155.

23. Baron, Robert A., and Donn Byrne, *Social Psychology: Understanding Human Interaction*, 2d ed. Boston: Allyn and Bacon, 1977.

24. Bateson, Gregory, *Steps to an Ecology of Mind*. New York: Ballantine Books, 1972.

25. Bateson, Gregory. *Mind and Nature: A Necessary Unity*. New York: Bantam Books, 1979.

26. Bateson, Gregory, Don D. Jackson, Jay Haley, and John H. Weakland, "Toward a Theory of Schizophrenia," in *Double Bind: The Foundation of the Communicational Approach to the Family*. Carlos E. Sluzki and Donald C. Ransom (eds.). New York: Grune and Stratton, 1976.

27. Bavelas, Janet Beavin, "Situations That Lead to Disqualification." *Human Communication Research* 9, No. 2 (Winter 1983):130–145.

28. Bavelas, Janet Beavin, and Beverly J. Smith, "A Method for Scaling Verbal Disqualification," *Human Communication Research* 8, No. 3, (Spring 1982):214–227.

29. Baxter, Leslie A. Personal correspondence, March 22, 1978. Department of Communications, Lewis and Clark College, Portland, OR.

30. Baxter, Leslie A., "Self-disclosure as a Relationship Disengagement Strategy: An Exploratory Investigation." *Human Communication Research* 5, No. 3 (Spring 1979):215–222.

31. Baxter, Leslie A., "Towards a Dialectical Understanding of Interpersonal Relationships: Research and Theory in the 1980's," Keynote address, Ninth Annual Communication Conference, California State University, Fresno, CA, 1982.

32. Baxter, Leslie A., "Relationship Disengagement: An Examination of the Reversal Hypothesis." *Western Journal of Speech Communication* 47, No. 2 (Spring 1983):85–98.

33. Baxter, Leslie A., "Strategies for Ending Relationships: Two Studies." *Western Journal of Speech Communication* 46, No. 3 (Summer 1982):223–241.

34. Baxter, Leslie A. Personal correspondence, March 1984.

35. Baxter, Leslie A., "An Investigation of Compliance-Gaining as Polite-

ness." *Human Communication Research* **10**, No. 3 (Spring 1984):427–456.

36. Baxter, Leslie A., "Trajectories of Relationship Disengagement." *Journal of Social and Personal Relationships* **1**, No. 1 (March 1984):29–48.

37. Baxter, Leslie A., and Jeff Philpott, "Attribution-Based Strategies for Initiating and Terminating Friendships." *Communication Quarterly*, **30**, No. 3 (Summer 1982):217–224.

38. Baxter, Leslie A., and William W. Wilmot, "Communication Characteristics of Relationships with Differential Growth Rates." *Communication Monographs* **50**, No. 3 (September 1983):264–272.

39. Baxter, Leslie A., and William W. Wilmot, "Secret Tests: Social Strategies for Acquiring Information About the State of the Relationship." *Human Communication Research*, **11**, No. 2 (Winter 1984):171–201.

40. Baxter, Leslie A., and William W. Wilmot, "Taboo Topics in Close Relationships," *Journal of Social and Personal Relationships* **2**(1985):253–269.

41. Beach, Wayne, "Implications of the Dyadic Need for Reciprocity." Paper for Interpersonal Communication 590: Dyadic Communication, March 1974.

42. Beatty, Michael J., and Ralph R. Behnke, "An Assimilation Theory Perspective of Communication Apprehension." *Human Communication Research* **6**, No. 4 (Summer 1980):319–325.

43. Bell, Jeff, and Aza Hadas, "On Friendship." Paper presented to the WYOTANA Conference, University of Montana, June 1977.

44. Bell, Robert A., and John A. Daly, "The Affinity-Seeking Function of Communication." *Communication Monographs* **51**, No. 2 (June 1984):91–115.

45. Bellah, Robert N., Richard Madsen, William M. Sullivan, Ann Swidler, and Steven M. Tipton, *Habits of the Heart.* Berkeley: Univ. of California Press, 1985.

46. Bem, Daryl J. "Self-perception Theory," in *Advances in Experimental Social Psychology*, Vol. 6, Leonard Berkowitz (ed.). New York: Academic Press, 1972.

47. Bennis, Warren G., Edgar H. Schein, Fred I. Steele, and David E. Berlew, *Interpersonal Dynamics*, 2d ed. Homewood, IL: Dorsey Press, 1968.

48. Bennis, Warren G., David E. Berlew, Edgar H. Schein, and Fred I. Steele (eds.), *Interpersonal Dynamics: Essays and Readings on Human Interaction*, 3d ed. Homewood, IL: Dorsey Press, 1973.

49. Berg, John H., and Richard L. Archer, "The Disclosure-Liking Relationship: Effects of Self-perception, Order of Disclosure, and Topical Similarity." *Human Communication Research* **10**, No. 2 (Winter 1983):269–281.

50. Berger, Charles A., "Task Performance and Attributional Communication as Determinants of Interpersonal Attraction." *Speech Monographs* **40**, No. 4 (November 1973):280–286.

51. Berger, Charles R., "Proactive and Retroactive Attribution Processes in Interpersonal Communications." *Human Communication Research* **2**, No. 1 (Fall 1975):33–50.

52. Berger, Charles R., "Interpersonal Communication Theory and Research: An Overview," in *Communication Yearbook I*, Brent D. Ruben (ed.). New Brunswick, NJ: International Communication Association, 1977, pp. 217–228.

53. Berger, Charles R., and J. J. Bradac, *Language and Social Knowledge: Uncertainty in Interpersonal Relations.* London: Edward Arnold, 1982.

54. Berger, Charles R., and William Douglas, "Studies in Interpersonal Epistemology: III. Anticipated Interaction, Self-monitoring, and Observational Context Selection." *Communication Monographs* **48**, No. 3 (September 1981):183–196.

55. Berger, Charles R., Royce R. Gardner, Glen W. Clatterbuck, and Linda S. Schulman, "Perceptions of Information Sequencing in Relationship Development." *Human Communication Research* **3**, No. 1 (Fall 1976):29–46.

56. Berger, Milton M. (ed.), *Beyond the Double Bind: Communication and Family Systems, Theories, and Techniques with Schizophrenics.* New York: Brunner/Mazel, 1978.

57. Berlo, David, *The Process of Communication.* New York: Holt, Rinehart and Winston, 1960.

58. Bernal, G., and J. Baker, "Toward a Metacommunicational Framework of Couple Interactions," *Family Process* **18**, No. 3 (1979):293–302.

59. Berscheid, Ellen, and Elaine Hatfield Walster, *Interpersonal Attraction.* Reading, MA: Addison-Wesley, 1969.

60. Berscheid, Ellen and Elaine Hatfield Walster, *Interpersonal Attraction,* 2d ed. Reading, MA: Addison-Wesley, 1978.

61. Bleiberg, Aaron H., and Harry E. Leubling, *Parents' Guide to Cleft Palate Rehabilitation.* Jericho, NY: Exposition Press, 1971.

62. Bochner, Art, "On Taking Ourselves Seriously: An Analysis of Some Persistent Problems and Promising Directions in Interpersonal Research." *Human Communication Research* **4**, No. 2 (Winter 1978):179–191.

63. Bochner, Arthur P., "On the Efficacy of Openness in Close Relationships," in Michael Burgoon (ed.), *Communication Yearbook* 5. New Brunswick, NJ: International Communication Association/Transaction Books, 1982, pp. 109–124.

64. Bochner, Arthur P., Edmund P. Kaminski, and Mary Anne Fitzpatrick, "The Conceptual Domain of Interpersonal Communication Behavior: A Factor-Analytic Study." *Human Communication Research* **3**, No. 4 (Summer 1977):291–302.

65. Bohannan, Paul, "Divorce Chains, Households of Remarriage, and Multiple Divorcers," in *Divorce and After,* Paul Bohannan (ed.). Garden City, NY: Doubleday, Anchor Books, 1971.

66. Bornstein, P. H., P. J. Bach, J. F. Heider, and J. Ernst (1981). "Clinical

Treatment of Marital Dysfunction: A Multiple-Baseline Analysis." *Behavioral Assessment* **3,** 335–343.

67. Boszormenyi-Nagy, Ivan, and Geraldine M. Spark, *Invisible Loyalties: Reciprocity in Intergenerational Family Therapy.* New York: Harper & Row, 1973.

68. Bowen, Murray, "Family Psychotherapy with Schizophrenia in the Hospital and in Private Practice," in *Intensive Family Therapy: Theoretical and Practical Aspects,* Ivan Boszormenyi-Nagy and James L. Framo (eds.). New York: Harper & Row, 1965, pp. 213–243.

69. Bower, Donald W., and Victor A. Christopherson, "University Student Cohabitation: A Regional Comparison of Selected Attitudes and Behavior." *Journal of Marriage and the Family* **39,** No. 3 (August 1977):447–452.

70. Bradac, James J., Charles H. Tardy, and Lawrence A. Hosman, "Disclosure Styles and a Hint at Their Genesis." *Human Communication Research* **6,** No. 3 (Spring 1980):228–238.

71. Bradford, Larry, "The Death of a Dyad." Paper presented to the Northwestern University Speech Communication and Association Doctoral Honors Seminar on the Growth and Disintegration of Interpersonal Communication Systems: Theory, Methodology, and Research, Evanston, IL, February 1977.

72. Braiker, Harriet B., and Harold H. Kelley, "Conflict in the Development of Close Relationships," in *Social Exchange in Developing Relationships,* Robert Burgess and Ted Huston (eds.). New York: Academic Press, 1979, pp. 135–168.

73. Brandt, David R. "On Linking Social Performance with Social Competence: Some Relations Between Communicative Style and Attributions of Interpersonal Attractiveness and Effectiveness." *Human Communication Research* **5,** No. 3 (Spring 1979):223–237.

74. Brewer, Robert E., and Marilynn B. Brewer, "Attraction and Accuracy of Perception in Dyads." *Journal of Personality and Social Psychology* **8,** No. 2 (1968):188–193.

75. Bronowski, Jacob, "The Logic of the Mind," in *Man and the Science of Man,* William R. Coulson and Carl R. Rogers, eds. Columbus, OH: Charles E. Merrill, 1968, pp. 31–49.

76. Broome, Benjamin J., "The Attraction Paradigm Revisited: Responses to Dissimilar Others." *Human Communication Research* **10,** No. 1 (Fall 1983):137–151.

77. Bruner, Jerome S., David Shapiro, and Renato Tagiuri, "The Meaning of Traits in Isolation and in Combination," in *Person Perception and Interpersonal Behavior,* Renato Tagiuri and Luigi Petrullo (eds.). Stanford, CA: Stanford University Press, 1958, pp. 277–288.

78. Budd, Richard W., and Brent D. Ruben, *Approaches to Human Communication.* New York: Spartan Books, 1972.

79. Burgoon, Judee K., and Thomas Saine, *The Unspoken Dialogue: An Introduction to Nonverbal Communication.* Boston: Houghton Mifflin, 1978.

80. Burgoon, Judee K., David B. Buller, Jerod L. Hale, and Mark A.

deTurck, "Relational Messages Associated with Nonverbal Behaviors." *Human Communication Research* **10,** No. 3 (Spring 1984):351–378.

81. Burhans, David T., "Coalition Game Research: A Reexamination." *American Journal of Sociology* **79,** No. 2 (September 1973):389–408.

82. Burleson, Brant R., "Social Cognition, Empathic Motivation, and Adults' Comforting Strategies," *Human Communication Research* **10,** No. 2 (Winter 1983):295–304.

83. Byrne, Donn, "Attitudes and Attraction," in *Advances in Experimental Social Psychology,* Vol. 4, Leonard Berkowitz (ed.). New York: Academic Press, 1969, pp. 35–89.

84. Byrne, Donn, *The Attraction Paradigm.* New York: Academic Press, 1971.

85. Byrne, Donn, and Barbara Blaylock, "Similarity and Assumed Similarity of Attitudes Between Husbands and Wives." *Journal of Abnormal and Social Psychology* **67,** No. 6 (1963):636–640.

86. Cahn, Dudley D., "Interpersonal Communication and Transactional Relationships Clarification and Application." *Communication Quarterly* **24,** No. 4 (Fall 1976):38–44.

87. Cahn, Dudley D., and Jack T. Hanford, "Perspectives on Human Communication Research: Behaviorism, Phenomenology, and an Integrated View." *Western Journal of Speech Communication* **48,** No. 3 (Summer 1984):277–292.

88. Caldwell, Mayta Ann, and Letitia A. Peplau, "Sex Differences in Friendship." Paper presented to the Western Psychological Association Convention, Seattle, April 1977.

89. Camden, Carl, Michael T. Motley, and Ann Wilson, "White Lies in Interpersonal Communication: A Taxonomy and Preliminary Investigation of Social Motivations." *Western Journal of Speech Communication* **48,** No. 4 (Fall 1984):309–325.

90. Capella, J. N. "Mutual Influence in Expressive Behavior." *Psychological Bulletin* **89**(1981):101–132.

91. Capella, Joseph N., "The Relevance of the Microstructure of Interaction to Relationship Change." *Journal of Social and Personal Relationships* **1,** No. 1 (June 1984):239–264.

92. Caplow, Theodore, *Two Against One: Coalitions in Triads.* Englewood Cliffs, NJ: Prentice-Hall, 1968.

93. Capra, Fritjof, *The Tao of Physics,* 2d ed. New York: Bantam Books, 1983.

94. Carson, Robert C., *Interaction Concepts of Personality.* Chicago: Aldine, 1969.

95. Cavior, Norman, Karen Miller, and Stanley H. Cohen, "Physical Attractiveness, Attitude Similarity, and Length of Acquaintance as Contributors to Interpersonal Attraction among Adolescents." *Social Behavior and Personality* **3,** No. 2 (1975):133–141.

96. Cegala, Donald J., "Affective and Cognitive Manifestations of Interaction Involvement During Unstructured and Competitive Interactions." *Communication Monographs* **51,** No. 4 (December 1984):320–338.

97. Chertkoff, Jerome M., "Sociopsychological Views on Sequential Effects in Coalition Formation." *American Behavioral Scientist* **18**, No. 4 (March/April 1975):451–471.

98. Chesebro, James W. (ed.) *Gayspeak: Gay Male and Lesbian Communication.* New York: Pilgrim Press, 1981.

99. Chown, Sheila M., "Friendship in Old Age," in *Personal Relationships,* Vol. II, Steve Duck and Robin Gilmour (eds.). New York: Academic Press, 1981. pp. 232–246.

100. Cissna, Kenneth N., "Interpersonal Confirmation: A Review of Current Theory and Research." Paper presented to the Central States Speech Association Convention, Chicago, 1976.

101. Clignet, Remi, *Many Wives, Many Powers: Authority and Power in Polygymous Families.* Evanston, IL: Northwestern University Press, 1970.

102. Cody, Michael J., "A Typology of Disengagement Strategies and an Examination of the Role Intimacy, Reactions to Inequity and Relational Problems Play in Strategy Selection." *Communication Monographs* **49**, No. 3 (September 1982):148–170.

103. Cody, Michael J., Mary Lou Woelfel, and William J. Jordan, "Dimensions of Compliance-Gaining Situations." *Human Communication Research,* **9**, No. 2 (Winter 1983):99–113.

104. Cohen, Yehudi A., "Patterns of Friendship," in *Social Structure and Personality,* Yehudi A. Cohen (ed.). New York: Holt, Rinehart and Winston, 1961, pp. 351–386.

105. Conville, Richard L., "Second-Order Development in Interpersonal Communication." *Human Communication Research* **9**, No. 3 (Spring 1983):195–207.

106. Cooley, Charles Horton, "The Social Self: On the Meanings of 'I,' " in *The Self in Social Interactions, Vol. I: Classic and Contemporary Perspectives,* Chad Gordon and Kenneth J. Gergen (eds.). New York: Wiley, 1968, pp. 87–91.

107. Coombs, Robert H., "Social Participation, Self-concept, and Interpersonal Valuation," *Sociometry* **32**, No. 3 (1969):273–286.

108. Costello, Daniel E., "Health Communication Theory and Research: An Overview," in *Communication Yearbook I,* Brent D. Ruben (ed.). New Brunswick, NJ: International Communication Association, 1977, pp. 557–567.

109. Cote, John, "A Conceptualization of Dyads and Triads." Paper for Interpersonal Communication 590: Dyadic Communication, February 1974.

110. Courtright, John A., Frank E. Millar, and L. Edna Rogers-Millar, "Domineeringness and Dominance: Replication and Expansion." *Communication Monographs* **46**, No. 3 (August 1979):179–192.

111. Cox, E. Sam, "A Survey of the Literature Concerning Double Bind Theory." Paper presented to Western Speech Communication Association Convention, Fresno, CA, 1985.

112. Cozby, Paul, "Self-disclosure: A Literature Review." *Psychological Bulletin* **79**, No. 2 (February 1973):73–90.

113. Cronbach, Lee J., "Processes Affecting Scores on 'Understanding of Others,' and 'Assumed Similarity.'" *Psychological Bulletin* **52** (1955):177–193.

114. Cupach, William R., and Brian H. Spitzberg, "Trait Versus State: A Comparison of Dispositional and Situational Measures of Interpersonal Communication Competence." *Western Journal of Speech Communication* **47**, No. 4 (Fall 1983):364–379.

115. Davis, Kingsley E., *Human Society.* New York: Macmillan, 1948.

116. Davis, Murray S., *Intimate Relations.* New York: Free Press, 1973.

117. Delia, Jesse G., "Change of Meaning Processes in Impression Formation." *Communication Monographs* **43** (June 1976):142–157.

118. Delia, Jesse G., "Some Tentative Thoughts Concerning the Study of Interpersonal Relationships and Their Development." *Western Journal of Speech Communication* **44**, No. 2 (Spring 1980):97–103.

119. Delia, Jesse G., Ruth Anne Clark, and David E. Switzer, "The Content of Informal Conversations as a Function of Interactants' Interpersonal Cognitive Complexity." *Communication Monographs*, **46**, No. 4 (November 1979):274–281.

120. Delia, Jesse G., Andrew H. Gonyea, and Walter H. Crockett, "Individual Personality Constructs in the Formation of Impressions." Paper presented to Speech Communication Association Convention, Chicago, 1970.

121. Delia, Jesse G., Susan L. Kline, and Brant R. Burleson, "The Development of Persuasive Communication Strategies in Kindergartners Through Twelfth-Graders." *Communication Monographs* **46**, No. 4 (November):241–256.

122. Dell, Paul F., and Harold A. Goolishian, "Order Through Fluctuation: An Evolutionary Epistemology for Human Systems." *Australian Journal of Family Therapy* **2**, No. 4 (1981):175–184.

123. Denzin, Norman K., "Rules of Conduct and the Study of Deviant Behavior: Some Notes on Social Relationship," in *Social Relationships*, G. McCall et al. Chicago: Aldine-Atherton, 1970, pp. 62–94.

124. Derlega, Valerian J., and Alan L. Chaikin, *Sharing Intimacy: What We Reveal to Others and Why.* Englewood Cliffs, NJ: Prentice-Hall, 1975.

125. DeSaint-Exupery, Antoine, *The Little Prince.* New York: Harcourt Brace Jovanovich, 1943.

126. Dettering, Richard, "The Syntax of Personality." *ETC: A Review of General Semantics* **26** (June 1969):139–156.

127. Dickens, Wenda J., and Daniel Perlman, "Friendship over the Life-Cycle," in *Personal Relationships*, Vol. II, Steve Duck and Robin Gilmour, New York: Academic Press, 1981, pp. 91–122.

128. Dienstag, Eleanor, "The Myth of Creative Divorce." *Psychology Today* (April 1977):49–50, 93.

129. Donohue, William A., "Development of a Model of Rule Use in Negotiation Interaction." *Communication Monographs* **48**, No. 2 (June 1981):106–120.

130. Douglas, William, "Scripts and Self-monitoring: When Does Being a High Self-monitor Really Make a Difference?" *Human Communication Research* **10**, No. 1 (Fall 1983):81–96.

131. Douvan, Elizabeth, "Interpersonal Relationships: Some Questions and Observations," in *Close Relationships*, George Levinger and Harold L. Raush (eds.). Amherst, MA: University of Massachusetts Press, 1977, pp. 17–32.

132. Drewery, James, "An Interpersonal Perception Technique," *British Journal of Medical Psychology* **42** (1969):171–181.

133. Duck, Steven, *Personal Relationships and Personal Constructs*. New York: Wiley, 1973.

134. Duck, Steven, "Interpersonal Communication in Developing Acquaintance," in *Explorations in Interpersonal Communication*, Gerald R. Miller (ed.). Beverly Hills, CA: Sage Publications, 1976, pp. 126–147.

135. Duck, Steve (ed.), *Personal Relationships, Vol. IV: Dissolving Personal Relationships*. New York: Academic Press, 1982.

136. Duck, Steven, "A Topography of Relationship Disengagement and Dissolution," in *Personal Relationships, Vol. IV: Dissolving Personal Relationships*, Steve Duck (ed.), New York: Academic Press, 1982, pp. 1–30.

137. Duck, Steve and Robin Gilmour (eds). *Personal Relationships, Vol. I, Studying Personal Relationships*. New York: Academic Press, 1981.

138. Duck, Steve, Andrew Lock, George McCall, Mary Anne Fitzpatrick, and James C. Coyne, "Social and Personal Relationships: A Joint Editorial." *Journal of Social and Personal Relationships*, **1**, No. 1 (1984):1–10.

139. Duvall, Shelley, and Robert A. Wicklund, *A Theory of Objective Self Awareness* New York: Academic Press, 1972.

140. Edwards, John N., and Alan Booth, "Sexual Behavior In and Out of Marriage: An Assessment of Correlates." *Journal of Marriage and the Family* **38**, No. 1 (February 1976):73–81.

141. Ehrlich, Howard J., and David B. Graeven, "Reciprocal Self-disclosure in a Dyad." *Journal of Experimental Social Psychology* **7** (1971):389–400.

142. Elliott, Norman, "Communicative Development from Birth." *Western Journal of Speech Communication* **48**, No. 2 (Spring 1984):184–196.

143. Fahs, Michael L., "The Effects of Self-disclosing Communication and Attitude Similarity on Reduction of Interpersonal Conflict." *Western Journal of Speech Communication* **45**, No. 1 (Winter 1981):38–50.

144. Faules, Don F., and Dennis C. Alexander, *Communication and Social Behavior: A Symbolic Interaction Perspective*. Reading, MA: Addison-Wesley, 1978.

145. Feffer, Melvin, and Leonard Suchotliff, "Decentering Implications of Social Interactions." *Journal of Personality and Social Psychology* **4**, No. 4 (1966):415–422.

146. Festinger, Leon, "A Theory of Social Comparison Processes." *Human Relations* **2**, No. 2 (May 1954):117–140.

147. Festinger, Leon, S. Schachter, and K. Back, *Social Pressures in Informal Groups: A Study of Human Factors in Housing.* New York: Harper & Row, 1950.

148. Fischer, Claude S., *To Dwell Among Friends: Personal Networks in Town and City.* Chicago: University of Chicago Press, 1982.

149. Fischer, Paul H., "An Analysis of the Primary Group." *Sociometry* **16** (August 1953):272–276.

150. Fisher, B. Aubrey, and G. Lloyd Drecksel, "A Cyclical Model of Developing Relationships: A Study of Relational Control Interaction." *Communication Monographs* **50**, No. 1 (March 1983):66–78.

151. Fisher, Walter R., "Reaffirmation and Subversion of the American Dream." *Quarterly Journal of Speech* **59**, No. 2, (1973):160–167.

152. Fitzpatrick, Mary Anne, "A Typological Approach to Communication in Relationships," in *Communication Yearbook I*, Brent D. Ruben (ed.). New Brunswick, NJ: International Communication Association, 1977, pp. 263–275.

153. Fitzpatrick, Mary Anne, and Patricia Best, "Dyadic Adjustment in Relational Types: Consensus, Cohesion, Affectional Expression, and Satisfaction in Enduring Relationships." *Communication Monographs* **46**, No. 3 (August 1979):167–178.

154. Fitzpatrick, Mary Anne, and Julie Indvik, "Implicit Theories in Enduring Relationships: Psychological Gender Differences in Perceptions of One's Mate." *Western Journal of Speech Communication* **46**, No. 4 (Fall 1982):311–325.

155. Fitzpatrick, Mary Anne, and Julie Indvik, "The Instrumental and Expressiveness Domains of Marital Communication." *Human Communication Research* **8**, No. 3 (Spring 1982):195–213.

156. Fogarty, Thomas F., "System Concepts and the Dimensions of Self," in *Family Therapy: Theory and Practice*, Philip J. Guerin, Jr. (ed.). New York: Gardner Press, 1976, pp. 144–153.

157. Frankl, Viktor E., *Man's Search for Meaning: An Introduction to Logotherapy.* New York: Simon and Schuster (Pocket Books), 1972.

158. Frentz, Thomas S., and Thomas B. Farrell, "Language-Action: A Paradigm for Communication." *Quarterly Journal of Speech* **62**, No. 4 (December 1976):333–349.

159. Frentz, Thomas S., and Janice H. Rushing, "Fulfilling Closeness and Distance Needs Through Consensual Relationship Definitions and Communicative Vibration." Paper presented to the Western Speech Communication Association Convention, 1979.

160. Gadlin, Howard, "Private Lives and Public Order: A Critical View of the History of Intimate Relations in the United States," in *Close Relationships*, George Levinger and Harold L. Raush (eds.). Amherst, MA: University of Massachusetts Press, 1977, pp. 33–72.

161. Galvin, Kathleen M., "An Analysis of Communication Instruction in Current Marital Interaction Programs." Paper presented at the Speech Communication Association Convention, 1978.

162. Galvin, Kathleen M., and Bernard J. Brommel, *Family Communication: Cohesion and Change,* 2d edition. Glenview, IL: Scott, Foresman, 1986.

163. Gamson, W. A., "Experimental Studies of Coalition Formation," in *Advances in Experimental Social Psychology,* Vol. 1, Leonard Berkowitz (ed.). New York: Academic Press, 1964, pp. 82–110.

164. Garfield, John C., Steven L. Weiss, and Ethan A. Pollack, "Effects of the Child's Social Class on School Counselors' Decision Making." *Journal of Counseling Psychology* 20, No. 2 (1973):166–168.

165. Gergen, Kenneth J., "Interaction Goals and Personalistic Feedback as Factors Affecting the Presentation of Self." *Journal of Personality and Social Psychology* 1 (1965):413–424.

166. Gergen, Kenneth J., "Personal Consistency and the Presentation of Self," in *The Self in Social Interaction, Vol. I: Classic and Contemporary Perspectives,* Chad Gordon and Kenneth J. Gergen (eds.). New York: Wiley, 1968, pp. 299–308.

167. Gergen, Kenneth J., *The Concept of Self.* New York: Holt, Rinehart and Winston, 1971.

168. Gilbert, Shirley J., "Effects of Unanticipated Self-disclosure on Recipients of Varying Levels of Self-esteem: A Research Note." *Human Communication Research* 3, No. 4 (Summer 1977):368–371.

169. Gilbert, Shirley J., and David Horenstein, "The Communication of Self-disclosure: Level Versus Valence." *Human Communication Research* 1, No. 4 (Summer 1975):316–322.

170. Gilbert, Shirley J., and Gale G. Whiteneck, "Toward a Multi-dimensional Approach to the Study of Self-disclosure." *Human Communication Research* 2, No. 4 (Summer 1976):347–355.

171. Gilbert, Richard, Andrew Christensen, and Gayla Margolin, "Patterns of Alliances in Nondistressed and Multiproblem Families." *Family Process* 23, No. 1 (March 1984):75–87.

172. Glass, D. C., "Changes in Liking as a Means of Reducing Cognitive Discrepancies Between Self-esteem and Aggression." *Journal of Personality* 32 (1964):530–549.

173. Glass, Shirley P., and Thomas L. Wright, "The Relationship of Extramarital Sex, Length of Marriage, and Sex Differences on Marital Satisfaction and Romanticism: Athanasiou's Data Reanalyzed." *Journal of Marriage and the Family* 39, No. 4 (November 1977):691–703.

174. Glasser, William, *Reality Therapy.* New York: Harper & Row, 1965.

175. Glenn, Norval D., and Charles N. Weaver, "The Marital Happiness of Remarried Divorced Persons." *Journal of Marriage and the Family* 39, No. 2 (May 1977):331–337.

176. Glenwick, David S., and Susan K. Whitbourne, "Beyond Despair and Disengagement: A Transactional Model of Personality Development in Later Life." *International Journal of Aging and Human Development* 8, No. 3 (1977–78):261–267.

177. Glick, Paul C., "Updating the Life Cycle of the Family." *Journal of Marriage and the Family* 39, No. 1 (1977):5–13.

178. Goffman, Erving. *The Presentation of Self in Everyday Life.* Garden City, NY: Doubleday, Anchor Books. 1959.

179. Golas, Thaddeus, *The Lazy Man's Guide to Enlightenment.* Palo Alto, CA: The Seed Center, 1971.

180. Gordon, Chad, and Kenneth J. Gergen (eds.), *The Self in Social Interaction, Vol. I: Classic and Contemporary Perspectives.* New York: Wiley, 1968.

181. Gottman, John M., *Marital Interaction: Experimental Investigations.* New York: Academic Press, 1979.

182. Gottman, John M., "Emotional Responsiveness in Marital Conversations." *Journal of Communication* 32, No. 8 (Summer 1982):108–120.

183. Gouldner, Alvin W., "The Norm of Reciprocity: A Preliminary Statement." *American Sociological Review* 25 (April 1960):161–178.

184. Gray, Farnum, Paul S. Graubard, and Harry Rosenberg, "Little Brother Is Changing You." *Psychology Today,* March 1974.

185. Greenblatt, Lynda, James E. Hasenauer, and Vicki S. Freimuth, "Psychological Sex Type and Androgyny in the Study of Communication Variables: Self-disclosure and Communication Apprehension." *Human Communication Research,* 6, No. 2 (Winter 1980):117–129.

186. Greeley, Andrew M., *The Friendship Game.* Garden City, NY: Doubleday, 1970.

187. Greenburg, Dan, *How to Be a Jewish Mother.* Los Angeles: Price, Stern, Sloan, 1964.

188. Greene, John O., "Evaluating Cognitive Explanations of Communicative Phenomena." *Quarterly Journal of Speech* 70, No. 3 (August 1984):241–254.

189. Gudykunst, William B., and Tsukasa Nishida, "Individual and Cultural Influences on Uncertainty Reduction." *Communication Monographs* 51, No. 1 (March 1984):23–36.

190. Guthrie, E. R., *The Psychology of Human Conflict.* New York: Harper & Row, 1938.

191. Haley, Jay, "An Interactional Description of Schizophrenia." *Psychiatry* 22 (1959):321–332.

192. Haley, Jay, *Strategies of Psychotherapy.* New York: Grune and Stratton, 1963.

193. Haley, Jay, *Problem-Solving Therapy: New Strategies for Effective Family Therapy.* San Francisco: Jossey-Bass, 1977.

194. Hare, A. Paul, *Handbook of Small Group Research.* New York: Free Press, 1965.

195. Hare-Mustin, Rachel T., "Treatment of Temper Tantrums by a Paradoxical Intervention." *Family Process* 14, No. 4 (December 1975):481–485.

196. Harris, Linda, "The Effects of Interaction Management and Background Similarity on Perceived Communication Competence and Attraction During Initial Interaction." Paper presented to the Doctoral Honors Seminar, Northwestern University, February 1977.

197. Harris, Linda, "Analysis of Paradoxical Logic: A Case Study." *Family Process* **19** (1980):19–33.

198. Hart, Roderick P., and Don M. Burks, "Rhetorical Sensitivity and Social Interaction." *Speech Monographs* **39**, No. 2 (June 1972):75–91.

199. Hart, Roderick R., Robert E. Carlson, and William F. Eadie, "Attitudes Toward Communication and the Assessment of Rhetorical Sensitivity." *Communication Monographs* **47**, No. 1 (March 1980):1–22.

200. Haslett, Beth, "Acquiring Conversational Competence." *Western Journal of Speech Communication* **48**, No. 2 (Spring 1984):107–124.

201. Haslett, Beth, "Preschoolers' Communicative Strategies in Gaining Compliance from Peers: A Developmental Study." *Quarterly Journal of Speech* **69**, No. 1 (February 1983):84–99.

202. Hastof, Albert H., David J. Schneider, and Judith Polefka, *Person Perception.* Reading, MA: Addison-Wesley, 1970.

203. Hatfield, Elaine, "Passionate Love, Companionate Love, and Intimacy," in *Intimacy*, M. Fisher and G. Stricker (eds.). New York: Plenum, 1982, pp. 267–292.

204. Hatfield, Elaine, and Jane Traupmann, "Intimate Relationships: A Perspective from Equity Theory," in *Personal Relationships*, Vol. I, Steve Duck and Robin Gilmour (eds.). New York: Academic Press, 1981, pp. 165–178.

205. Hays, Robert B., "The Development and Maintenance of Friendship." *Journal of Social and Personal Relationships* **1**, No. 1 (March 1984):75–98.

206. Hecht, Michael L., "Toward a Conceptualization of Communication Satisfaction." *Quarterly Journal of Speech* **64** (1978):47–62.

207. Hecht, Michael L. "The Conceptualization and Measurement of Interpersonal Communication Satisfaction." *Human Communication Research* **4**, No. 3 (Spring 1978):251–264.

208. Hecht, Michael L., "Satisfying Communication and Relationship Labels: Intimacy and Length of Relationship as Perceptual Frames of Naturalistic Conversations." *Western Journal of Speech Communication* **48**, No. 3 (Summer 1984):201–216.

209. Hecht, Michael, Tara Shepherd, and M. Joanne Hall, "Multivariate Indices of the Effects of Self-disclosure." *Western Journal of Speech Communication* **43**, No. 4 (Fall 1979):235–245.

210. Heider, Fritz, *The Psychology of Interpersonal Relations.* New York: Wiley, 1958.

211. Heine, Patricke Johns, *Personality in Social Theory.* Chicago: Aldine-Atherton, 1971.

212. Hendrick, Clyde, "The Study of Interpersonal Attraction." *Acta Symbolica* **2**, No. 1 (1971):15–17.

213. Hicks, Mary W., and Marilyn Platt, "Marital Happiness and Stability: A Review of the Research in the Sixties." *Journal of Marriage and the Family* **32**, No. 4 (November 1970):553–573.

214. Hill, Charles T., Zick Rubin, and Letitia Anne Peplau, "Breakups Before Marriage: The End of 103 Affairs." *Journal of Social Issues* **32**, No. 1 (1976).

215. Hinde, Robert A., "The Bases of a Science of Interpersonal Relationships," in *Personal Relationships* Vol. I, Steve Duck and Robin Gilmour (eds.). New York: Academic Press, 1981, pp. 1–22.

216. Hinde, Robert A., *Towards Understanding Relationships.* London: Academic Press, 1979.

217. Hocker, Joyce L., "The Prevention of Family Dysfunction and the Profession of Communication." Paper presented at the Western Speech Communication Association Convention, Fresno, CA, February 1985.

218. Hocker, Joyce L., "Does Self-help Work?: Improving Marital Satisfaction and Communication Skills in Enrichment Couples Using a Self-help Manual." Paper presented at the Western Speech Communication Association Convention, Tucson, AZ, February 1986.

219. Hocker, Joyce L., "Improving Marital Satisfaction and Communication Skills in Enrichment Couples Using a Self-help Manual." Unpublished Ph.D. dissertation, Clinical Psychology, University of Montana, 1985.

220. Hocker, Joyce L., and William W. Wilmot, *Interpersonal Conflict*, 2nd ed. Dubuque, IA: William C. Brown, 1985.

221. Hofstadter, Douglas R., *Godel, Escher, Bach: The Eternal Golden Braid.* New York: Basic Books, 1979.

222. Homans, George C., *Social Behavior: Its Elementary Forms.* New York: Harcourt Brace Jovanovich, 1961.

223. Honeycutt, James M., Mark L. Knapp, and William G. Powers, "On Knowing Others and Predicting What They Say." *Western Journal of Speech Communication* **47,** No. 2 (Spring 1983):138–156.

224. Honeycutt, James M., and Robert W. Norton, "The Couple Versus the Spouse as the Unit of Analysis in Marital Research." Paper presented at the International Communication Association Convention, Boston, MA, May 1982.

225. Hopper, Robert, and Robert A. Bell, "Broadening the Deception Construct," *Quarterly Journal of Speech*, **70,** No. 3 (August 1984):288–302.

226. Hora, T., "Tao, Zen, and Existential Psychotherapy." *Psychologia* **2** (1959):236–242.

227. Huesmann, L. Rowell, and George Levinger, "Incremental Exchange Theory: A Formal Model for Progression in Dyadic Interaction," in *Advances in Experimental Social Psychology*, Vol. 9, Leonard Berkowitz and Elaine Walster (eds.). New York: Academic Press, 1976, pp. 191–229.

228. Hugenberg, Sr., Lawrence W. and Mark J. Schaefermeyer, "Soliloquy as Self-disclosure." *Quarterly Journal of Speech* **69,** No. 2 (May 1983):180–190.

229. Humphreys, Christmas, *Buddhism.* Harmondsworth, England: Penguin Books, 1951.

230. Huston, Ted L., Catherine A. Surra, Nancy M. Fitzgerald, and Rodney M. Cate, "From Courtship to Marriage: Mate Selection as an Interpersonal Process," in *Personal Relationships*, Vol. II, Steve Duck and Robin Gilmour (eds.). New York: Academic Press, 1981, pp. 53–88.

231. Ichheiser, Gustav, *Appearances and Realities: Misunderstanding in Human Relations.* San Francisco: Jossey-Bass, 1970.

232. Infante, Dominic A., and William I. Gorden, "Subordinate and Superior Perceptions of Self and One Another: Relations, Accuracy, and Reciprocity of Liking." *Western Journal of Speech Communication* 43, No. 3 (Summer 1979):212–223.

233. Jablin, Fredric M., "Superior's Upward Influence, Satisfaction, and Openness in Superior–Subordinate Communication: A Reexamination of the 'Pelz Effect.'" *Human Communication Research* 6, No., 3 (Spring 1980):210–220.

234. Jablin, Fredric M., "Formal Structural Characteristics of Organizations and Superior–Subordinate Communication." *Human Communication Research* 8, No. 4 (Summer 1982):338–347.

235. Jackson, Don D., "Family Interaction, Family Homeostasis and Some Implications for Conjoint Family Psychotherapy," in *Individual and Familial Dynamics*, Jules H. Masserman (ed.). New York: Grune and Stratton, 1959.

236. Jackson, Sally, "Conversational Implicature in Children's Comprehension of Reference." *Communication Monographs* 48, No. 3 (September 1981):237–249.

237. Jacobson, N. S., "A Component Analysis of Behavioral Marital Therapy: The Relative Effectiveness of Behavior Change and Communication/ Problem-Solving Training." *Journal of Consulting and Clinical Psychology*, 52 (1984):295–305.

238. James, John, "The Distribution of Free-Forming Small Group Size." *American Sociological Review* 18, No. 15 (October 1953):569–570.

239. James, William, *The Principles of Psychology*, Vol. I. New York: Holt, 1890.

240. Jones, Edward E., David E. Kanhouse, Harold H. Kelley, Richard E. Nisbett, Stuart Valins, and Bernard Weiner, *Attribution: Perceiving the Causes of Behavior.* Morristown, NJ: General Learning Corporation, 1971.

241. Jones, Edward E., and Richard E. Nisbett, "The Actor and the Observer: Divergent Perceptions of the Causes of Behavior," in *Attribution: Perceiving the Causes of Behavior*, Edward E. Jones et al. Morristown, NJ: General Learning Corporation, 1971, pp. 79–94.

242. Jourard, Sidney, *The Transparent Self.* New York: D. Van Nostrand, 1964.

243. Kantor, David, and William Lehr, *Inside the Family: Toward a Theory of Family Process.* San Francisco: Jossey-Bass, 1975.

244. Katriel, Tamar, and Gerry Philipsen, "What We Need Is Communication: 'Communication' as a Cultural Category in Some American Speech." *Communication Monographs* 48, No. 4 (December 1981): 301–317.

245. Kayser, Egon, Thomas Schwinger, and Ronald L. Cohen, "Layperson's Conceptions of Social Relationships: A Test of Contract Theory." *Journal of Social and Personal Relationships* 1, No. 4 (December 1984):433–458.

246. Kellermann, Kathy, "The Negativity Effect and Its Implication for Initial

Interaction." *Communication Monographs* **51,** No. 1 (March 1984):37–55.

247. Kelley, Harold H., "Attribution in Social Interaction," in *Attribution: Perceiving the Causes of Behavior,* Edward E. Jones et al. Morristown, NJ: General Learning Corporation, 1972.

248. Kelley, H. H., E. Berscheid, A. Christensen, J. Harvey, T. L. Huston, G. Levinger, E. McClintock, L. A. Peplau, and D. R. Peterson, "Analyzing Close Relationships," in *Close Relationships,* H. H. Kelley et al. (eds.). New York: W. H. Freeman, 1983, pp. 20–67.

249. Kelley, Harold H., Ellen Berscheid, Andrew Christensen, John H. Harvey, Ted L. Huston, George Levinger, Evie McClintock, Letitia Anne Peplau, and Donald R. Peterson, *Close Relationships.* New York: W. H. Freeman, 1983.

250. Kelley, Robert L., W. J. Osborne, and Clyde Hendrick, "Role-Taking and Role-Playing in Human Communication." *Human Communication Research* **1,** No. 1 (Fall 1974):62–74.

251. Kelly, Carol, Ted Huston, and Rodney M. Cate, "Premarital Relationship Correlates of the Erosion of Satisfaction in Marriage." *Journal of Social and Personal Relationships* **2,** No. 2 (June 1985):167–178.

252. Kelly, George A., *A Theory of Personality: The Psychology of Personal Constructs.* New York: W. W. Norton, 1963.

253. Kelly, Lynne, "A Rose by Any Other Name Is Still a Rose: A Comparative Analysis of Reticence, Communication Apprehension, Unwillingness to Communicate, and Shyness." *Human Communication Research* **8,** No. 2 (Winter 1982):99–113.

254. Kennedy, Carol W., and Carl T. Camden, "A New Look at Interruptions." *Western Journal of Speech Communication* **47,** No. 1 (Winter 1983):45–58.

255. Kerckhoff, A. C., and K. E. Davis, "Value Consensus and Need Complementarity in Mate Selection." *American Sociological Review* **27** (1962):295–303.

256. Kidd, Virginia, "Happily Ever After and Other Relationship Styles: Advice on Interpersonal Relations in Popular Magazines, 1951–1973." *Quarterly Journal of Speech* **61** (February 1975):31–39.

257. Kinch, John W., "A Formalized Theory of the Self-Concept," in *Symbolic Interaction,* 2d ed., Jerome Manis and Bernard N. Meltzer (eds.). Boston: Allyn and Bacon, 1972, pp. 245–252.

258. King, Stephen W., and Kenneth K. Sereno, "Conversational Appropriateness as a Conversational Imperative." *Quarterly Journal of Speech* **70,** No. 3 (August 1984):264–273.

259. Klemmer, E. T., and F. W. Snyder, "Measurement of Time Spent Communicating." *Journal of Communication* **22** (June 1972):142–158.

260. Knapp, Mark L., *Interpersonal Communication and Human Relationships.* Boston: Allyn and Bacon, 1984.

261. Knapp, Mark L., Donald G. Ellis, and Barbara A. Williams, "Perceptions of Communication Behavior Associated with Relationship Terms." *Communication Monographs* **47,** No. 4 (November 1980):262–278.

262. Knapp, Mark L., Roderick P. Hart, G. W. Friedrich, and G. M. Shulman, "The Rhetoric of Goodbye: Verbal and Nonverbal Correlates of Leave Taking." *Speech Monographs* **40** (1973):182–198.

263. Knapp, Mark L., John M. Wiemann, and John A. Daly, "Nonverbal Communication: Issues and Appraisal." *Human Communication Research* **4**, No. 3 (Spring 1978):271–280.

264. Krain, Mark, "Communication as a Process of Dyadic Organization and Development." *Journal of Communication* **23** (December 1973):392–408.

265. Krivonos, P. D. and M. L. Knapp, "Initiating Communication: What Do You Say When You Say Hello?" *Central States Speech Journal* **26** (1975):115–125.

266. Krueger, Dorothy Lenk, "Pragmatics of Dyadic Decision Making: A Sequential Analysis of Communication Patterns." *Western Journal of Speech Communication* **47**, No. 2 (Spring 1983):99–117.

267. Kurth, Suzanne B., "Friendships and Friendly Relations," in *Social Relationships*, G. McCall et al. Chicago: Aldine-Atherton, 1970, pp. 136–170.

268. L'Abate, Luciano, "Prevention as a Profession: Toward a New Conceptual Frame of Reference," in *Prevention in Family Services*, David R. Mace (ed.). Beverly Hills, CA: Sage Publishing, 1983.

269. La Gaipa, John J., "Children's Friendships," in *Personal Relationships*, Vol. I, Steve Duck and Robin Gilmour (eds.). New York: Academic Press, 1981, pp. 161–185.

270. La Gaipa, John J., "A Systems Approach to Personal Relationships," in *Studying Personal Relationships*, Vol. I, Steve Duck and Robin Gilmour (eds.). New York: Academic Press, 1981, pp. 67–89.

271. Laing, R. D., *Self and Others*, 2d ed. New York: Pantheon Books, 1969.

272. Laing, R. D., *Knots.* New York: Random House, Vintage Books, 1970.

273. Laing, Ronald D., "Mystification, Confusion, and Conflict," in *Intensive Family Therapy.* Ivan Boszormenyi-Nagy and James L. Framo (eds.). New York: Harper & Row, 1965, pp. 343–363.

274. Laing, R. D., H. Phillipson, and A. R. Lee, *Interpersonal Perception.* Baltimore: Perennial Library, 1966.

275. La France, Marianne, and Clara Mayo, "A Review of Nonverbal Behaviors of Women and Men." *Western Journal of Speech Communication* **43**, No. 2 (Spring 1979):96–107.

276. Lander, Louise, "Why Some People Seek Revenge Against Doctors." *Psychology Today* (July 1978):88–94, 104.

277. Lang, Kurt, and Gladys Engel Lang, *Collective Dynamics.* New York: Thomas Y. Crowell, 1961.

278. Lange, Jonathan I., and Theodore G. Grove, "Sociometric and Autonomic Responses to Three Levels of Self-disclosure in Dyads." *Western Journal of Speech Communication* **45**, No. 4 (Fall 1981):355–362.

279. Leary, Mark R., "The Conceptual Distinctions Are Important: Another Look at Communication Apprehension and Related Constructs." *Human Communication Research* **10**, No. 2 (Winter 1983):305–312.

280. Leary, Timothy, "The Theory and Measurement Methodology of Inter-personal Communication." *Psychiatry* **18** (May 1955):147–161.

281. Leathers, Dale G., "The Impact of Multichannel Message Inconsistency on Verbal and Nonverbal Decoding Behaviors." *Communication Monographs* **46**, No. 2 (June 1979):88–100.

282. Lecky, Prescott, *Self-consistency: A Theory of Personality*. Forth Myers Beach, FL: Island Press, 1945.

283. Lederer, W. J., and Don D. Jackson, *Mirages of Marriage*. New York: W. W. Norton, 1968.

284. Lee, Loren, "Sequences in Separation: A Framework for Investigating Endings of the Personal (romantic) Relationship." *Journal of Social and Personal Relationships* **1**, No. 1 (March 1984):49–73.

285. Levine, James A., "Real Kids Vs. the 'Average' Family." *Psychology Today* (June 1978):14–15.

286. Levinger, George, "Marital Cohesiveness and Dissolution: An Integrative Review." *Journal of Marriage and the Family* **27**, No. 1 (February 1965):19–28.

287. Levinger, George, "A Social Psychological Perspective on Marital Dissolution." *Journal of Social Issues* **32**, No. 1 (1976):21–47.

288. Levinger, George, "The Embrace of Lives: Changing and Unchanging," in *Close Relationships*, George Levinger and Harold L. Raush (eds.). Amherst, MA: University of Massachusetts Press, 1977, pp. 1–16.

289. Levinger, George, "Re-Viewing the Close Relationship," in *Close Relationships*, George Levinger and Harold L. Raush (eds.). Amherst, MA: University of Massachusetts Press, 1977, pp. 137–161.

290. Levinger, George, "Development and Change" in *Close Relationships*, Kelley et al. (eds.). New York: W. H. Freeman, 1983, pp. 315–359.

291. Levinger, George, "Marital Cohesiveness at the Brink: The Fate of Applications for Divorce," in *Divorce and Separation*, George Levinger and Oliver C. Moles (eds.). New York: Basic Books, 1979, pp. 137–150.

292. Levinger, George, David J. Senn, and Bruce W. Jorgenson, "Progress toward Permanence in Courtship: A Test of the Kerckhoff–Davis Hypotheses." *Sociometry* **33**, No. 4 (1970):427–443.

293. Levinger, George, and James Breedlove, "Interpersonal Attraction and Agreement." *Journal of Personality and Social Psychology* **3**, No. 4 (1966):367–372.

294. Levinger, George, and J. Diedrick Snoek, "Attraction in Relationship: A New Look at Interpersonal Attraction," in *Attraction in Relationships*, G. Levinger and J. Snoek, Morristown, NJ: General Learning Press, 1972, pp. 1–22.

295. Levinger, George, and Oliver C. Moles, "In Conclusion Threads in the Fabric." *Journal of Social Issues* **32**, No. 1 (1976):193–207.

296. Levinger, George, and Raush, Harold L. *Close Relationships: Perspectives on the Meaning of Intimacy*. Amherst, MA: University of Massachusetts Press, 1977.

297. Lewis, Robert A. and Spanier, Graham B., "Theorizing about the Quality and Stability of Marriage," in *Contemporary Theories About the Fam-*

ily: Research Based Theories, Vol. I, Wesley R. Burr, Reuben Hill, F. Ivan Nye, and Ira L. Reiss (eds.). New York: Basic Books, 1979.

298. Lewis, Robert A., "A Longitudinal Test of a Developmental Framework for Premarital Dyadic Formation." *Journal of Marriage and the Family* **35,** No. 1 (February 1973):16–25.

299. Lewis, Robert A. (ed.), *Men in Difficult Times.* Englewood Cliffs, NJ: Prentice-Hall, 1981.

300. Lin, Nan, "Communication Effects: Review and Commentary," in *Communication Yearbook I,* Brent D. Ruben (ed.). New Brunswick, NJ: International Communication Association, 197i, pp. 55–72.

301. Lloyd, Sally A. and Rodney M. Cate, "The Developmental Course of Conflict in Dissolution of Premarital Relationships," *Journal of Social and Personal Relationships* **2,** No. 2 (June 1985):179–194.

302. Loeff, R. G., "Differential Discrimination of Conflicting Emotional Messages by Normal, Delinquent, and Schizophrenic Adolescents." University Microfilms No. 66–1470, 1966 (Cited in Schuham, 1967).

303. Luft, Joseph, *Of Human Interaction.* Palo Alto, CA: National Press Books, 1969.

304. Lustig, Myron W., and Stephen W. King, "The Effect of Communication Apprehension and Situation on Communication Strategy Choices." *Human Communication Research* **7,** No. 1 (Fall 1980):74–82.

305. Luthman, Shirley Gehrke, *The Dynamic Family.* Palo Alto, CA: Science and Behavior Books, 1974.

306. Mace, David R. (ed.), *Prevention in Family Services: Approaches to Family Wellness.* Beverly Hills, CA: Sage Publishing, 1983.

307. Mace, David R., "The Marriage Enrichment Movement," in *Prevention in Family Services,* David R. Mace (ed.). Beverly Hills, CA: Sage, 1983, pp. 98–109.

308. Mangam, I. L., "Relationships at Work: A Matter of Tension and Tolerance," in *Personal Relationships,* Vol. I, Steve Duck and Robin Gilmour (eds.). New York: Academic Press, 1981, pp. 197–214.

309. Markman, H. J. "Application of a behavioral model of marriage in predicting relationship satisfaction of couples planning marriage." *Journal of Consulting and Clinical Psychology* **47,** (1979):743–749.

310. Markus, Hazel, and Keith Sentis, "The Self in Social Information Processing," in *Psychological Perspectives on the Self,* Jerry Suls (ed.). New York: Lawrence Erlbaum, 1982, pp. 41–70.

311. Marlowe, David, and Kenneth J. Gergen, "Personality and Social Interaction," in *The Handbook of Social Psychology, Vol. III: The Individual in a Social Context,* Gardner Lindzey and Elliot Aronson (eds.). Reading, MA: Addison-Wesley, 1969, pp. 590–665.

312. Frankl, Viktor E. *Man's Search for Meaning.* New York: New American Library, Signet Books, 1967.

313. Mazur, Ronald, *The New Intimacy: Open-Ended Marriage and Alternative Lifestyles.* Boston: Beacon Press, 1973.

314. McCall, George J., "Communication and Negotiated Identity." *Communication* **2,** No. 2 (1976):173–184.

315. McCall, George J., "The Social Organization of Relationships," in *Social Relationships*, G. McCall et al. Chicago: Aldine-Atherton, 1970, pp. 3–34.

316. McCall, George J., and J. L. Simmons, *Identities and Interactions*. New York: Free Press, 1966.

317. McCall, Michael M., "Boundary Rules in Relationships and Encounters," in *Social Relationships*, G. McCall et al. Chicago: Aldine-Atherton, 1970, pp. 35–61.

318. McClintock, Evie, "Interaction," in *Close Relationships*, H. H. Kelley et al. (eds.). New York: W. H. Freeman, 1983, pp. 68–109.

319. McCroskey, James C., "Oral Communication Apprehension: A Summary of Recent Theory and Research." *Human Communication Research* **4,** No. 1 (Fall 1977):78–96.

320. McCroskey, James C., John A. Daly, Virginia P. Richmond, and Raymond L. Falcione, "Studies of the Relationship Between Communication Apprehension and Self-Esteem." *Human Communication Research* **3,** No. 3 (Spring 1977):269–277.

321. McCroskey, James C., Virginia P. Richmond, John A. Daly, and Barbara G. Cox, "The Effects of Communication Apprehension on Interpersonal Attraction." *Human Communication Research* **2,** No. 1 (Fall 1975):51–65.

322. McGuire, Michael T., "Dyadic Communication, Verbal Behavior, Thinking, and Understanding, Vol. I: Background Problems and Theory." *Journal of Nervous and Mental Disease* **152,** NO. 4 (April 1971):223–241.

323. McLaughlin, Margaret L., and Michael J. Cody, "Awkward Silences: Behavioral Antecedents and Consequences of the Conversational Lapse." *Human Communication Research* **8,** No. 4 (Summer 1982):299–316.

324. Mead, Margaret, "Anomalies in American Postdivorce Relationships," in *Divorce and After*, Paul Bohannan (ed.). Garden City, NY: Doubleday, Anchor Books, 1971, pp. 107–125.

325. Merton, Robert K., *Social Structure*. New York: Free Press, 1957.

326. Mettetal, Gwendolyn, and John M. Gottman, "Reciprocity and Dominance in Marital Interaction," in *Family Intervention, Assessment and Theory*, Vol. I, John P. Vincent (ed). New York: JAI Press, 1980.

327. Millar, Frank E., III, "A Transactional Analysis of Marital Communication Patterns; An Exploratory Study." Unpublished Ph.D. dissertation, Michigan State University, 1973.

328. Millar, Frank E., and L. Edna Rogers, "A Relational Approach to Interpersonal Communication," in *Explorations in Interpersonal Communication*, Gerald R. Miller (ed.). Beverly Hills, CA: Sage Publications, 1976, pp. 87–103.

329. Millar, Frank E., L. Edna Rogers, and Janet Beavin Bavelas, "Identifying Patterns of Verbal Conflict in Interpersonal Dynamics." *Western Journal of Speech Communication* **48,** No. 3 (Summer 1984):231–246.

330. Millar, L. Edna Rogers, and Frank E. Millar III, "A Transactional Defi-

nition and Measure of Power." Paper presented to the Speech Communication Association Convention, Washington, DC, December 1977.

331. Miller, Arthur A., "Reactions of Friends to Divorce," in *Divorce and After,* Paul Bohannan (ed.). Garden City, NY: Doubleday, Anchor Books, 1971, pp. 63–86.

332. Miller, Gerald R. (ed.), *Explorations in Interpersonal Communication.* Beverly Hills, CA: Sage Publications, 1976.

333. Miller, Gerald R., and Malcolm R. Parks, "Communication in Dissolving Relationships," in *Personal Relationships Vol. 4: Dissolving Personal Relationships.* Steve Duck (ed.). New York: Academic Press, 1982.

334. Miller, Gerald R., and Mark Steinberg, *Between People: A New Analysis of Interpersonal Communication.* Chicago: Science Research Associates, 1975.

335. Miller, Larry D., "Correspondence Between Self and Other Perceptions of Communication Dominance." *Western Journal of Speech Communication* 44, No. 2 (Spring 1980):120–131.

336. Mills, Theodore M., "Power Relations in Three-Person Groups." *American Sociological Review* 18, (1953):351–357.

337. Minuchin, Salvador, *Families and Family Therapy.* Cambridge, MA: Harvard University Press, 1974.

338. Mischel, T., *Personality and Assessment.* New York: Wiley, 1968.

339. Mischel, T., "Continuity and Change in Personality." *American Psychologist* 11 (1969):1012–1018.

340. Montgomery, Barbara M., and Robert W. Norton, "Sex Differences and Similarities in Communicator Style." *Communication Monographs* 48, No. 2 (June 1981):121–134.

341. Morton, Teru L., and Mary Ann Douglas, "Growth of Relationships," in *Personal Relationships,* Vol. II, Steve Duck and Robin Gilmour (eds.). New York: Academic Press, 1981, 3–26.

342. Morton, Teru L., James F. Alexander, and Irwin Altman, "Communication and Relationship Definition," in *Explorations in Interpersonal Communication,* Gerald R. Miller (ed.). Beverly Hills, CA: Sage Publications, 1976, pp. 105–125.

343. Moran, Gary, "Dyadic Attraction and Orientational Consensus." *Journal of Personality and Social Psychology* 4, No. 1 (1966):94–99.

344. Mortenson, C. David, *Communication: The Study of Human Interaction.* New York: McGraw-Hill, 1972.

345. Moss, J. Joel, Frank Apolonio, and Margaret Jensen, "the Premarital Dyad During the Sixties," *Journal of Marriage and the Family* 33, No. 1 (February 1971):50–69.

346. Naremore, Rita C., "On the Functional Analysis of Social Class Differences in Modes of Speech." *Speech Monographs* 36 (1969):77–1020.

347. Navran, Leslie, "Communication and Adjustment in Marriage." *Family Process* 6, (1967):173–184.

348. Newcomb, Michael D., "Heterosexual Cohabitation Relationships," in *Personal Relationships,* Vol. I, Steve Duck and Robin Gilmour (eds.). New York: Academic Press, 1981, pp. 131–164.

349. Newcomb, Theodore M., "An Approach to the Study of Communicative Acts." *Psychological Review* **60** (1953):393–404.

350. Newcomb, Theodore M., *The Acquaintance Process.* New York: Holt, Rinehart and Winston, 1961.

351. Newcomb, Theodore M., "Stabilities Underlying Changes in Interpersonal Attraction." *Journal of Abnormal and Social Psychology* **66** (1963):376–386.

352. Newman, Helen M., "Talk about a Past Relationship Partner: Metacommunicative Implications." Unpublished paper, Department of Communications, Hunter College, New York, 1984.

353. Newman, Helen M., "Interpretation and Explanation: Influences on Communicative Exchanges Within Intimate Relationships." *Communication Quarterly* **29**, No. 2 (Spring 1981):123–131.

354. Newman, Helen M., and Ellen J. Langer, "Post-Divorce Adaptation and the Attribution of Responsibility." *Sex Roles* **7**, No. 3 (1981): 223–232.

355. Nierenberg, Gerald I., and Henry Calero, *Meta-Talk.* New York: Trident Press, 1973.

356. Nisbett, Richard E., and Stuart Valins, "Perceiving the Causes of One's Own Behavior," in *Attribution: Perceiving the Causes of Behavior,* Edward E. Jones et al. Morristown, NJ: General Learning Corporation, 1971, pp. 63–78.

357. Nofsinger, Robert E., "The Demand Ticket: A Conversational Device for Getting the Floor," *Speech Monographs* **42**, No. 1 (March 1975): 1–9.

358. Norton, Arthur J., and Paul C. Glick, "Marital Instability: Past, Present, and Future." *Journal of Social Issues* **32**, No. 1 (1976):5, 20.

359. Norton, Robert W., and Loyd Pettegrew, "Attentiveness as a Style of Communication: A Structural Analysis." *Communication Monographs* **46**, No. 1 (March 1979):13–26.

360. Nussbaum, Jon F., "Perceptions of Communication Content and Life Satisfaction Among the Elderly." *Communication Quarterly* **32**, No. 4 (Fall 1983):313–319.

361. Nussbaum, Jon F., "Relational Closeness of Elderly Interaction: Implications for Life Satisfaction." *Western Journal of Speech Communication* **47**, No. 3 (Summer 1983):229–243.

362. O'Donnell-Trujillo, Nick, and Katherine Adams, "Heheh in Conversation: Some Coordinating Accomplishments of Laughter." *Western Journal of Speech Communication* **47**, No. 2 (Spring 1983):175–191.

363. Ofshe, Richard, and Lynne Ofshe, "Social Choice and Utility in Coalition Formation." *Sociometry* **32**, No. 3 (1969):330–337.

364. Ofshe, Lynne, and Richard Ofshe, *Utility and Choice in Social Interaction.* Englewood Cliffs, NJ: Prentice-Hall, 1970.

365. O'Keefe, B. J., and J. G. Delia, "Construct Comprehensiveness and Cognitive Complexity as Predictors of the Number of Strategic Adaptation of Arguments and Appeals in a Persuasive Message." *Communication Monographs* **46**, No. 4 (November 1979):231–240.

366. Olson, David H. L., *Treating Relationships.* Lake Mills, IA: Graphic Publishing Co., 1976.

367. Olson, David H., "Insiders' and Outsiders' View of Relationships: Research Studies," in *Close Relationships*, Levinger and Raush (eds.), 1977, pp. 115–135.

368. Olson, David H., "How Effective Is Marriage Preparation," in *Prevention in Family Services*, David R. Mace (ed.). Beverly Hills, CA: Sage Publications, 1983, pp. 65–75.

369. O'Neill, Nena, and George O'Neill, *Open Marriage.* New York: M. Evans, 1972.

370. Osterkamp, Marilynn B., "Communication During Initial Interactions: Toward a Different Model." *Western Journal of Speech Communication* 44, No. 2 (Spring 1980):108–113.

371. Owen, William Foster, "Interpretive Themes in Relational Communication." *Quarterly Journal of Speech* 70, No. 3 (August 1984):274–287.

372. Owen, William Foster, "The Verbal Expression of Love as Metacommunication in Personal Relationships." Unpublished manuscript, 1985.

373. Parks, Malcolm R., "Towards an Axiomatic Theory of Complementarity and Symmetry." Unpublished paper for Communication 806, Department of Communication, Michigan State University, 1974.

374. Parks, Malcolm R., "Dyadic Communication from the Perspective of Small Group Research." Paper presented to Central States Speech Association, Milwaukee, WI, 1974.

375. Parks, Malcolm R., "Relational Communication: Theory and Research." *Human Communication Research* 3, No. 4 (Summer 1977):372–381.

376. Parks, Malcolm R., "Anomia and Close Friendship Communication Networks." *Human Communication Research* 4, No. 1 (Fall 1977):48–57.

377. Parks, Malcolm R., "A Test of the Cross-Situational Consistency of Communication Apprehension" *Communicaton Monographs* 47, No. 3 (August 1980):220–232.

378. Parks, Malcolm R., "Ideology in Interpersonal Communication: Off the Couch and Into the World," in *Communication Yearbook* 5, Michael Burgoon (ed.). New Brunswick, N.J.: International Communication Association/Transaction Books, 1982, pp. 79–107.

379. Parks, Malcolm R., and Mara B. Adelman, "Communication Networks and the Development of Romantic Relationships: An Expansion of Uncertainty Reduction Theory." *Human Communication Research* 10, No. 1 (Fall 1983):55–79.

380. Parks, M. R., C. M. Stan, and L. L. Eggert, "Romantic Involvement and Social Network Involvement." *Social Psychology Quarterly* 46, 1983:116–131.

381. Parks, M. R., and William W. Wilmot, "Three Research Models of Communication: Action, Interaction and Transaction." Paper presented at the annual convention of the Western Speech Communication Association, Seattle, WA, November 1975.

382. Parry, John, *The Psychology of Human Communication.* New York: American Elsevier, 1967.

383. Pawlby, Susan J., "Infant–Mother Relationships," in *Personal Relationships,* Vol. II, Steve Duck and Robin Gilmour (eds.). New York: Academic Press, 1981, pp. 123–139.

384. Pearce, W. Barnett, and Forrest Conklin, "A Model of Hierarchical Meanings in Coherent Conversation and a Study of Indirect Responses." *Communication Monographs* **46,** No. 2 (June 1979):75–87.

385. Pearce, W. B., V. E. Cronen, Kenneth Johnson, Greg Jones, and Robert Raymond, "The Structure of Communication Rules and Form of Conversation: An Experimental Simulation." *Western Journal of Speech Communication* **44,** No. 1 (Winter 1980):20–34.

386. Pearce, W. Barnett, and Steward M. Sharp, "Self-Disclosing Communication." *Journal of Communication* **23** (December 1973):409–425.

387. Peters, Thomas J., and Robert H. Waterman, Jr., *In Search of Excellence: Lessons from America's Best Run Companies.* New York: Harper & Row, 1982.

388. Petronio, Sandra, "Communication Strategies to Reduce Embarrassment Differences Between Men and Women." *Western Journal of Speech Communication* **48,** No. 1 (Winter 1984):28–38.

389. Petronio, Sandra S., "The Effect of Interpersonal Communication on the Woman's Family Role Satisfaction." *Western Journal of Speech Communication* **46,** No. 3 (Summer 1982):208–222.

390. Phillips, Gerald M., "Rhetoritherapy Versus the Medical Model: Dealing with Reticence." *Communication Education* **26** (January 1977):34–43.

391. Phillips, Gerald M., and Nancy J. Metzger, *Intimate Communication.* Boston: Allyn and Bacon, 1976.

392. Piaget, Jean, *Judgment and Reasoning in the Child.* London: Routledge and Kegan Paul, 1928.

393. Piaget, Jean, *Play, Dreams and Imitation in Childhood.* New York: W.W. Norton, 1962.

394. Przybyla, D. P. J., and Donn Byrne, "Sexual Relationships," in *Personal Relationships,* Vol. I, Steve Duck and Robin Gilmour (eds.). New York: Academic Press, 1981, pp. 109–130.

395. Putnam, Linda L., and Tricia S. Jones, "Reciprocity in Negotiations: An Analysis of Bargaining Interaction." *Communication Monographs* **49,** No. 3 (September 1982):171–191.

396. Ragan, Sandra L., and Robert Hopper, "Ways to Leave Your Lover: A Conversational Analysis of Literature." *Communication Quarterly* **32,** No. 4 (Fall 1984):310–317.

397. Rawlins, William K., "Openness as Problematic in Ongoing Friendships: Two Conversational Dilemmas." *Communication Monographs* **50,** No. 1 (March 1983):1–13.

398. Rawlins, William K., "Negotiating Close Friendship: The Dialectic of Conjunctive Freedoms." *Human Communication Research* **9,** No. 3 (Spring 1983):255–266.

399. Reardon, Kathleen Kelley, "Conversational Deviance: A Structural Model." *Human Communication Research* **9,** No. 1 (Fall 1982):59–74.

400. Riccillo, Samuel C., "Modes of Speech as a Developmental Hierarchy: A Descriptive Study." *Western Journal of Speech Communication* **47,** No. 1 (Winter 1983):1–15.

401. Richmond, Virginia P., "The Relationship Between Trait and State Communication Apprehension and Interpersonal Perceptions During Acquaintance Stages," *Human Communication Research* **4,** No. 4 (Summer 1978):338–349.

402. Ridley, Carl A., and Arthur W. Avery, "Social Network Influence on the Dyadic Relationship," in *Social Exchange in Developing Relationships,* Burgess and Huston (eds.), 1979, pp. 223–246.

403. Riesman, David, *The Lonely Crowd.* New Haven, CT: Yale University Press, 1950.

404. Ringuette, E. L., "Double Binds, Schizophrenics and Psychological Testing: Letters from Schizophrenics and Nonschizophrenic Patients." *Psychological Reports* **51,** No. 3 (December 1982):693–694.

405. Ritter, Ellen M., "Social Perspective-Taking Ability, Cognitive Complexity and Listener-Adapted Communication in Early and Late Adolescence." *Communication Monographs* **46,** No. 1 (March 1979):40–51.

406. Rogers, Carl R., *Client-Centered Therapy.* Boston: Houghton Mifflin, 1951.

407. Rogers, L. Edna, "Dyadic Systems and Transactional Communication in a Family Context." Unpublished Ph.D. dissertation, Michigan State University, 1972.

408. Rogers, L. Edna, and Richard V. Farace, "Analysis of Relational Communication in Dyads: New Measurement Procedures." *Human Communication Research* **1,** No. 3 (Spring 1975):222–239.

409. Rogers-Millar, L. Edna, and Frank E. Millar, III, "Domineeringness and Dominance: A Transactional View." *Human Communication Research* **5,** No. 3 (Spring 1979):238–246.

410. Romey, William D., *Risk–Trust–Love: Learning in a Humane Environment.* Columbus, OH: Charles E. Merrill, 1972.

411. Rosenberg, Morris, "Psychological Selectivity in Self-esteem Formation," in *Attitude, Ego-Involvement, and Change,* Carolyn W. Sherif and Muzafer Sherif (eds.). New York: Wiley, 1967, pp. 26–50.

412. Rosenfeld, Lawrence R., "Self-disclosure Avoidance: Why I Am Afraid to Tell You Who I Am." *Communication Monographs* **46,** No. 1 (March 1979):63–74.

413. Rosenfeld, Lawrence R. and W. Leslie Kendrick, "Choosing to Be Open: An Empirical Investigation of Subjective Reasons for Self-disclosure." *Western Journal of Speech Communication* **48,** No. 4 (Fall 1984):326–346.

414. Rosenhan, D. L., "On Being Sane in Insane Places." *Science* **179** (January 1973):250–258.

415. Rosenthal, Robert, "The Pygmalion Effect Lives." *Psychology Today,* September 1973.

416. Rosenthal, Robert, and Lenore Jacobsen, *Pygmalion in the Classroom.* New York: Holt, Rinehart and Winston, 1968.

417. Ruben, Brent D., "General System Theory: An Approach to Human Communication," in *Approaches to Human Communication*, Richard W. Budd and Brent D. Ruben. New York: Spartan Books, 1972, pp. 120–144.

418. Ruddock, Ralph, *Roles and Relationships*. London: Routledge and Kegan Paul, 1969.

419. Ruesch, Jurgen, "Synopsis of the Theory of Human Communication." *Psychiatry* **16**, No. 3 (August 1953):215–243.

420. Ruesch, Jurgen, "Psychiatry and the Challenge of Communication." *Psychiatry* **17**, No. 1 (February 1954):1–18.

421. Ruesch, Jurgen, *Disturbed Communication*. New York: W. W. Norton, 1957.

422. Ruesch, Jurgen, *Therapeutic Communication*. New York: W. W. Norton, 1961.

423. Ruesch, Jurgen, "The Tangential Response," in *Psychopathology of Communication*, P. H. Hoch and J. Zubin (eds.). New York: Grune and Stratton, 1958, pp. 354–364.

424. Ruesch, Jurgen, and Gregory Bateson, *Communication; The Social Matrix of Psychiatry*. New York: W. W. Norton, 1968.

425. Ruesch, Jurgen, and A. Rodney Prestwood, "Interaction Processes and Personal Codification." *Journal of Personality* **18** (1950):391–430.

426. Rushing, Janice Hocker, "Impression Management as Communicative Action: A Nonverbal Strategy in Interpersonal Encounters." Paper presented to the Western Speech Communication Association Convention, San Francisco, November 1976.

427. Rushing, Janice Hocker, "The Rhetoric of the American Western Myth." *Communication Monographs* **50**, No. 1 (March 1983), 14–32.

428. Rushing, Janice Hocker, and Thomas S. Frentz, "The Rhetoric of 'Rocky': A Social Value Model of Criticism." *Western Journal of Speech Communication* **42** (Spring 1978):63–72.

429. Samovar, Larry D., Robert P. Brooks, and Richard Porter, "A Survey of Adult Communication Activities." *Journal of Communication* **19** (December 1969):301–307.

430. Sanford, John A., *Dreams: God's Forgotten Language*. Philadelphia: J. B. Lippincott, 1968.

431. Sarbin, Theodore R., Ronald Taft, and Daniel E. Bailey, *Clinical Inference and Cognitivie Theory*. New York: Holt, Rinehart and Winston, 1960.

432. Satir, Virginia, *Conjoint Family Therapy*, rev. ed. Palo Alto, CA: Science and Behavior Books, 1967.

433. Satir, Virginia, *Peoplemaking*. Palo Alto, CA: Science and Behavior Books, 1972.

434. Scheff, Thomas J., "Toward a Sociological Model of Consensus." *American Sociological Review* **32** (February 1967):32–46.

435. Scheflen, Albert E., "Regressive One-to-One Relationships." *Psychiatric Quarterly* **34**, No. 4 (1960):692–709.

436. Scheflen, Albert E., and Alice Scheflen, *Body Language and the Social Order.* Englewood Cliffs, N.J.: Prentice-Hall, 1972.

437. Schlenker, Barry R., *Impression Management: The Self-concept, Social Identity and Interpersonal Relations.* Monterery, CA: Brooks/Cole Publishing Co., 1980.

438. Schlien, John M., "Phenomenology and Personality," in *Concepts of Personality,* Joseph W. Wepman and Ralph W. Heine (eds.). Chicago: Aldine-Atherton, 1963, pp. 291–330.

439. Schofield, Margot J. and Norman F. Kafer, "Children's Understanding of Friendship Issues: Development by Stage or Sequence?" *Journal of Social and Personal Relationships* **2**, No. 2 (June 1985):151–165.

440. Schopler, John, and John C. Compere, "Effects of Being Kind or Harsh to Another on Liking." *Journal of Personality and Social Psychology* **20**, No. 2 (1971):155–159.

441. Schuham, Anthony I., "The Double-Bind Hypothesis a Decade Later." *Psychological Bulletin* **68**, No. 6 (1967):409–416.

442. Schutz, Alfred, *Collected Papers, Vol. II: Studies in Social Theory,* Arvid Broderson (ed.). Martinus Nijhoff, 1964.

443. Schutz, William C., *The Interpersonal Underworld.* Palo Alto, CA: Science and Behavior Books, 1966.

444. Scott, Michael D., and Lawrence R. Wheeless, "Instructional Communication Theory and Research: An Overview," in *Communication Yearbook I,* Brent D. Ruben (ed.). New Brunswick, N.J.: International Communication Association, 1977, pp. 495–511.

445. Searles, Harold F., "The Effort to Drive the Other Person Crazy—An Element in the Aetiology and Psychotherapy of Schizophrenia." *The British Journal of Medical Psychology* **32**, Pt. 1 (1959):1–18.

446. Secord, Paul F., and Carl W. Backman, "Personality Theory and the Problem of Stability and Change in Individual Behavior: An Interpersonal Approach." *Psychological Review* **68** (1961):21–33.

447. Seligman, M. E. P., *Helplessness: On Suppression, Development, and Death.* San Francisco: Freeman, 1975.

448. Selman, Robert L., and Anne P. Selman, "Children's Ideas About Friendship: A New Theory." *Psychology Today* (October 1979):71–80, 114.

449. Shaver, Kelly G., *An Introduction to Attribution Processes.* Cambridge, MA: Winthrop Publishers, 1975.

450. Shaw, Mark R., "Taken-for-Granted Assumptions of Applicants in Simulated Selection Interviews." *Western Journal of Speech Communication* **47**, No. 2 (Spring 1983):138–156.

451. Shepperson, Vance L., "Difference in Family Coalitions and Hierarchies Between Normals and Neurotics." *Family Relations* **30** (July 1981):361–365.

452. Shibutani, Tamotsu, *Society and Personality: An Interactionist Approach to Social Psychology.* Englewood Cliffs, N.J.:Prentice-Hall, 1961.

453. Shostrum, Everett, and James Kavanaugh, *Between Man and Woman.* New York: Bantam Books, 1971.

454. Shulman, Norman, "Life-Cycle Variations in Patterns of Close Relationships." *Journal of Marriage and the Family* **37**, No. 4 (November 1975):813–821.

455. Sieburg, Evelyn, "Interpersonal Confirmation: A Paradigm for Conceptualization and Measurement." San Diego: United States International University, ERIC Document No. ED 098 634, 1975.

456. Sieburg, Evelyn, and Carl Larson, "Dimensions of Interpersonal Response." Paper presented to International Communication Association Convention, Phoenix, AZ, April 22–24, 1971.

457. Sillars, Alan L., "Attributions and Communication in Roommate Conflicts." *Communication Monographs* **47**, No. 3 (August 1980):180–200.

458. Sillars, Alan L., "Attributions and Interpersonal Conflict Resolution," in *New Directions in Attribution Research*, Vol. 3, John H. Harvey, William Ickes, and Robert F. Kidd (eds.). Hillsdale, N.J.: Lawrence Erlbaum, 1981, pp. 279–305.

459. Sillars, Alan, L., Gary R. Pike, Tricia S. Jones, and Mary A. Murphy, "Communication and Understanding in Marriage," *Human Communication Research* **10**, No. 3 (Spring 1984):317–350.

460. Sillars, Alan L., and Michael D. Scott, "Interpersonal Perception Between Intimates: An Integrative Review." *Human Communication Research* **10**, No. 1 (Fall 1983):153–176.

461. Simmel, Georg, "The Number of Members as Determining the Sociological Form of the Group, I." *American Journal of Sociology* **8**, No. 1 (July 1902):1–46.

462. Skipper, James K., Jr., and Gilbert Nass, "Dating Behavior: A Framework for Analysis and an Illustration." *Journal of Marriage and the Family* **30** (1966):412–420.

463. Slater, Philip E., "Contrasting Correlates of Group Size," *Sociometry* **21**, No. 2 (June 1958):129–139.

464. Sluzki, Carlos E., and Janet Helmick Beavin, "Simetría y Complementaridad: Una Definición Operacional y una Tipología de Parajas." *Acta Psiquiatrica y Psicológica de America Latina* **11** (1965):321–330.

465. Sluzki, Carlos E., Janet Beavin, Alejandro Tarnopolsky, and Eliseo Veron, "Transactional Disqualification." *Archives of General Psychiatry* **16** (April 1967):494–504.

466. Sluzki, Carlos E., and Eliseo Veron, "The Double Bind as a Universal Pathogenic Situation." *Family Process* **10** (1971):397–410.

467. Smith, David, "Everyone Talks About Process but No One Does Anything About It." Paper presented to Speech Communication Association Convention, San Francisco, 1971.

468. Smith, Dennis R., and L. Keith Williamson, *Interpersonal Communication: Roles, Rules, Strategies, and Games.* Dubuque, IA: Wm. C. Brown, 1977.

469. Smith, R. M., S. M. Schoffner, and J. P. Scotte, "Marriage and Family Enrichment: A New Professional Area." *The Family Coordinator* **28** (1979):87–93.

470. Speck, Ross V., and Carolyn L. Attneave, *Family Networks.* New York: Random House, Vintage Books, 1973.

471. Speigel, John P., "The Social Roles of Doctor and Patient in Psycho-analysis and Psychotherapy," in *Personality and Social Systems*, Neil J. Smelser and William T. Smelser (eds.). New York: Wiley, 1963, pp. 600–607.

472. Spitzberg, Brian H., and Michael L. Hecht, "A Component Model of Relational Competence." *Human Communication Research* 10, No. 4 (Summer 1984):575–599.

473. Spitzberg, Brian H., and William R. Cupach. *Interpersonal Communication Competence*. Beverly Hills, CA: Sage Publications, 1984.

474. Stafford, Laura, and John A. Daly, "Conversational Memory: The Effects of Recall Mode and Memory Expectancies on Remembrances of Natural Conversations." *Human Communication Research* 10, No. 3 (Spring 1984): 379–402.

475. Stech, Ernest L., "A Grammar of Conversation with a Quantitative Empirical Test." *Human Communication Research* 5, No. 2 (Winter 1979):158–170.

476. Steeves, H. Leslie, "Developing Coorientation Measures for Small Groups." *Communication Monographs* 51, No. 2 (June 1984):185–192.

477. Steiner, Claude, "The Rescue Triangle." *Issues in Radical Therapy* 1, No. 4 (Fall 1973):3–4.

478. Steinglass, Peter, "The Conceptualization of Marriage from a Systems Theory Perspective," in *Marriage and Marital Therapy*, Thomas O. Paolino and Barbara S. McCrady (eds.). New York: Brunner Mazel, 1987, pp. 298–364.

479. Stinnett, Nicholas, "Strong Families: A Portrait, " in *Prevention in Family Services*, David R. Mace (ed.). Beverly Hills: Sage Publications, 1983, pp. 27–38.

480. Stuart, Richard B., *Helping Couples Change: A Social Learning Approach to Marital Therapy*. New York: Guilford Press, 1980.

481. Suinn, R. M., and J. Geiger, "Stress and the Stability of Self and Other Attitudes." *Journal of General Psychology* 73 (1965):177–180.

482. Sullivan, Harry Stack, *Conceptions of Modern Psychiatry*. New York: W. W. Norton, 1940.

483. Sullivan, Harry Stack, *The Interpersonal Theory of Psychiatry*. New York: W. W. Norton, 1953.

484. Sunnafrank, Michael, "Attitude Similarity and Interpersonal Attraction in Communication Processes: In Pursuit of an Ephemeral Influence." *Communication Monographs* 50, No. 4 (December 1983):273–284.

485. Sunnafrank, Michael, "A Communication-Based Perspective on Attitude Similarity and Interpersonal Attraction in Early Acquaintance." *Communication Monographs* 51, No. 4 (December 1984):372–380.

486. Sunnafrank, Michael, "Attitude Similarity and Interpersonal Attraction During Early Communicative Relationships: A Research Note on the Generalizability of Findings to Opposite-Sex Relationships." *Western Journal of Speech Communication* 49, No. 1 (Winter 1985):73–80.

487. Sunnafrank, Michael J., and Gerald R. Miller, "The Role of Initial Conversations in Determining Attraction to Similar and Dissimilar Strangers." *Human Communication Research* 8, No. 1 (Fall 1981):16–25.

488. Suttles, Gerald P., "Friendship as a Social Institution," in *Social Relationships*, G. McCall et al. Chicago: Aldine-Atherton, 1970, pp. 95–135.

489. Swensen, Clifford H., Jr., *Introduction to Interpersonal Relations.* Glenview, IL: Scott, Foresman, 1973.

490. Sykes, Richard E., "Initial Interaction Between Strangers and Acquaintances: A Multivariate Analysis of Factors Affecting Choice of Communication Partners." *Human Communication Research* **10**, No. 1 (Fall 1983):27–53.

491. Sypher, Beverly Davenport, and Howard E. Sypher, "Seeing Ourselves as Others See Us: Convergence and Divergence in Assessments of Communication Behavior." Paper presented at the Speech Communication Association Convention, Louisville, Kentucky, 1982.

492. Tagiuri, Renato, "Social Preference and Its Perception," in *Person Perception and Interpersonal Behavior*, Renato Tagiuri and Luigi Petrullo (eds.). Stanford, CA: Stanford University Press, 1958, pp. 316–336.

493. Tagiuri, Renato, "Person Perception," in *The Handbook of Social Psychology, Vol. III: The Individual in a Social Context*, Gardner Lindzey and Elliot Aronson (eds.). Reading, MA: Addison-Wesley, 1969, pp. 395–449.

494. Tagiuri, Renato, and Luigi Petrullo (eds.), *Person Perception and Interpersonal Behavior.* Stanford, CA: Stanford University Press, 1958.

495. Talley, Mary A., and Virginia Peck Richmond, "The Relationship Between Psychological Gender Orientation and Communicator Style." *Human Communication Research* **6**, No. 4 (Summer 1980):326–339.

496. Tardy, Charles H., and Lawrence A. Hosman, "Self-monitoring and Self-disclosure Flexibility: A Research Note." *Western Journal of Speech Communication* **46**, No. 1 (Winter 1982):92–97.

497. Taylor, F. Kraupl, "Awareness of One's Social Appeal." *Human Relations* **9**, No. 1 (1956):47–56.

498. Taylor, F. Kraupl, "Display of Dyadic Emotions." *Human Relations* **10**, No. 3 (1957):257–262.

499. Taylor, Howard F., *Balance in Small Groups.* New York: D. Van Nostrand, 1970.

500. Teger, A. I., "The Effect of Early Cooperation on the Escalation of Conflict." *Journal of Experimental Social Psychology* **6** (1970):187–204.

501. Teyber, Edward, "Structural Family Relations: Primary Dyadic Alliances and Adolescent Adjustment." *Journal of Marital and Family Therapy* **9**, No. 1, (1983):89–99.

502. Thibaut, John W., and Harold H. Kelley, *The Social Psychology of Groups*, New York: Wiley, 1959.

503. Thornton, Arland, "Children and Marital Stability." *Journal of Marriage and the Family* **39**, No. 3 (August 1977):531–540.

504. Tipton, Leonard P., "Agreement and Accuracy in Dyadic Communication." Paper presented to International Communication Association, Phoenix, AZ, 1971.

505. Toffler, Alvin, *Future Shock.* New York: Bantam, 1970.

506. Travis, Robert P., and Patricia Y. Travis, "Preparing Couples for Mid-

Life and the Later Years," in *Prevention in Family Services*, David R. Mace (ed.). Beverly Hills, CA: Sage Publications, 1983, pp. 87–97.

507. Turner, R. E., C. Edgely, and G. Olmstead, "Information Control in Conversation: Honesty Is Not Always the Best Policy." *Kansas Journal of Sociology* 11 (1975):69–89.

508. Turney-High, Harry Holbert, *Man and System: Foundations for the Study of Human Relations.* New York: Appleton-Century-Crofts, 1968.

509. Vernon, Glen M., *Human Interaction: An Introduction to Sociology*, 2d ed. New York: Ronald Press, 1972.

510. Vernon, M. D., *The Psychology of Perception.* Baltimore: Penguin Books, 1962.

511. Von Foerster, Heinz. *Observing Systems.* Seaside, CA: Intersystems Publications, 1981.

512. Von Neumann, John, and Oskar Morgenstern, *Theory of Games and Economic Behavior.* Princeton, NJ: Princeton University Press, 1944.

513. Von Wiese, Leopold, *Systematic Sociology.* Translated by Howard Becker. New York: Wiley, 1932.

514. Walster, Elaine, "The Effect of Self-esteem on Liking for Dates of Various Social Desirabilities." *Journal of Experimental Social Psychology* 6 (1970):248–253.

515. Walster, Elaine, Ellen Berscheid, and G. William Walster, "New Directions in Equity Research," in *Advances in Experimental Social Psychology*, Vol. 9, Leonard Berkowitz and Elaine Walster (eds.). New York: Academic Press, 1976, pp. 1–42.

516. Watkins, John, *The Therapeutic Self*, New York: Human Sciences Press, 1978.

517. Watkins, John, *The Two Hands of God: The Myths of Polarity.* New York: Macmillan, Collier Books, 1963.

518. Watzlawick, Paul, *The Language of Change.* New York: Basic Books, 1978.

519. Watzlawick, Paul, Janet Helmick Beavin, and Don D. Jackson, *The Pragmatics of Human Communication.* New York: W. W. Norton, 1967.

520. Watzlawick, Paul, John Weakland, and Richard Fisch, *Change: Principles of Problem Formation and Problem Resolution.* New York: W. W. Norton, 1974.

521. Weick, Karl E., *The Social Psychology of Organizing* (2d ed.). Reading, MA: Addison-Wesley, 1979.

522. Weinstein, Eugene A., and Paul Deutschberger, "Some Dimensions of Altercasting." *Sociometry* 26 (December 1963):454–466.

523. Weiss, Lawrence, and Marjorie F. Lowenthal, "Perceptions and Complexities of Friendship in Four Stages of the Adult Life Cycle." *Proceedings of the 81st Annual Convention of the American Psychological Association.* Montreal, Canada, 1973, Vol. 8, pp. 773–774.

524. Weiss, Robert S., "The Fund of Sociability." *Trans-Action* 6 (July/August 1969):36–43.

525. Weiss, Robert S., *Marital Separation.* New York: Basic Books, 1975.

526. Weisskopf-Joelson, Edith, "Some Comments on a Viennese School of Psychiatry." *The Journal of Abnormal and Social Psychology* **51** (1955):701–703.

527. Wender, Paul H., "Communicative Unclarity: Some Comments on the Rhetoric of Confusion." *Psychiatry* **30** (1967):332–349.

528. Wheeler, Ladd, and John Nezlek, "Sex Differences in Social Participation." *Journal of Personality and Social Psychology* **35,** No. 10, (1977):742–754.

529. Wheeless, Lawrence R., "Self-disclosure and Interpersonal Solidarity: Measurement, Validation, and Relationships." *Human Communication Research* **3,** No. 1 (Fall 1976):47–61.

530. Wheeless, Lawrence R., and Janis Grotz, "Conceptualization in Measurement of Reported Self-disclosure." *Human Communication Research* **2,** No. 4 (Summer 1976):338–346.

531. Wheeless, Lawrence R., and Janis Grotz, "The Measurement of Trust and Its Relationship to Self-Disclosure." *Human Communication Research* **3,** No. 3 (Spring 1977):250–257.

532. Wheeless, L. R., V. Eman Wheeless, and Raymond Baus, "Sexual Communication, Communication Satisfaction, and Solidarity in the Developmental Stages of Intimate Relationships." *Western Journal of Speech Communication* **48,** No. 3 (Summer 1984):217–230.

533. White, Geoffrey M., "Conceptual Universals in Interpersonal Language," *American Anthropologist* **82,** No. 4 (December 1980):759–781.

534. Whyte, William H., Jr., *The Organization Man.* Garden City, N.Y.: Doubleday, Anchor Books, 1957.

535. Wicklund, Robert A., "How Society Uses Self-Awareness," in *Psychological Perspectives on the Self,* Jerry Suls (ed.). Vol. I, New York: Lawrence Erlbaum, 1982, pp. 209–230.

536. Wiemann, John M., "Explication and Test of a Model of Communicative Competence." *Human Communication Research* **3,** No. 3 (Spring 1977):195–213.

537. Wiemann, John M., "A Summary of Current Research in Communicative Competence." Paper presented to the Speech Communication Association Convention, Washington, D.C., 1977.

538. Wiemann, John M. "A Description of Competent and Incompetent Communication Behavior." Paper presented to the Speech Communication Association Convention, Washington, D.C., December 1977.

539. Wilden, Anthony, and Tim Wilson, "The Double-Bind: Logic, Magic, and Economics," in *Double Bind: The Foundation of the Communicational Approach to the Family,* Carlos E. Sluzki and Donald C. Ransom (eds.). New York: Grune and Stratton, 1976, pp. 263–286.

540. Wilder, Carol, "The Palo Alto Group: Difficulties and Directions of the Interactional View for Human Communication Research." *Human Communication Research* **5,** No. 2 (Winter 1979):171–186.

541. Will, Otto, "Human Relations and the Schizophrenia Reaction." *Psychiatry* **22** (1959):205–223.

542. Willis, Richard H., "Coalitions in the Tetrad." *Sociometry* **25,** No. 4 (December 1962):358–376.

543. Wilmot, William W., "Metacommunication: A Re-examination and Extension," in *Communication Yearbook 4.* D. Nimmo (ed.). New Brunswick: Transaction Books, 1980, pp. 61–69.

544. Wilmot, William W., and Leslie A. Baxter, "Reciprocal Framing of Relationship Definitions and Episodic Interaction." *Western Journal of Speech Communication* 47, No. 3 (Summer 1983):205–217.

545. Wilmot, William W., and Leslie A. Baxter, "Defining Relationships: The Interplay of Cognitive Schemata and Communication." Paper presented to the Western Speech Communication Association Convention, Seattle, WA, 1984.

546. Wilmot, William W., and Donal A. Carbaugh, "Long Distance Lovers: Predicting the Dissolution of their Relationships." *Journal of the Northwest Communication Association* 14, No. 1 (Spring 1986):43–59.

547. Wilmot, William W., Donal A. Carbaugh, and Leslie A. Baxter, "Communicative Strategies Used to Terminate Romantic Relationships," *The Western Journal of Speech Communication* 49 (Summer 1985):204–216.

548. Wolff, Kurt H. (ed. and trans.), *The Sociology of Georg Simmel,* New York: Free Press, 1950.

549. Wood, Julia T., "Communication and Relational Culture: Bases for the Study of Human Relationships." *Communication Quarterly* 30, No. 2 (Spring 1982):75–83.

550. Wood, J. T., and C. R. Conrad, "Paradox in the Experiences of Professional Women." *Western Journal of Speech Communication* 47 (1983):305–322.

551. Woodman, Loring, *Perspectives in Self-Awareness: Essays on Human Problems.* Columbus, OH: Charles E. Merrill, 1973.

552. Word, Carl O., Mark P. Zanna, and Joel Cooper, "The Nonverbal Mediation of Self-Fulfilling Prophecies in Interracial Interactions." *Journal of Experimental Social Psychology* 10 (1974):109–120.

553. Worthy, Morgan, Albert C. Gary, and Gay M. Kahn, "Self-disclosure as an Exchange Process." *Journal of Personality and Social Psychology* 13, No. 1 (1969):59–63.

554. Wright, Paul H., "A Model and a Technique for Studies of Friendship." *Journal of Experimental Social Psychology* 5 (1969):295–309.

555. Wylie, Ruth C., *The Self-concept: A Critical Survey of Pertinent Research Literature.* Lincoln: University of Nebraska Press, 1961.

556. Yablonsky, Lewis, "The Sociometry of the Dyad." *Sociometry* 18 (1955):613–616.

557. Yerby, Janet, and Nancy L. Buerkel-Rothfuss, "Communication Patterns, Contradictions, and Family Functions." Paper presented at the annual convention, Speech Communication Association, Louisville, Kentucky, November, 1982.

558. Zakahi, Walter R., and Robert L. Duran, "All the Lonely People: The Relationship Among Loneliness, Communicative Competence, and Communication Anxiety." *Communication Quarterly* 30, No. 3 (Summer 1982):203–209.

559. Zakahi, Walter R., and Robert L. Duran, "Loneliness, Communicative Competence, and Communication Apprehension: Extension and Replication." *Communication Quarterly* **33**, No. 1 (Winter 1985):50–60.

560. Zelditch, M., Jr., "Role Differentiation in the Nuclear Family: A Comparative Study," in *Family, Socialization and Interaction Process*, T. Parsons and R. F. Bales (eds.). Glencoe, IL: Free Press, 1955, pp. 307–351.

561. Ziller, Robert C., *The Social Self.* New York: Pergamon Press, 1973.

562. Zimbardo, Philip, *Shyness.* Reading, MA: Addison-Wesley, 1977.

Author Index

This index is keyed to the preceding references.

Subject Index

About the Author

WILLIAM W. WILMOT is professor and chair of the Department of Interpersonal Communication at the University of Montana. He received his B.A. from the University of Wyoming, and M.A. and Ph.D. degrees from the University of Washington. He has published numerous articles in professional journals and is co-author of *Interpersonal Conflict* (Wm. C. Brown, 2nd edition, 1985). He is a past president of the Western Speech Communication Association, and frequently serves as a speaker, trainer, and consultant.